MILLER'S

antiques art & collectibles ON THE WEB

Phil Ellis holds a Masters degree in History and is an experienced antiques writer who contributes to several publications. For over 10 years, he worked as Assistant Editor on the weekly *Antiques Magazine*.

Simon Edwards is the technical director of computer security firm DeadSecure. He has previously worked as the online editor for a number of websites including *PC Pro*, *Computer Buyer*, and *Computer Shopper*. He has previously worked as a news editor on *Computer Buyer* and has spent much time investigating computer hacker activity. He has appeared on Sky TV and live radio, providing comment on current Internet issues and offering advice to technically-challenged audiences. He is the author of *The Good Website Guide 2002* (Mitchell Beazley, 2002).

Joyce Hanes has been in the antiques world since 1972 and, with her husband, runs a successful antiques business in Connecticut, exhibiting at fairs and shows throughout the United States. She is a dealer member of the American Ceramics Circle and is a founder member of The Antiques Council. Joyce has been writing on antiques for the last ten years and is a keen user and supporter of the Internet.

MILLER'S

antiques art & collectibles ON THE WEB

CONTRIBUTORS

Phil Ellis

Simon Edwards

Joyce Hanes

MILLER'S ANTIQUES, ART, & COLLECTIBLES ON THE WEB

Contributors: Phil Ellis, Simon Edwards, and Joyce Hanes

First published in Great Britain in 2000 by Miller's,
a division of Mitchell Beazley,
imprints of Octopus Publishing Group Ltd,
2-4 Heron Quays, London E14 4JP
This revised edition published 2002

Commissioning Editor **Anna Sanderson**
Executive Art Editor **Rhonda Fisher**
Designer **Victoria Bevan, Peter Gerrish**
Jacket Design **Colin Goody, Victoria Bevan**
Editor **Claire Musters**
Editorial Assistant **Rose Hudson**
Proofreader **Sue Harper**
Indexer **Hilary Bird**
Production **Angela Couchman**

A CIP catalogue record for this book is available from the British Library

ISBN 1 84000 570 X

Set in Frutiger and Helvetica
Produced and printed by Bath Press, Bath

CONTENTS

USING THIS BOOK

This new edition of *Miller's Antiques, Art, & Collectibles on the Web* has been completely updated and revised. It is divided into three sections, opening with a basic introduction to the Internet: what it is, how it operates, and how to make it work best for you. There are hints and tips on how to search efficiently plus general information about buying and selling on the Internet, whether at auction or through a dealer. Advice is given on how to set up your own home page, create an auction listing, and much more. A glossary (see page 276) clarifies specialist terms for the novice.

The second section contains lists of general sites on antiques and collectibles. Here you will find publications, auction houses (including online ones), museums, trade associations, plus those offering services such as auction searches, stolen property registers etc. If a site is particularly specialist you will find it in the relevant subject category in the third section. For ease of use the book has been sorted into subject areas and the sites listed alphabetically. However you can use the index (see page 279) to search for particular organizations or subject areas. The "Worth a Look" feature at the end of each section highlights sites throughout the book that merit further inspection.

The third section lists almost 60 specialist subject areas with a selection of sites, from dealers and specialist auctions to museums and other resource sites. Many sites offer links to related subjects. All the sites listed in the book were active at the time of going to press but, due to the nature of the Internet, things are always changing and we apologize for any inconvenience this may cause if you find sites have changed their location or ceased to exist since we produced this book. However, we can assure you that within these pages you will find a selection of the best of what is available online now and, as the world wide web continually extends its net, this book also gives a taste of what is to come.

Please note that, while all addresses have "http://" in front, it is not necessary to type this into the address bar – your computer should do this automatically – and we have not added these into the addresses given. However, not all sites begin with "www" and in this book this prefix has only been given when it is actually part of the address.

If you would like to recommend a site for possible inclusion in the next edition of *Miller's Antiques, Art, & Collectibles on the Web* please photocopy and return the form on page 288 or email us at: **millerswebguide@mitchell-beazley.co.uk**.

WHAT IS THE WEB?

The Internet is a massive global network of computers that provides a number of services, some of which are directly useful to the public. These include the world wide web, email, online chat, and newsgroups. The web is the colourful and noisy part of the Internet that everyone talks about. It's the place where you can find pages of information containing pictures, files that play music through your computer, and software programs that you can download and run at home.

There are millions of pages on the web, and each has a unique address. An address is likely to look something like: www.anysite.com. You will have seen such addresses, also known as URLs (Uniform Resource Locator), on adverts in newspapers, on TV, and on the sides of buses. Pages are grouped into areas called sites. This book contains reviews of approximately 1,000 sites, and you'll find the appropriate addresses printed above each one.

USING THE WEB

You can visit a website by connecting to the Internet, typing the site's address into a program called a web browser, and waiting for the information to be displayed on your computer screen. Your computer will probably have come with a web browser already on it. The two main ones are Microsoft's Internet Explorer and Netscape's browser. Whether you use a PC or a Mac, you'll be able to choose one of these to access the Internet.

Once you've found a site that you like, you can follow links on its pages to display further pages within the site. Some links might even take you to other sites altogether. Usually, but not always, a link will be a button or some underlined text. (Hover your mouse over a link to see where it leads to. The web address, or "URL", will appear at the bottom of your browser's display.)

Sometimes the author of a website will use special tools when creating a page, either to create impressive effects, or to make his/her own life easier. In these cases you may have to use another bit of software, in addition to your web browser, called a plugin. Plugins kick into action automatically when needed, so you'll only have to download and install them once – and then you can forget about them. If you don't have the right plugins installed when you visit a site you will often be given the option to download them straight away. This can be annoying and time-consuming, so don't waste your time doing this for every site that you visit – just the ones that you know you want to get information from. Flash, Shockwave, and QuickTime are the three most common plugins that are worth bothering with.

There are some terms that you will come across on the web, and in this book, that may be new and confusing to you. It doesn't help that some people use the same terms to mean different things! Here, when we refer to being online, we mean that you have connected to the Internet, probably using a modem. When you find a picture, a piece of software, or check your email, you download the data from the Internet to your computer. Strictly speaking you also download web pages when you visit a website. These are stored in a special place on your hard disk for a while and will then get replaced with other pages every so often. Your web browser program controls how long the information is stored for and how frequently it is replaced.

Downloading Pages from the Web

You can also command your web browser to download a particular web page, and store it anywhere you like on your computer or floppy disk. This is useful if you want to refer back to pages of information later and don't want the bother of connecting to the Internet. You can read downloaded pages while disconnected (offline). There are a number of ways to download pages for offline use, using your browser. Here's how to use Internet Explorer to do so.

Find the page you want and click the File option on your Browser's toolbar, selecting "Save As..." from the menu. Choose a folder on your computer where the page will be saved and pick "Web Page, HTML only" from the "Save as type:" box. Click "OK" to store the text from the page on your computer. If you want to store the pictures too, choose "Web Page, complete" from the "Save as type:" box.

Sometimes you might come across a site where you want to read lots of pages, but don't want to stay online to do so. In cases like these you can use special programs to download the whole site, or parts of it. Microsoft Internet Explorer can make sites available offline without any help from other software. Go to the site and add it to your list of Favourites by clicking on the Favourites menu on the toolbar and choose the "Add to Favourites..." option. You'll be confronted by a box that contains an option to "Make Available Offline". Click in the box and then on the "Customize" button. You can tell Internet Explorer to burrow down through links on the site and store other pages on your computer for offline browsing. You can choose how many levels down the program will dig, and it makes sense to keep this figure quite low because websites are constructed in layers, or levels, and some have lots of these – imagine them as a pyramid shape. The first layer is the first page you see when you visit the site. As you click on links, which may be buttons, pieces of text, or images, you visit other pages that exist on the lower layers. Each of these layers will contain articles and pages with more links to deeper layers. If you decide to follow every single link on every page you will find the number of total pages you visit will grow exponentially at every click. The first page might take you to five or six different areas, but these areas could link you to 30 sub-categories, or even other websites. These other pages and sites could, theoretically, link to the rest of the Internet after following a few links. So it makes sense, when sampling a website for offline browsing, to restrict how many links your software is allowed to follow. Too few and you might as well not have bothered, but if you ask for too many then you'll have to wait ages for a mixture of both useful and useless information to be downloaded. A good way to start is to tell the program to visit just one level down. This way only newer articles and the updated first page will be copied to your computer. You can then see news announcements and read the basic stories. Any links from the news stories will obviously be unavailable, so you'll need to reconnect to the Internet to follow any of them.

Another way to read web pages offline is to print them out. Any good quality inkjet printer or low-cost laser printer will do the job, allowing you to read the information without staring at a screen and straining your eyes.

If you wish to keep returning to certain pages and sites you can create a list on your computer, often called a "Bookmarks" or "Favourites" list. When you find a place you like press Control-D or "Apple Key"-D (if you're using Microsoft Internet Explorer or Netscape's browser on a PC or Mac respectively) and the page's address will be saved. You can now return to that place with ease, and won't need to search the whole Internet each time. Don't be too eager to create a bookmark for every page you think you might need, though. The list can become unmanageably long very quickly and you'll end up finding that using a search engine will be faster than trawling through your own index!

SEARCHING THE INTERNET

The web is very big, extremely useful, but exceedingly disorganized. Unlike a public library, where all of the books are categorized and indexed, the web has very little structure and you can spend a large chunk of your time looking for useful pieces of information. Fortunately there are a number of simple ways to search for things on the web, using search engines and directories.

DIRECTORIES AND SEARCH ENGINES

Although there is no single, central index on the Internet there are a number of smaller ones, called search engines, that regularly scan the web and create their own indices. You can use one of these to look for sites in your area of interest. Because this process is run automatically by computers the results are not always very discriminating, but by using powerful searching techniques, such as those described below, we can harness the search engines' power to find the best stuff and discard the useless sites.

Directories, on the other hand, are created by people and contain more limited, but usually more relevant, information. You can browse these by category, for example "Art Deco" or "Miniatures and Figurines", or search the whole (or parts of) the directory using a built-in search facility.

Using a Directory

Web directories provide the simplest way to find information on the web. A directory is a site that has lists of other Internet sites. They are organized into broad groups, with each one containing sets of narrower categories. These in turn contain even more specific headings. If you want to find out about thimbles, for example, you should browse through the available categories until you find one called something like "Collectibles". There will be sub-categories for you to burrow down into and satisfy your particular interest. Often, directories have a basic search feature. Use it to find the main category you need, then use your intuition and common sense to follow the rest of the links.

Yahoo! (www.yahoo.com) is a superior web directory. To show how it works, we are using it here to search for information on thimbles. Initially you might enter something like "thimbles" into the search box and press the Search button to start your search for information (see Fig 1). The Antiques and Collectibles > Thimbles section is probably a likely candidate (see Fig 2), and clicking on it brings up a list of useful-looking sites, and other sub-categories (see Fig 3). A site's title and address can often give a clue as to how official and/or useful it's going to be.

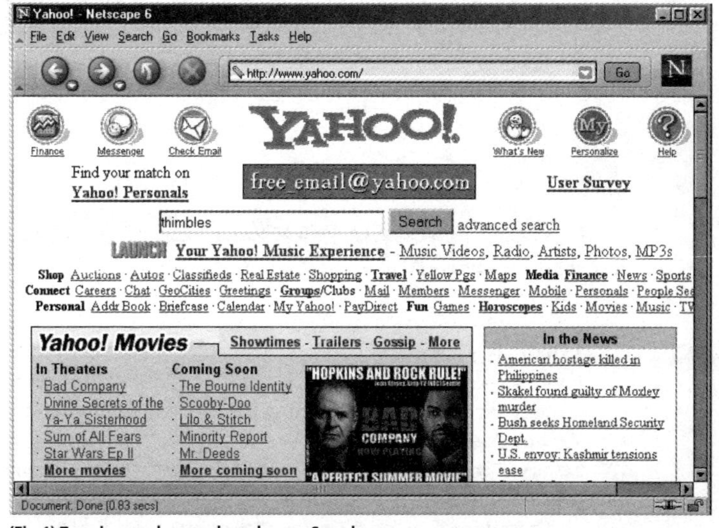

(Fig 1) Type in your keywords and press Search.

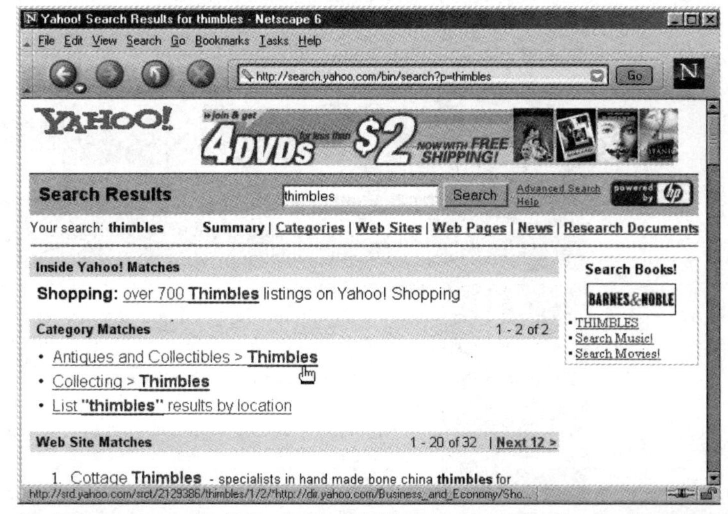

(Fig 2) Find a category that looks suitable and click on its link to see a list of useful sites.

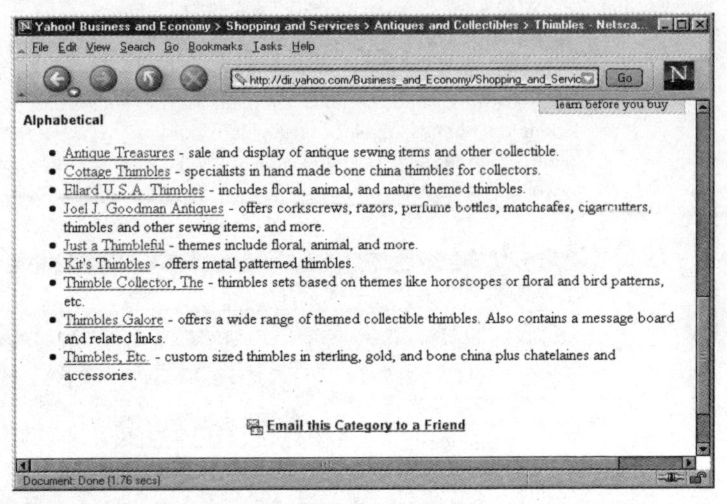

(Fig 3) And here is a list of dealers all waiting to sell you the thimble of your dreams.

Local Information

If you are seeking out information on local businesses then the easiest method is to use the electronic equivalent of the local telephone directory – try the Antique Dealers Directory at www.antique-dealers-directory.co.uk (see Fig 4). Many will go further than just providing telephone numbers and addresses; resource sites like iCollector (www2.icollector.com) provide links to online auctions, dealers, galleries, and all sorts of other useful resources.

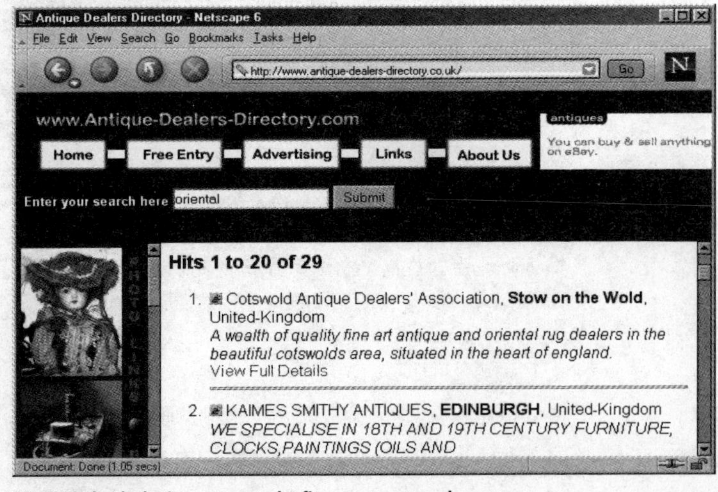

(Fig 4) Find a dealer in your area who fits your exact needs.

Using a Search Engine

Powerful but slightly unpredictable, a search engine is almost as likely to turn up pages from the secret corners of the web as it is to find a large antique dealer's site. Try searching for "antiques" and you'll see what I mean. You'll be faced with a huge number of pages containing information from museums through to jokes. In fact, any page that the search engine has discovered to contain the word "antiques" will be listed. Don't be put off, though. Read the next few paragraphs and you'll be able to pare away the pages you don't want, to reveal the juicy bits that you do.

The secret to a successful search is to be specific, and those who ask the best questions get the best answers. One of the superior general search engines is www.google.com. Try typing "antique clock" and press Search (see Fig 5). The number of sites has decreased dramatically and the chance of picking up relevant pages is looking more likely. But there are still thousands of pages listed. Now try "antique clock "expert repair"". The inverted commas have been placed round the additional subject we've added in here because they are always needed when using a phrase containing more than one word. Continue to whittle down the results until your list is of manageable proportions. Use "longcase" to whittle down the list further (see Fig 6).

Initially your screen will only show a few of the possibly thousands of pages that the search engine has found as a result of your specific search request. You can call up the next few links by pressing the Next command that is always located at the bottom of the page (see Fig 7).

(Fig 5) Start off with a general word or phrase before narrowing down your search. The phrase "antique clock" has generated around 192,000 results, most of which are useless.

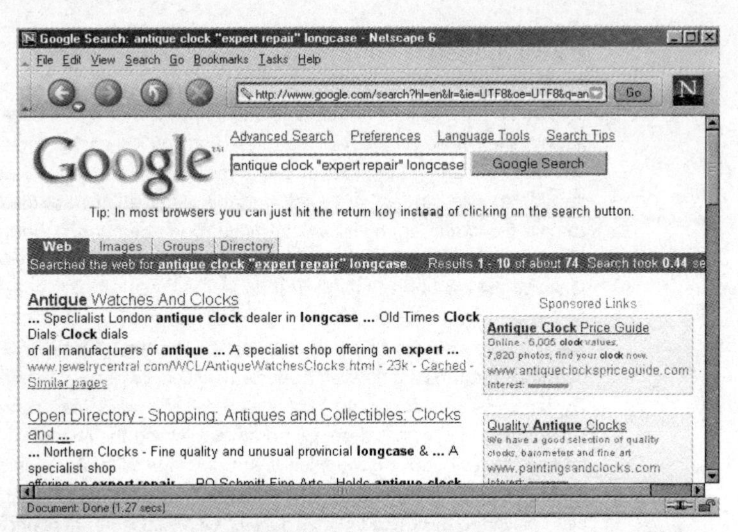

(Fig 6) Add some more keywords to help the search engine. We now have only around 74 pages listed – a much more manageable amount.

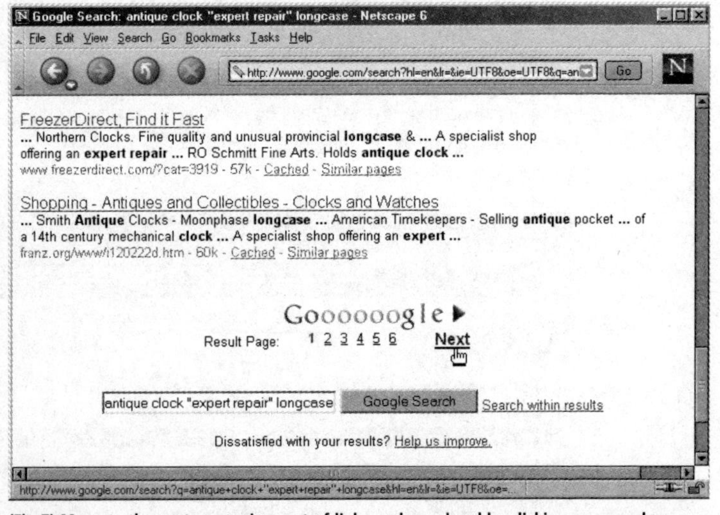

(Fig 7) Move to the next or previous set of links, or leap ahead by clicking on a number.

Advanced Searching

You can really narrow down your Internet searches by using a standard set of commands that are known as Boolean operators. The most common are AND, OR, and AND NOT. Google and Alta Vista also use the "+" sign instead of the word AND, while "-" counts as a NOT. A search for "+beanie +baby -auction" will, for example, save you a lot of time that you'd otherwise waste trawling through useless pages as you've provided lots of detail about what you are looking for (see Fig 8). Some search engines also support extra features like NEAR, which will find keywords that appear within a certain number of words from each other. When you are using these commands, try searching for exact phrases. If you are looking for a unique or nearly unique item, and you know its name, then enclose it in inverted commas and give it a try. Search for "+"beanie baby" +"bucky the beaver" +picture +sale", and the list that you will get back will be very specific – probably including links to pictures of the item that you can view online or download for use later.

Don't waste your valuable searching time clicking through thousands of really irrelevant links. Practise these advanced techniques to save time in the long run.

(Fig 8) Just 22 links in this list means we can check each one to find the best within minutes.

NEWSGROUPS

Newsgroups, also known as Usenet, is an area of the Internet where people ask and answer questions, exchange files, and express opinions. It is really a huge selection of electronic bulletin boards, each dedicated to often very specific subjects. Newsgroups have been around for a very long time, and the system is not as pretty or easy to use as the web. It can be very useful, though, and once you've given it a try you may well find you prefer it.

USING A NEWSREADER

There are two main ways to harness the power of Internet newsgroups. To use them properly you should use a special newsreader program. You are likely to have one already installed on your computer in the shape of Microsoft Outlook Express or Netscape Messenger, both of which are reasonably powerful email programs with news capabilities. A better option is to use a dedicated newsreader such as Forté Free Agent, which is easier to use and has a more powerful set of features.

Your newsreader will need to be set up before it will work properly. This involves connecting to the Internet and downloading a very large list of all the available newsgroups. Check with your Internet Service Provider (ISP) that you have access to a newsgroup service, and write down the name of the news server. It will look something like: news.myisp.com. Newsreader programs tend to work in similar ways, but you should read the instructions with your version carefully to find out how to use it "offline". This means that you can connect to the Internet, download messages, and disconnect again quickly, so you can relax and read the discussions without worrying about the phone bill.

Picking a Newsgroup

First, find a list of likely-looking groups. Subscribe to each one to create a shortlist – this is a bit like your web browser's Favourites or Bookmarks. Subscribing to a newsgroup doesn't cost anything and no one will know that you are following the discussions until you start contributing. It is a good idea to monitor a group for a while before you start sending in your questions, just to make sure that the other users are friendly and likely to help.

Connect to the Internet and download the "message headers" in each group. These are short subject lines that indicate what the messages are about. You

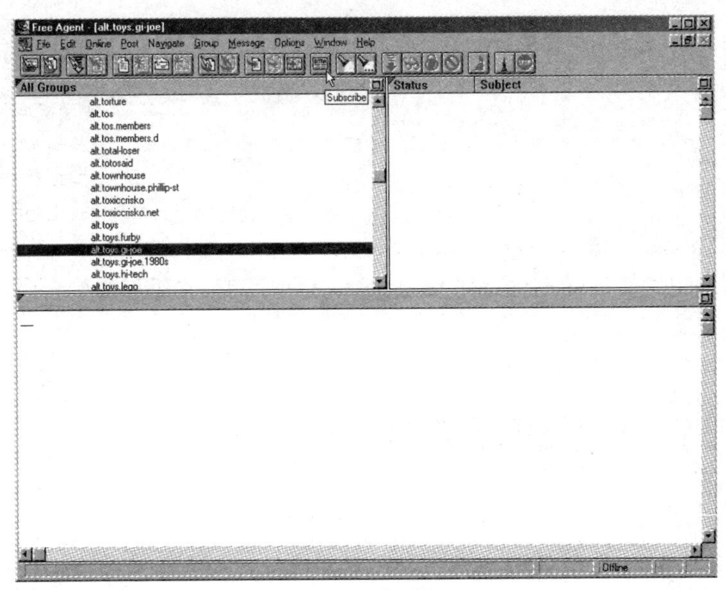

(Fig 9) Browse through the groups and create a shortlist.

can ignore any irrelevant-looking ones and go straight for the juicy threads (see Fig 9). Downloading a few hundred headers takes little time, even over a slow connection. Disconnect from the Internet again.

Spend some time reading the headers and select each one that you think looks interesting (see Fig 10), marking it for retrieval. This means that the next time that you connect the actual message will be downloaded.

Connect again and download any news headers as well as the messages you have already marked. Disconnect and read the messages (see Fig 11), marking any interesting new headers, and continue this routine occasionally throughout the day.

When you want to ask a question or provide someone with an answer you'll need to send your message to the news server. This is actually done using email, but your newsreader program should be able to make things easy for you, so specify the name of your ISP's outgoing email server in the appropriate place (see Fig 12).

If you want to send a message to a group from Free Agent then click on the group's entry on the left and choose New Usenet Message from the toolbar's Post menu. Alternatively just press "P". Type in the text you want and press the Send Now button, ensuring that you are connected to the Internet.

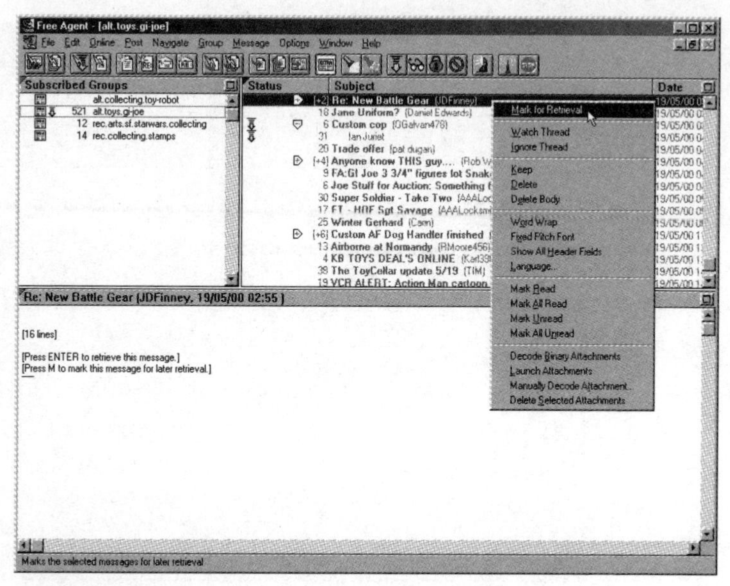

(Fig 10) Mark interesting-looking messages for retrieval.

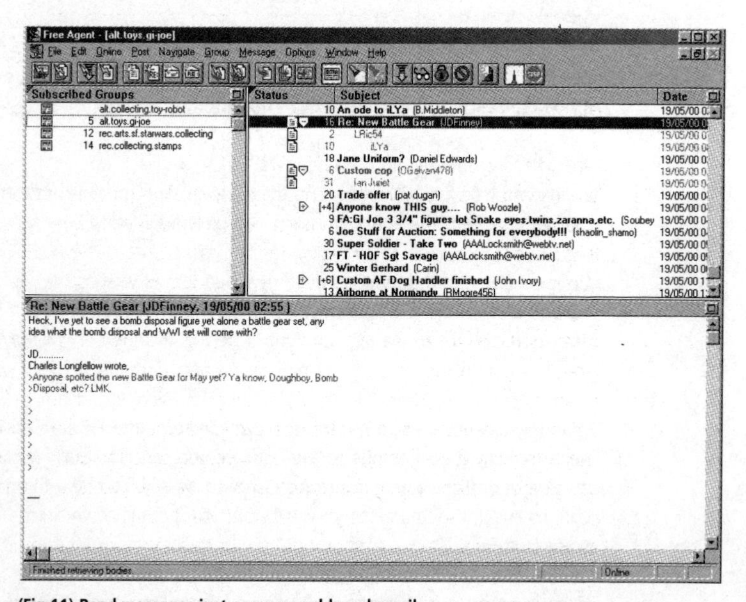

(Fig 11) Read messages just as you would read email.

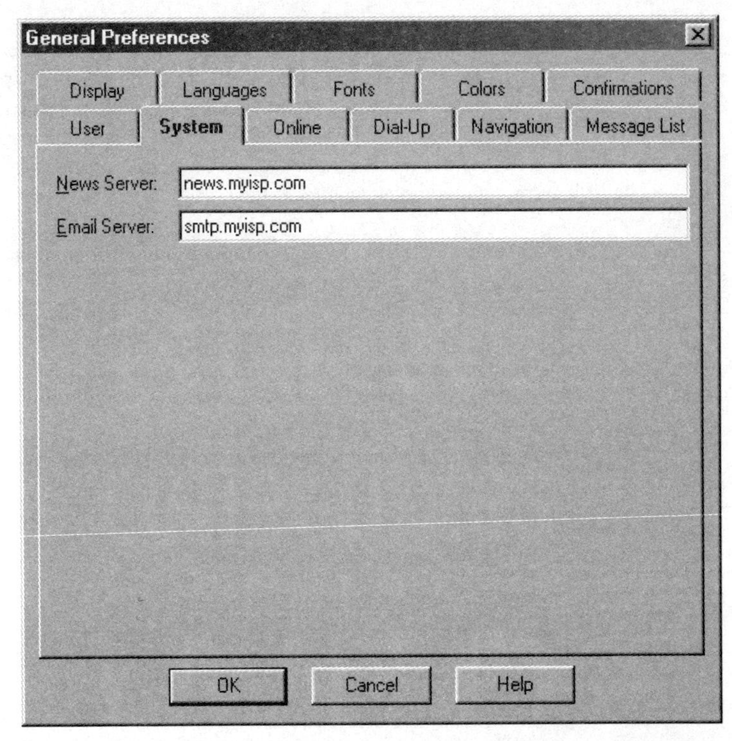

(Fig 12) Enter your email server's address so that you can post messages to the newsgroup.

You can reply to someone else's message by clicking on that message in the right-hand side of the window and choosing Follow-Up Usenet Message from the toolbar's Post menu – or just press "F". Then press Send Now.

Dos and Don'ts

Usenet relies on the goodwill of its users to be successful, as it's no one's duty to answer well, truthfully, or at all. It is therefore very important to be polite when using a newsgroup because people who would otherwise be helpful can turn nasty if they think they detect a wrong tone to your message. There are certain dos and don'ts for using Usenet. The main ones are listed below:

- Be polite, courteous, and grateful when someone answers your question – even if you know they are wrong. You'll only discourage others from responding to you at a later date if you sound aggressive or rude.

- Provide as much relevant information as you can about your problem or question. This also applies if you are answering someone else's questions.

- Tolerate other users. While some people will attack others (and possibly you) with scathing remarks, prejudiced opinions, and general silliness, it makes no sense for you to fight back in the same way. Other users will just see you as rising to the bait at best, and in the same league as the offending user at worst. And this would obviously affect the way in which you are treated by them in future newsgroup messages.

- If you must use Microsoft Outlook Express or another email program to post messages to newsgroups, then make sure you turn off the HTML-formatting option first. This will make life easier for those users who don't have HTML-compatible newsreaders (if you don't do this the message they receive will be surrounded by lots of garbled text), and it will also reduce the overall size of your final message.

- Type your message in very carefully, avoiding obvious spelling mistakes, poor punctuation, and grammatical errors. This will make life easier for everyone, but particularly for those newsgroup users who don't have English as their first language.

- Don't send annoyed messages to a group if your previous question was ignored. Either no one knew the answer or, alternatively, perhaps the answer to your question has actually already appeared in a Frequently Asked Questions (FAQ) document, which is often available to download from the group. Check there before you get upset!

- Groups are either binary or non-binary. You can tell by the name – for example, Alt.binaries.music and alt.binaries.autographs are binary groups, whereas alt.collecting.autographs is not. Don't copy picture, sound, or other files to non-binary groups, as those in the group will not want to see such files appearing – it will force their software to download large files that they probably don't actually want anyway.

- Don't SHOUT. Using excessive capitalization within a message is equivalent to shouting, and a few people get very upset by this. Although all-caps text is hard to read it does seem strange that some get quite so upset as they sometimes do, but these ever-so-sensitive individuals are the ones whose help you are requesting – so always remember to be polite.

- Don't use humour unless you are really sure that your fellow group users will "get" you. If you must try to be funny you may want to rely on a "smiley" to avoid misunderstandings. This is a picture of a smiley face that is made out of text characters. It is a type of emoticon (see glossary on page 276), and these are used to denote emotions that can be difficult to express otherwise. For example, you could tease your friend Jon with the following: "Jon doesn't know anything about Roman coins :)"

Searching Usenet using Google

Unless you have a lot of spare time you are unlikely to want to read all of the articles in your chosen set of groups but you can still take advantage of other people's knowledge and goodwill by using the web-based service run by the Google search engine (www.google.com). It stores the electronic discussions that form Usenet, known as threads, and provides a powerful search function.

Visit the site at groups.google.com and enter your keywords into the search box at the top of the page (we'll use "GI Joe" and "vintage" in this example – see Fig 13). After a few seconds you'll see a list of discussions, rather than the websites you'd expect a normal search engine to provide.

Hopefully, a number of people will have asked similar questions to the ones you have yourself. Read these carefully and see what other people have written as replies. The keywords that are used to search with will appear in bold on the screen. This is so you can instantly see the context they appear in within the questions so that you can decide if they are relevant or not. If you cannot understand the answers, or need more detail, you can narrow down the search using the excellent Power Search option. This lets you specify words you do and don't want to appear, and you can specify to view only messages written within certain dates and in particular newsgroups. For example, if you are searching for auctions on vintage GI Joe sailor dolls, you can tell Google to search only the alt.toys.gi-joe groups, and specify a date within the last two or three months.

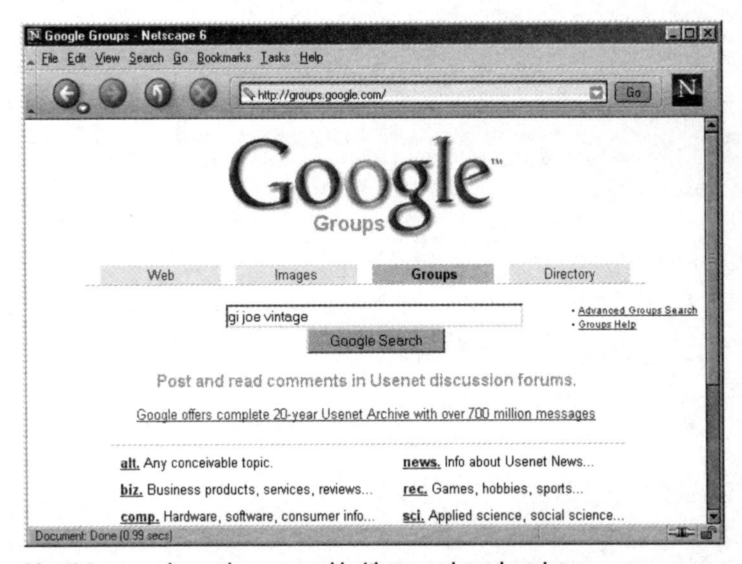

(Fig 13) Enter your keywords as you would with a normal search engine.

If you can't find enough detail to satisfy you, you can ask further questions, or add your own opinions to a discussion thread. This is possible using the reply feature (see Fig 14).

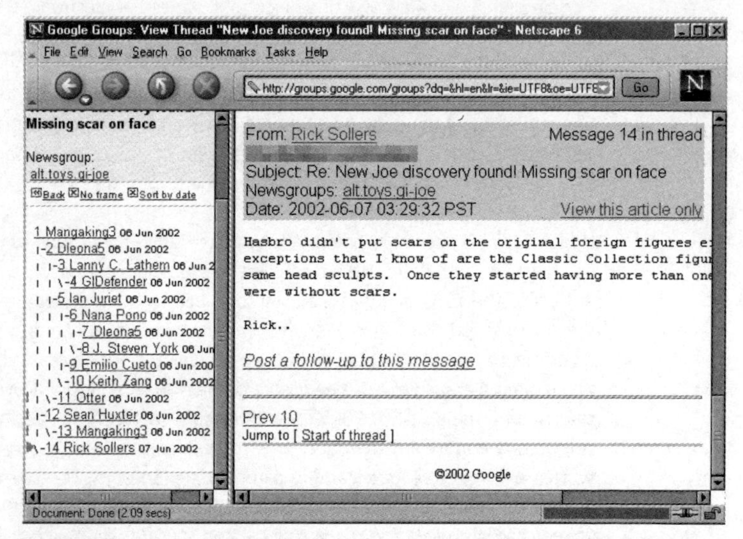

(Fig 14) Reply to ask further questions or add comments by clicking on "Post a follow-up to this message".

BUYING ONLINE

Using the Internet to buy goods and services has become very popular. Over the last few years the number of online shops has exploded and, no matter what you want to buy, it is very likely that there will be a website willing to sell it to you. This applies as much to antiques and collectibles as to anything else, and there are whole areas of the web devoted to providing the latest Beanie Baby or piece of antique jewellery, or, at the very least, direct access to those who deal in them.

INTERNET SHOPPING

Why buy from the Internet? You may be feeling left out. Perhaps you can't imagine why you'd want to buy something off a computer screen. And how do you even begin? You can't touch the merchandise and any descriptive pictures are likely to be small and lacking in detail. Maybe you are worried about how you're going to pay for things. After all, surely there is an invisible army of hackers just waiting to pounce on your credit card number the minute you send it over the Internet?

It is actually incredibly convenient and safe to use the Internet to buy things. You obviously can't examine the hallmarks closely, but if you are buying new collectible items you will already know what to expect anyway. In fact, if you have a particular item in mind, the Internet provides an excellent way to shop around while saving on shoe leather and patience. You can avoid the Saturday crowds and browse through shops online in a fraction of the time you could in the high street.

Buying from a website is like buying from a catalogue. If you're happy to part with money based on a stamp-sized picture in a magazine, why not when it's on a monitor? Also, the fact that the Internet is always up-to-the-minute means that prices can change for the better every day. However, as a buyer you need to be confident that you are getting what you pay for. Follow the rules on secure payments, then check out who you are buying from and what their terms and conditions are. Never click to confirm a transaction until you are satisfied.

In this book you will find a wide range of sites where you can purchase specialist items such as books and catalogues as well as traditional antiques and collectibles. If you are looking to buy a large piece of antique furniture it is unlikely that you will buy it straight off the Internet. But what the Internet will do for you is put you in touch with specialist dealers so that you can browse through their sites to view stock before making direct contact with them. Then, once you have contacted the dealer and have established a relationship with them, you will be able to communicate much more easily. The dealer can post digital images of new items that might be of interest directly to you via your computer. If you have formed a good relationship then you will be confident that what the dealer is offering is "right", just as if you were buying in their shop or at an antiques fair.

Your First Shopping Trip

How do you dip your toe into the Internet shopping centre? Your best option is to start off small. Buy something that will fit through your letterbox, like a book or a non-breakable item. That way you won't be worried about sending money off into the ether, and you won't have to wait in to receive a large package. There are plenty of places listed in this guide that will be happy to sell you a *Star Wars* figure or a silver thimble. You don't have to buy in bulk. When a parcel arrives, two or three days later, I guarantee you will be sold on the idea of using the Internet to shop.

Order tracking is an interesting feature that you'll find on all of the best sites. You identify yourself to the site using a unique user name and password, and the screen will tell you if your item has been placed into stock yet, whether or not it has actually been shipped out to you, and will also possibly give an estimated delivery date. Sometimes, when you order more than one thing, one item will be in stock while another needs to be ordered from the supplier. Use the order tracking facility to see exactly what's going on and you can avoid having to sit in a never-ending telephone queue waiting to speak to their customer services department.

Buying Tips

Given the choice, always use a credit card rather than a debit card. The former protects you when goods are faulty, or don't turn up, and the seller refuses to co-operate. You get your money back, and the credit card company chases the lost money itself. A debit card just provides a way to pay money from your bank account, and can be useful for small purchases, but you won't get any protection from fraudsters at all.

A good online shop will clearly publish its prices and include details of any tax you might have to pay. You should also be able to find out how much postage and packing will cost. Is insurance available? Find out. Reading the small print can be painful – there's usually loads of it – but it is essential that you know what you're letting yourself in for, particularly if you are dealing with an unfamiliar company.

Many stores will remember your details, so you won't have to type in your address and card number every time you buy something. If an online shop gives you a user name and password, make sure you keep it in a safe place. You won't want to lose it, and you certainly don't want someone else to find it and go on a spree at your expense. That said, the worst that can happen is that you'll receive a massive package one day. Any customer services department worth its salt will be happy to sort the mess out. It's no different from someone finding your catalogue card and ordering goods with it.

A well-run business in the high street will have a nice, big shop with excellent displays and polite staff. An Internet site can be made to look fantastic by anyone with a computer, some cheap software, and a half-decent eye for design. So how can you tell if an e-shop is all it appears? Some sites join schemes where they agree to follow a certain code of conduct and, in return, are permitted to display a logo that certifies them as good traders. This is intended to instill confidence in consumers, and generally it is a very helpful thing. Don't be taken in by any old certificate, though, as they can be falsely copied or created out of thin air. If in doubt, check the organization's website and see if the shop is listed. And if you haven't heard of an organization, then don't feel that you have to trust it. The Consumers' Association run a scheme called Which? Web Trader, and details of its services, as well as general advice, can be found at www.which.net/webtrader.

The familiar antiques trade associations still apply to a dealer with an Internet site (see pages 117–22 for examples of some of these) and they should instill the same confidence on the Internet as they do on the high street. But also remember that the same rules apply to buying antiques and collectibles on the Internet as on the high street – if the dealer is not accredited to a well-known organization or is only contactable by email then proceed with caution! Treat the transaction as you would if you were buying from a classified advert or a car boot sale. You may get a bargain but you may also get your fingers burned. The onus is on the customer to check out any dealer thoroughly before making a purchase online.

As with any mail-order transaction, the hardest part of Internet shopping is receiving the goods. Small items that come through the post will pose little or no problem, but order an antique four-poster bed and you will have to make sure that you're at home when the delivery man comes knocking. This is, however, no different from waiting for a large delivery from a high-street shop.

Importing

Buying online, whether through an online auction, website, or just mail order does not exempt you from paying import duties and tax. You need to stay abreast of the ever-changing laws. For example, if you plan on importing certain works of art, antiques, and collectors' pieces into the UK then you'll have to pay VAT. Until June 1999 you did not, and for a while there were different rates for different types of goods. Each country has different rules, and they are rarely straightforward. If in doubt check with your local customs office. The US Customs Service (www.customs.ustreas.gov) and the UK's HM Customs and Excise (www.hmce.gov.uk) websites both contain comprehensive import and export duty documents.

Before you establish how much importing an item will cost, you should also find out if it is even legal to bring it into the country. You might make the successful bid for an ivory picture, but it's not the seller's problem if it won't get through Customs or if the police come knocking at your door.

Security

There are plenty of Internet-aware criminals whose idea of fun and profit is to break into computer systems, particularly those that store your credit card details. But any good online store will take serious security precautions to keep this information safe. Even when you send your details to such shops over the web, the information will be transported using encryption. To do this the site has to make a special connection between itself and your computer, which encapsulates your name, address, and other details in secret code. This technology is called SSL (Secure Sockets Layer), and you can tell when it is in action because a small picture of a yellow padlock will appear at the bottom of your web browser. If you intend to sell goods directly from your website, and expect people to send in their banking details, you should add SSL to your site.

Just as you shouldn't flash your credit card around every here-today, gone-tomorrow high-street business, nor should you use your cards carelessly with unknown businesses operating on the Internet. If a company has no apparent phone number or physical address you should look elsewhere. An email address is not good enough should things go wrong and you wish to seek redress.

You may be worried that hackers will break into your computer to steal your credit card details directly from you. This is unlikely to happen, and the only real way that a hacker can gain control of your computer is if you are running "server" programs on your system. Most home PCs do not use this type of software. However, it is possible for a hacker to install server software using certain types of computer virus. The best defence against these is to avoid running files attached to email messages, unless you know what to expect. You should also make sure you install both an anti-virus and a personal firewall program. These programs are available for free or for as little as £30 each. Good anti-virus programs include those made by Symantec, McAfee, Kaspersky Labs, and AVG, while the Zone Alarm and BlackICE PC Protection firewalls are good value – the former being free.

Researching Prices

Whether you're ready to sell or buy from a web page or through an online auction you'll need to know roughly how much you can charge/should pay for your goods. There are price guidebooks available (*The Miller's Antiques Price Guide* being a notable example) and many online services that will appraise your belongings. You can often find these services as optional extras advertised on auction sites, and a quick browse through your favourite web directory will list a few. Try searching for "antique appraisal" to view examples.

Online appraisers will usually accept digital photos of items and base their evaluation on them. This lack of close inspection means that fakes, small flaws, and damaged pieces probably won't be noticed. If you want a comprehensive service then you should try one of the larger companies, such as Sotheby's or Christie's, or official trade associations like the British Antique Dealer's Association (BADA) at www.bada.org or America's National Association of Dealers in Antiques Inc at www.nadaweb.org. However, for a "hands-on" traditional valuation you must expect to pay considerably more than the usual £12.50/$20 fee charged by many online services. And don't base your insurance value on a figure quoted by an online appraiser.

Some specialist appraisal services for antiques and collectibles are:

www.appraisalday.com (Paul Royka of US *Antiques Roadshow* fame)
www.pcgs.com (professional coin-grading service)
www.psadna.com (autograph authenticators)
www.psacard.com (professional sports card authenticators)

The prices at online auctions are different from those paid at traditional auctions. It is worth doing some research before you buy or sell items online to see what the going prices are. Multiple auction sites, such as those listed below, allow you to build up a picture of the online market in particular items by seeing what has sold where and for how much:

www.auctionwatch.com
www.bidfind.com

Again, use the information available on sites such as these to find out more about the online market and how to get the best out of it.

Online price guides are useful indicators of how much you can charge or how much to bid at an auction, but they also sometimes feature galleries of stolen goods so that you can avoid buying hot property. Another quick search for "stolen antiques" will bring up a good list of sites that host images and descriptions of stolen works of art.

ONLINE AUCTIONS

Online auctions are a very accessible way to buy and sell collectible items. You have access to many more potential bidders and customers than could crowd into a hall, and that means you are more likely to sell items at higher prices or pick up something you like, if you are a buyer. Online auctions run all the time and, because they are on the Internet, they are available throughout the week, so you don't have to wait for a spare weekend to go hunting for the pieces that you want to add to your collection.

AUCTION HOUSES AND ONLINE SITES

Antiques and collectibles are included in online auctions held by the major auction houses as well as in more general online auction sites. In the former the descriptions of the lots and conditions of sale should be similar to those you encounter when bidding in person at a major auction house. When using these you can also have confidence that you are dealing with the experts in the field. Online auctions at the larger, more general, websites are quite different from conventional gatherings, so they need to be treated with a little more caution. First of all, you can't examine pieces on sale closely. There may be a photo and some descriptive text, as you would find in a catalogue, but that's as near to the object as you'll get unless you make the successful bid. Secondly, an online auction is likely to run for more than one afternoon. They usually run for days and even weeks, which can be both a good and a bad thing – buyers can get cold feet and run, while sellers may be seeking buyers from elsewhere simultaneously. Finally, the buyer, seller, and lot are not all in the same physical location, which means that the process of exchanging cash for goods, and the delivery of the goods is far from simple. (We discuss how to settle up within "Tips on Using Online Auctions", opposite.)

As with regular auctions, items being sold online in an auction will often have a hidden reserve price attached, so even though you may have placed the highest bid when the auction finishes, there is no guarantee that you have been successful in purchasing it.

How an Online Auction Works

Here's how it all works, from the bidder's point of view. Goods that are available for auction are listed on the auctioneer's website and anyone can make a bid by clicking on an item and offering a sum of money for it. You will also be able to see previous bids made by other people before you make your own bid, so obviously yours should be higher than those! The details of your bid are then printed on the page, which also gives others the chance to bid against you. Auction sites have, in the past, detected people bidding for items that they are actually selling, just to push the prices up. These people face suspension from the service.

Assuming the reserve price has been met or exceeded, the auction will conclude after a set period of time and the successful bidder will be notified by email. The seller and bidder should then go about the business of making the final transaction.

And here is where the problems can start. Let us assume that the seller is an honest dealer, who genuinely owns the item on sale, and the item is in as good a condition as he/she claimed when advertising it. Does the seller live nearby? If not, will he/she deliver to you or are you expected to pick up the goods? Will the item survive the postal service? Who will arrange the insurance for the transportation of very valuable items?

Tips on Using Online Auctions

Aside from the potential for fraud, there are some very real logistical problems when using an online auction. Buyers and sellers may come from all over the world, so it's wise to establish the ground rules first before you spend too much time consolidating your funds. It is also worth finding out a bit about who you are buying from. Remember that in many cases the fine-quality, good-condition, antique furniture advertised on a website will not have been examined by an impartial expert and so may turn out to be a reproduction, suffer from woodworm, or might even be stolen. If you are not buying from an auction house, or a well-known, affiliated company, then make sure that you treat the deal as if it were a classified advert and be as suspicious as you can stand to be.

Well-run auction sites will help you, the purchaser, by providing certain guarantees that are built upon agreements between the individual dealers and the site. For example, the Sotheby's auction site, which can be found at www.sothebys.com, demands that all its authorized sellers provide full refunds should an item that they sell prove to be a fake or turn out to be in a worse condition than was advertised. Additionally, all sellers are obliged to insure all of their own items throughout the delivery process to the buyer. The authenticity guarantee also runs for three years after the auction concludes, which gives buyers plenty of time to seek verification from an outside source. It is also always worth visiting the Frequently Asked Questions (FAQs) of any online auction site as in most of these you will find advice and tips on how to get the most out of online auctions.

It goes without saying that you shouldn't send money to a stranger, because should things go wrong and you end up without your carpet/chair/vase the auctioneers probably won't help, unless their guarantees state otherwise. Some claim to run self-policing communities, where offenders are given black marks against their names, but this will be of no comfort to you once your cheque has been cashed. Some auction sites have developed schemes where you send the money to them and they release it to the seller once they know you've received the goods and are happy with them. However, this is still much more common in the US than the UK at the moment. There are such "escrow" services available from third-party sites, though, such as Auctionpix (www.auctionpix.co.uk). The buyer pays the service, which then releases the funds to the seller on successful delivery of the goods.

Here are some other useful escrow sites:
www.escrow.com
www.tradesafe.com

There are three main things that you can do on an auction site. You can bid for an item, sell an item, and track the progress of your bid or sale. In the rest of the chapter we will go through the selling and bidding processes, step by step, using Sotheby's and QXL's websites as examples. Tracking is dealt with differently by different sites. Some will send you email messages regularly while others let you monitor bidding and selling from a web page. Most actually provide both options.

BIDDING

Registering

Before you can begin bidding you will need to register at the site that you have chosen. This means that you must identify yourself and enter your address and credit card details (see Fig 15). By registering you'll be able to take part in auctions and bid for items just by clicking on a button – which can prove rather too tempting sometimes! It also means that you must be serious when making bids. If you win you'll be expected to pay, and the site already has your credit card details so there's no backing out. If you are a seller then this is obviously a good thing, because you won't suffer from pranksters messing around and making false bids on your auction.

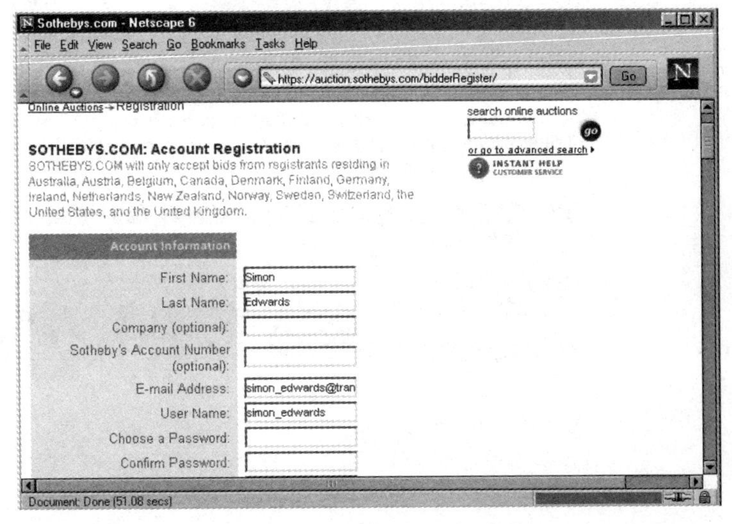

(Fig 15) Remember your password and username, but don't store them just anywhere – someone could use them to place high bids without you knowing. Keep them in a safe place, away from the computer.

Making a Bid

Before you can make a bid on the Internet, you first need to locate a site that has a piece that you are interested in buying. Most sites will allow you to browse through the lots or search for possible bargains using keywords. In this example we'll look for a nice, ancient native American artefact for my study, but we won't be too picky so we'll use the browsing option rather than search for a specific type (see Figs 16–23 and their accompanying descriptions).

(Fig 16) Click on a suitable category on the main page – in this case it will be "Ancient & Ethnographic Art". This will transport you to a virtual room in which there are auctions selling artefacts from all over the place.

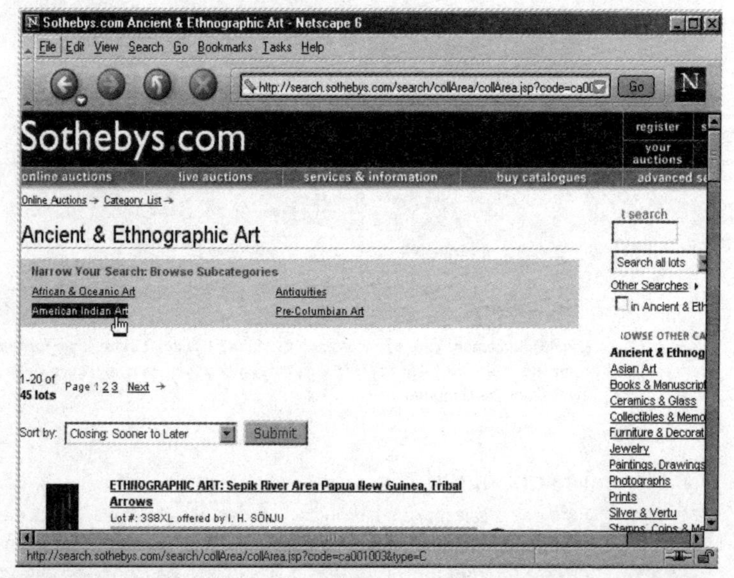

(Fig 17) There is a small selection of lots featured on the page, each showing an image of the lot and the highest bid to date, but none of them are in fact suitable for my study. At the top of the page, however, we can see some further sub-categories that may have something more appropriate. Here I've clicked on "American Indian Art".

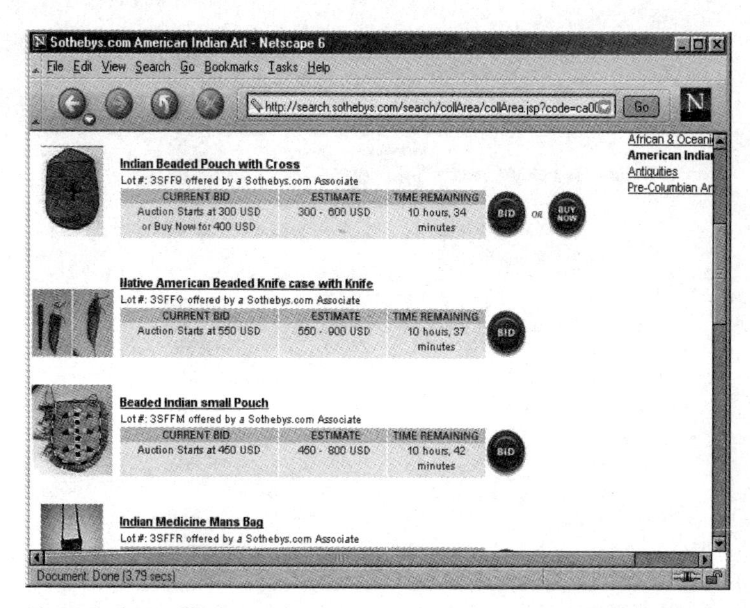

(Fig 18) That's more like it! Lots of American Indian items, some of which may fit within my budget and existing collection. With each lot you can see how much the experts believe it should fetch, how much has been bid so far, and how long the auction still has to run.

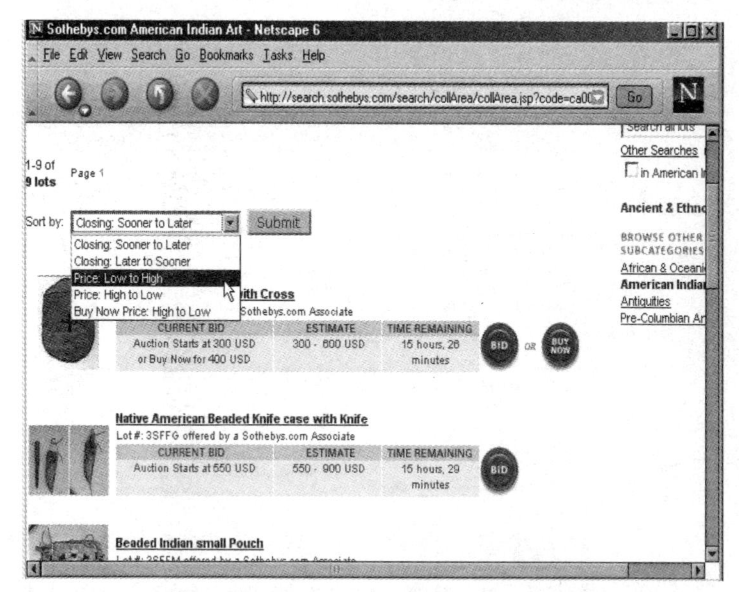

(Fig 19) You can sort the lots by different features, including bid value and auction closing date. Because I am bidding on a budget I have selected the "Price: Low to High" option. The first items I see are likely to be the least expensive, although this may not turn out to be the case once the auction has finished, of course.

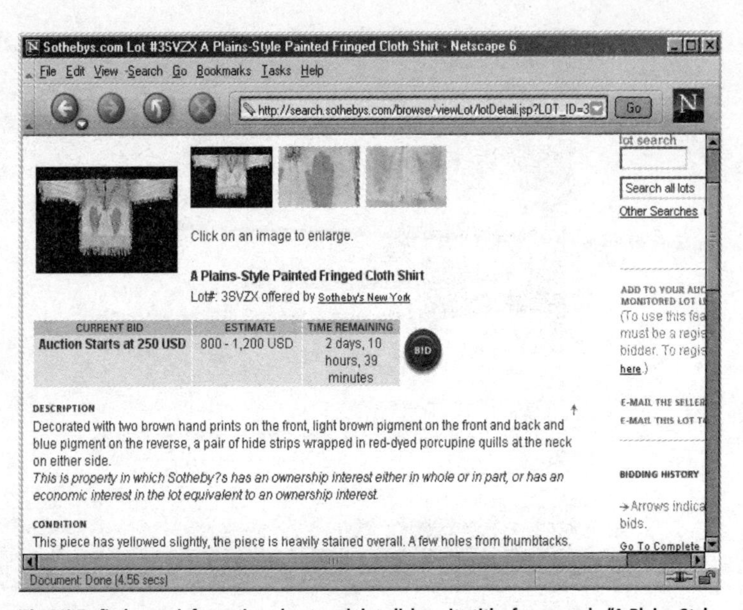

(Fig 20) To find more information about each lot click on its title, for example "A Plains-Style Painted Fringed Cloth Shirt". This takes you to a screen where you can see more detailed images and a full description. In this particular case, clicking on each picture displays a larger, clearer one from this site.

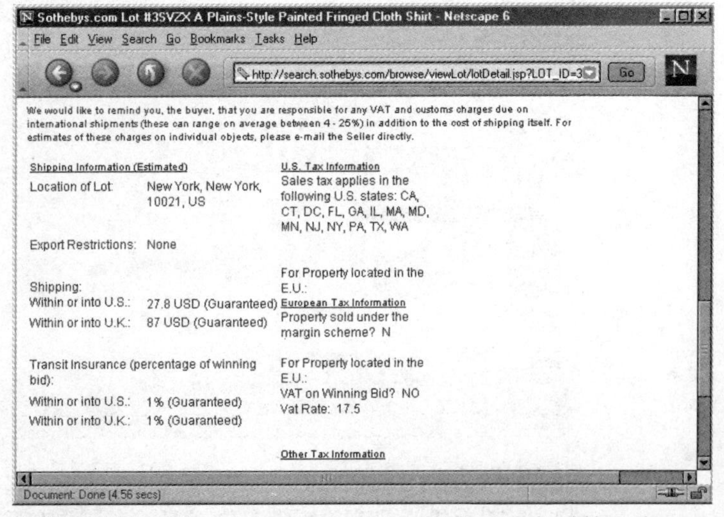

(Fig 21) The bidding history, measurements, and other details are also available on this page, as is shipping information including the location of the lot and the fees for transporting it to different countries.

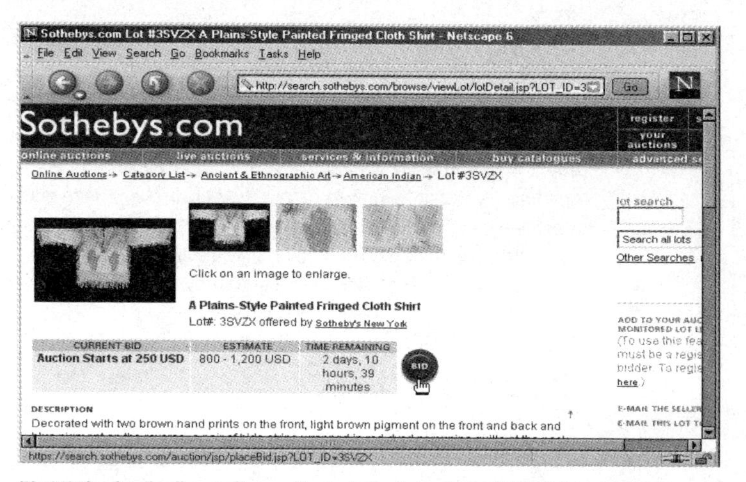

(Fig 22) The details all seem fine, so the next step is to place a bid. This is exceedingly simple to do. Just click on the Bid button beside the lot. You now have two choices: choose an amount to bid or specify the maximum amount you are prepared to bid.

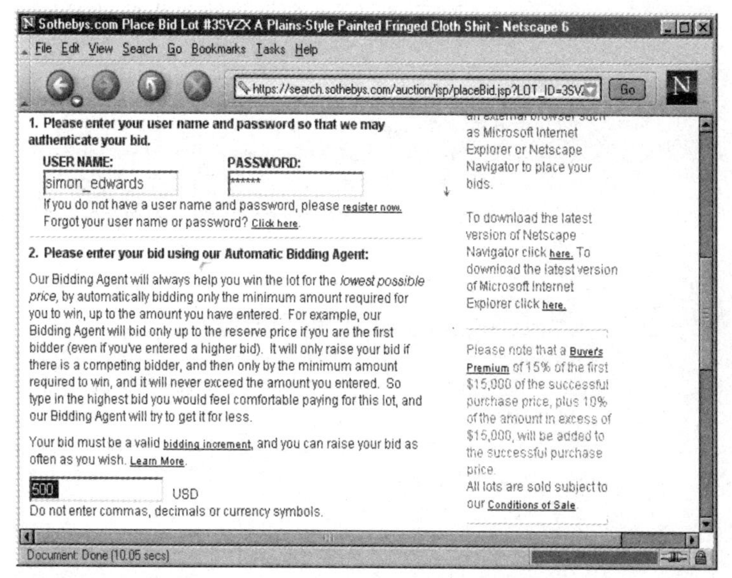

(Fig 23) If you want to keep returning to the auction over a period of hours or days, the first option of choosing a specific amount is best. However, if you won't be able to keep visiting the site, and would therefore rather the auction house bid for you, then you should choose the maximum bid option. Here, I've gone for the first option, and have placed a bid of $500. To prove that you are serious about buying the item that you have bid for, you'll have to enter your username and password. This will already have been set up when you first registered to bid with the auction site.

Tracking a Bid

Keep visiting the site to see how the auction is progressing (see Fig 24). How often you should do this really depends on the length of the auction. If it's likely to run for days and days then don't visit more than two or three times daily (unless you really want to, of course). Short auctions need more careful attention – you don't want to be out-bid because you were reading your email or making a cup of tea! If the auction site gives each auction a unique ID number then you should note down the relevant one – you'll be able to return quickly and easily from the main page to it by using the search facilities.

SELLING A PIECE

Before you can sell your own pieces on an auction site you will usually first have to register, providing your name, address, and credit card details as described previously. The reason for this is to prove that the sellers who use the Internet are responsible adults, rather than children just messing about, and to provide a safeguard against hoax sales. Most auction sites will also charge you a fee for successful auctions – the amount is usually a percentage of the sale's value.

Setting up an auction is easy and can be done very quickly. Make sure you don't rush through the process, though. Your advertisement will benefit from some careful planning. First, write a description of your item. Try to keep this reasonably short as most sites will limit the amount you can publish – 100 to 200 words should suffice. You will also need at least one picture, supplied in digital format.

Using Digital Images in Auctions

There are many different ways to turn prints into digital images. Your local photography labs can send off regular camera film or prints to be transferred to CD-ROM, or you could use a computer and scanner to create your own images. If you have access to a digital camera then so much the better. Keep shooting your piece until you get a good image of it, then download the digital picture to your computer's hard disk.

You may be surprised and disheartened to learn that not all digital images are the same. Unless you really want to get involved in the subtleties of file formats and photo editing then follow this straightforward advice – save all your pictures in JPEG format. You will have to use a photo-editing program at some point to "trim" the edges of your picture and resize it to a manageable format. The size of computer images is measured in two ways – file size and dimensions. Here's an explanation of this: we have created an auction on the

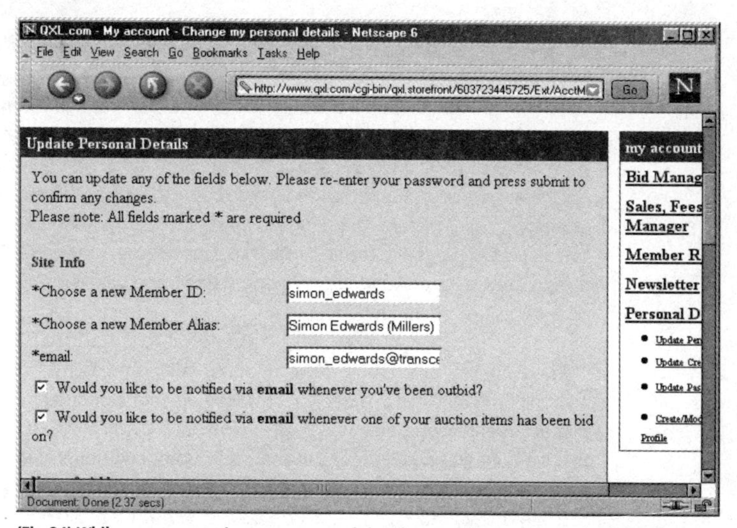

(Fig 24) While you are entering your personal details, you will also be asked a few other questions. Here I have chosen to receive email messages whenever I am outbid in an auction, and whenever someone bids on an item I am selling.

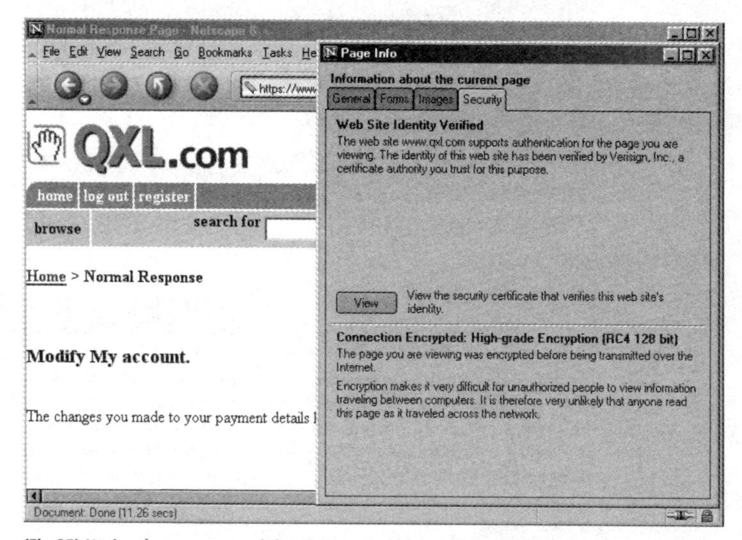

(Fig 25) Notice that my personal details have been sent to the auction site using a secure connection, to avoid casual hackers stealing credit card numbers and the like. The small yellow padlock at the bottom right part of the screen confirms this.

following pages, selling a bundle of plastic *Star Wars* figures, to explain how the auction process works. Our picture of the figures (see Fig 26), is 300 pixels wide and 300 pixels tall. (A pixel is the smallest element that a computer monitor can display.) This is a good dimensional size for use on the Internet because most people will be able to fit the image on their screen. The file containing the image takes up 9Kb of disk space – this is the file size. On the Internet, smaller pictures are generally best because they appear more quickly on people's computer screens. If we made the picture 1,000 pixels wide and 1,000 pixels tall it wouldn't fit on some screens and would also be larger, and therefore slower, to download.

There are plenty of free and low-cost photo-editing programs available, and you will probably already have one installed on your computer. You don't need to spend thousands on a professional package. In the past I've taken photographs of single items from the back, front, and underneath and used a photo-editing program to stick them all together in a montage. If your auction site only lets you upload one picture then this technique can help to show your item off to best effect.

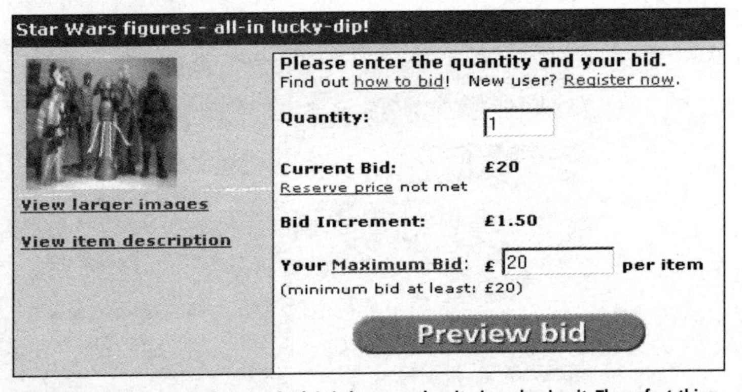

(Fig 26) If your picture looks squashed, it is because the site is reshaping it. The safest thing to do is to check an auction site first to see how other people's pictures are shaped. If they are all square then make yours square too, even if it means adding some white space to the sides or the top and bottom, as this is obviously the format that they use. Our own picture of the Star Wars figures (see Fig 33) may look small in the finished web page but clicking on it brings it up to the full size. The auction site has just created a smaller version to fit in with its page design.

The following pages explain the different stages of setting up your own online auction, using our *Star Wars* figures as the example. Follow the simple step-by-step windows shown (Figs 27–34), along with the accompanying captions that point out exactly what you should do at every stage, and you will soon be ready to create your own auction.

Creating an Auction

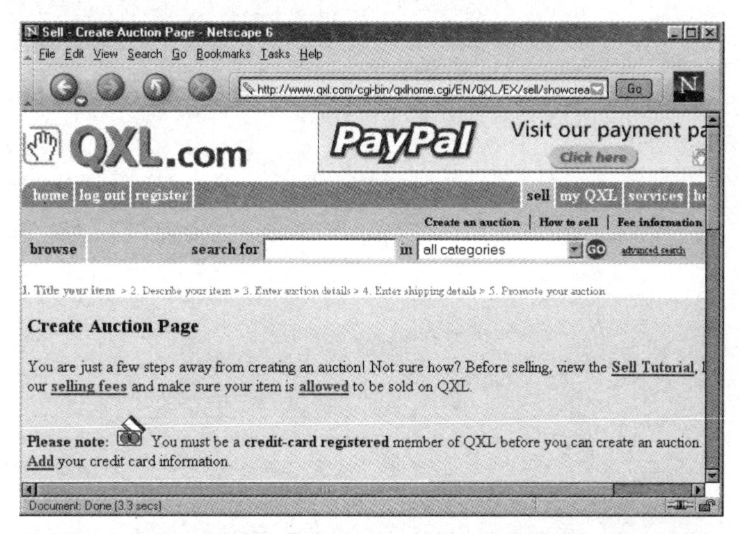

(Fig 27) Go to the part of the site where you can create new auctions (there will usually be an obvious link). At this point you should make sure you have everything you need – the words to describe your items, pictures if possible, and a clear expectation of how much you want to sell each piece for, including a reserve price.

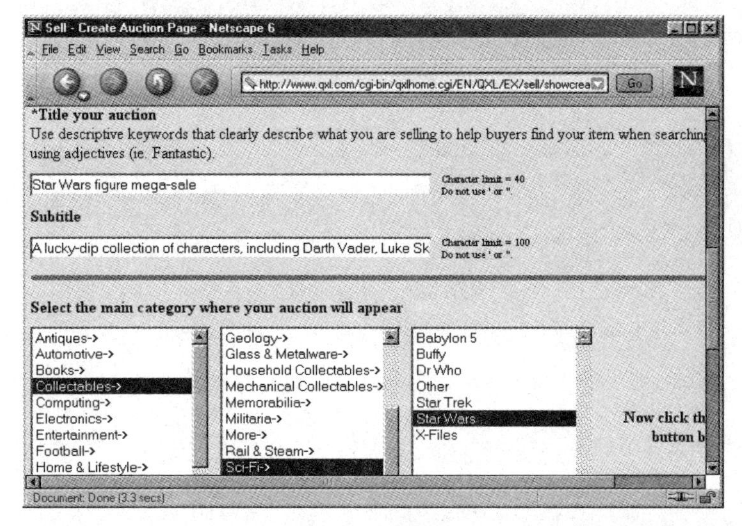

(Fig 28) Type in the details, ensuring that you don't make any typing errors. You may have an opportunity to fix things later, as they normally ask you to doublecheck the details before finally saving them, so don't panic if you do make a mistake. Choose the relevant categories for your item and others will find it easier to locate it when they visit the site.

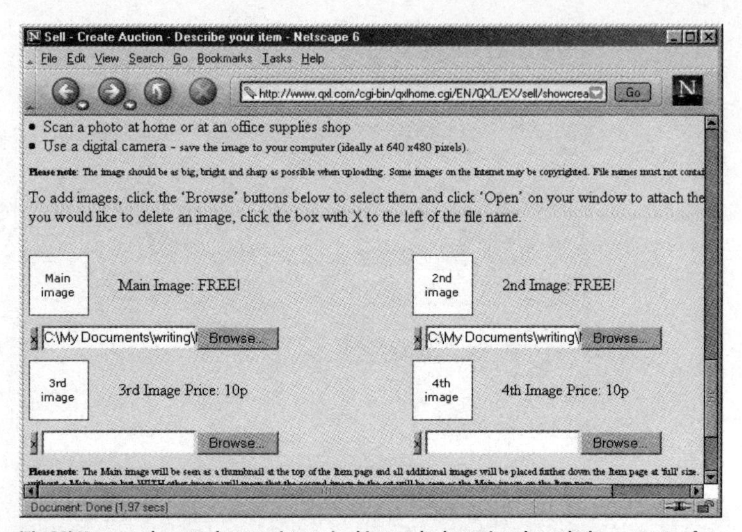

(Fig 29) You can also attach your picture, in this case by browsing through the contents of your hard disk until you find the right image. This will be sent to the auction site automatically when you finish entering the details. If you prefer, you may be able to link your auction to a photo on another website, possibly your own, which is a useful tool if you already have a site devoted to your collection.

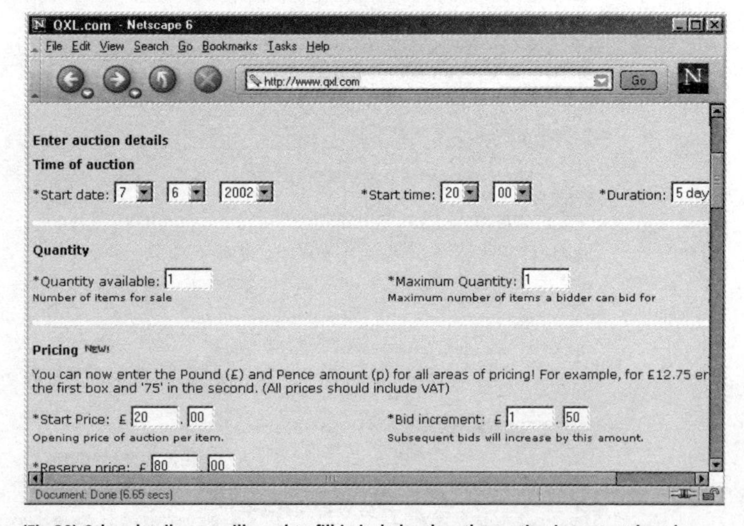

(Fig 30) Other details you will need to fill in include when the auction is to start, how long you would like it to continue for, and the starting bid. You can also set a reserve price and bidding increments, and indicate what type of payment is acceptable.

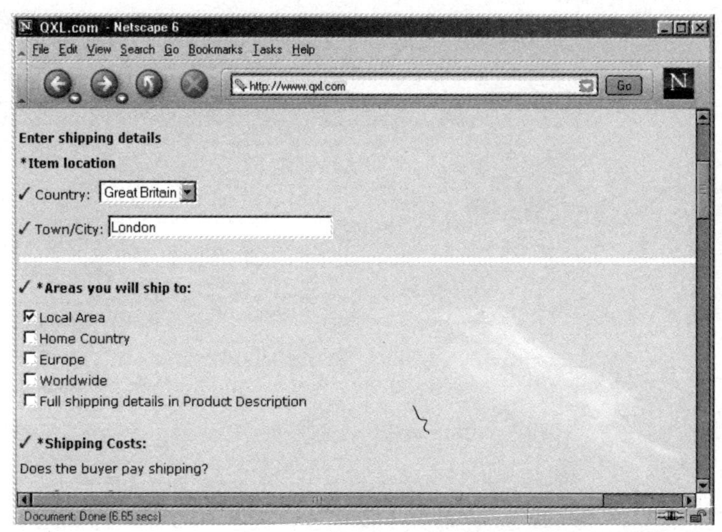

(Fig 31) When creating an auction, it is essential that you are clear about what you are taking responsibility for. On this page, you can specify shipping details such as where you will agree to ship to, and whether you or the buyer is paying the shipping costs. Don't forget your buyer could be on the opposite side of the world! After doing this, scroll down and click on the Submit button (not visible in this picture) to start the auction.

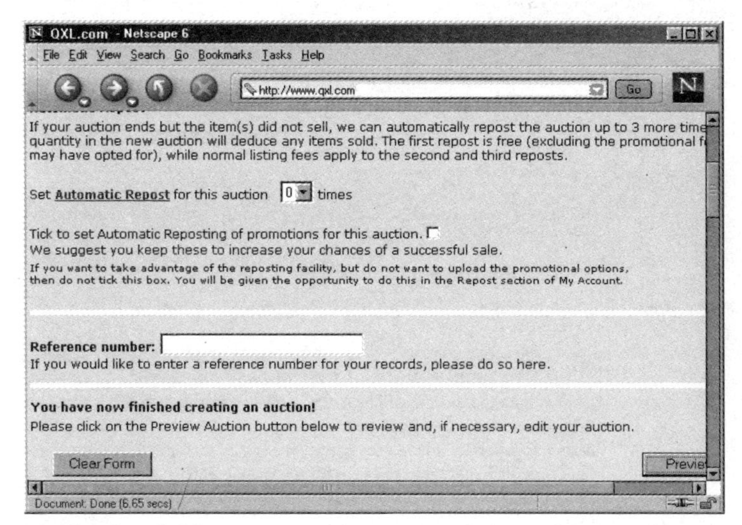

(Fig 32) At the end of the process you might come across the Automatic Repost option, which means your items can be put into further auctions if they do not sell immediately. Before you do this, make sure you are aware of what you are agreeing to in terms of fees. After confirmation of closure, you can click on an option to preview your auction.

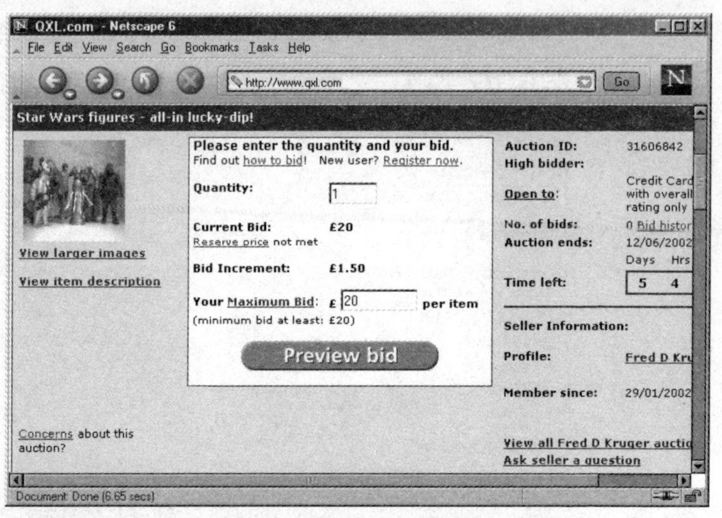

(Fig 33) The auction preview gives you a snapshot of what your potential buyers will see to tempt them to bid.

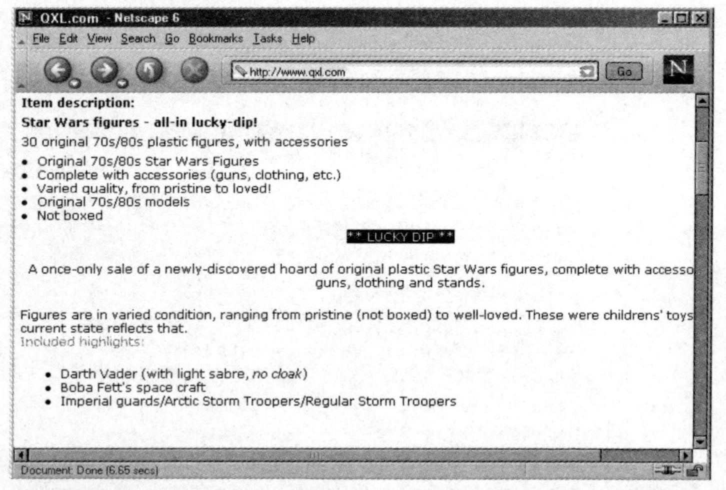

(Fig 34) Potential buyers will be greeted by a screen such as this when they click on "view item description". This illustrates how important it is to include a detailed and accurate description, particularly in very specialist areas of collecting. The more information given, the easier it should be to sell your item – include details about condition and packaging to avoid disappointment.

And there you have it – selling your item online really is straightforward. Once you have followed all these steps, the only thing that you will have left to do is to sit back and wait for the successful bid to be made!

CREATING YOUR OWN WEB PAGES

There are over a billion web pages on the Internet, and you too can make your own contribution. You can use your own home page for any number of things. You could start up a small online dealing business, publishing pictures of collectible items and including prices to allow people to order online or using the telephone. Or you could just create a personal site devoted to your collection of soda cans. The good news is, you don't have to be a computer programmer, you don't have to go to art school, and you have complete editorial control over your site's contents. This can, of course, be the bad news, too. The fact that people have the freedom to publish whatever they want accounts for quite a few badly designed and factually incorrect sites.

GETTING STARTED

To create a website you need an HTML (Hypertext Markup Language) editor program, some web space, and an FTP utility. You would use the editor to write the pages, the web space will hold your web pages in a place where other people are able to read them, and the FTP utility will move the pages from your hard disk to the web space.

It is very likely that your Internet account comes complete with some web space. The amount you have been allocated will, to some extent, affect what you can do but, because web pages take up very little space, even 1Mb will be enough for most people. Some ISPs allow as much as 200Mb or even an unlimited amount. If you don't have access to a web server, you can use one of the many free web space services available. Geocities (www.geocities.com) and Tripod (www.tripod.com) are popular choices.

You probably have an HTML editor too. Netscape's Internet package comes with a program called Composer, while Microsoft's Internet Explorer 5.0 includes FrontPage Express. Both programs can be used in much the same way as a word processor. You will find that you can resize and colour text, insert pictures, and save files. You can create links between pages, files, and even other websites. But if you find the features are too limited, you can buy commercial programs that offer much more and make designing a large site easier. If you are using a very up-to-date version of Windows or Internet Explorer you may not be able to find FrontPage Express on your computer. In this case, download and use a free package such as Amaya, available from www.w3.org/Amaya. Even professional web designers use these packages, although some prefer the expensive options such as Dreamweaver or FrontPage 2000.

What Does it all Mean?

HTML documents are a mixture of instructions for the computer and text for the website. The instructions for the computer are known as "tags" and are written within brackets, such as the word <TITLE>. When you look at an HTML document for the first time it may all seem totally incomprehensible, but the following explanations should help you understand what is what.

HTML documents start with the <html> tag and end with </html>. The text surrounded by the <title> and </title> tags appears at the very top of your web browser. The <body> and </body> tags denote the main contents of the page, which may include text, graphics, and other design elements.

Main headings are surrounded with the <h1> and </h1> tags. Different headings can be added using <h2>, <h3>, and so on up to <h6>. Paragraphs start and end with <p> and </p> respectively.

Links to other pages, websites, and so on are defined by the <a href> tag. To add in a link you will need to use the following: "<a href = "www.your link goes in here">" and you must close the relevant text with </a>. Graphics are inserted using the <img src> tag.

It's all very simple really – you will just need to spend some time getting used to the tagging system when you first start creating your own web pages. If you can't be bothered with all this technical jargon, FrontPage Express, Composer and Amaya will let you create pages quickly and simply, in much the same way as you'd write a letter in a word processor.

ORGANIZING YOUR WEB PAGES

Try to name your pages logically and keep images, files, and other elements in separate folders. This will make constructing your site easier, and you will have fewer problems with conflicting file names. For example, a file that contained details of your collection of stamps could be called "stamps.htm" and stored in a folder called "collections". Another file about Beanie Babies would be called something like "beanies.htm" but would still be stored in the "collections" folder. Alternatively, name each file "details.htm" and store one in a folder called "stamps" and the other in a folder called "beanies". Add another folder called "images" to each main folder and you've created a logical place to store digital images of your collection (see Fig 35). Always use lower case when naming files to avoid confusion and broken links.

Once you become more experienced you may want to look at the HTML code contained in the pages you have created. You can use any text editor, like Notepad or SimpleText, to open the files and change small details. There are many guides to writing in HTML available on the web. It is often a good idea

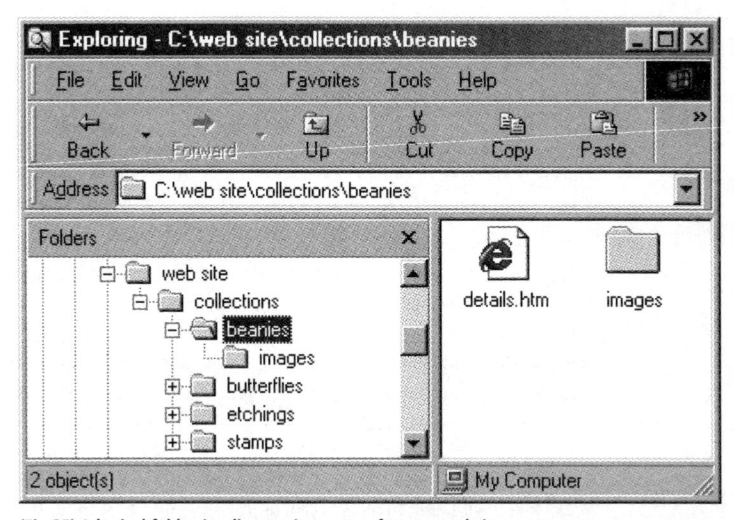

(Fig 35) A logical folder (or directory) structure for your website.

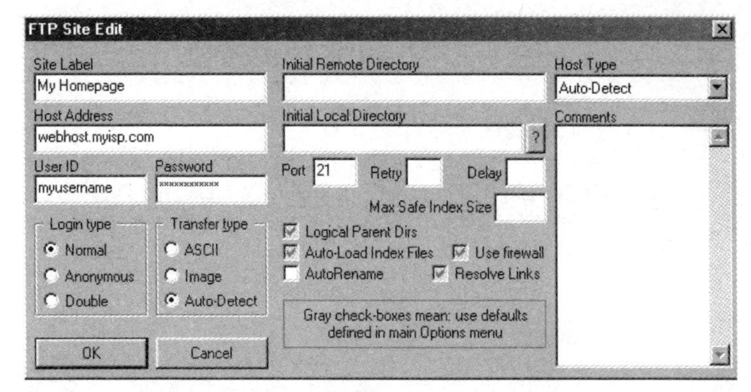

(Fig 36) Enter the details provided by your ISP to connect to your web space.

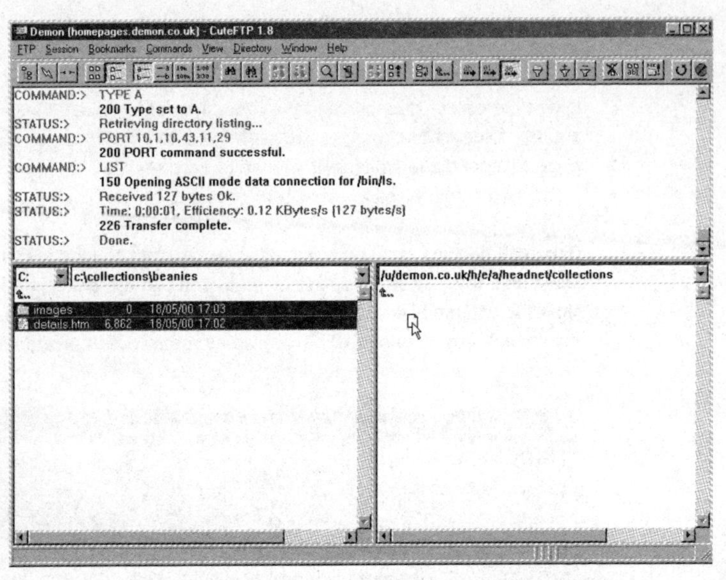

(Fig 37) Drag your files across to the website to make them available worldwide.

to use an authoring program like FrontPage to do most of the hard work, and then use a text editor to add extra bits in afterwards.

The pages will sit on your hard disk until you copy them to your web space. Test them thoroughly before sending them off as nothing looks more amateurish than spelling mistakes or pictures that are missing because of a broken link. Then use an FTP program to connect to your ISP's web server (see Figs 36–7). You will need your username, password, and the FTP server's address – all of these will have been provided by your Internet Service Provider (ISP).

A FEW DESIGN POINTS

Page Size

Remember that not everyone has the same-sized screen. If you design your pages using a large monitor running at a high resolution, your pages may appear mangled to someone with a smaller screen. It is generally accepted that pages should work with at least a resolution of 800 x 600 pixels.

Colours

Don't assume that everyone will be able to view full colour. If you use a colour palette containing the standard 256 colours you can be sure that everyone will see the same thing. Ideally you should switch your computer's display down when testing the site in order to identify any horrible clashes. (There is seldom a good reason to make your pages any colour other than white. If you really feel the need, at least restrict yourself to light colours, or your readers will have a hard time.)

Tables

Use tables to create sophisticated layouts. You can nest tables inside other tables to achieve almost any grid you desire. This is one of the few ways you can dictate how a page will look on other people's screens. A table-less page will change whenever a reader resizes the browser window.

Frames

Intelligent use of frames can revolutionize a website, making it very easy to use (see glossary on page 276 for an explanation of what frames are). Use frames to provide navigational tools, such as a toolbar, that remain in view all the time. However, remember that it is easy to go overboard with frames – try to keep your design simple.

Styles

Use cascading style sheets to control the look of your entire site with just one or two files. A single change to a style sheet can alter the colour, font type, and/or general layout of every page instead of you having to trawl through and make the changes wherever they occur. If you are planning to create a large site, such style sheets are essential.

Scripts

Programs, often known as CGI scripts, may be provided by your ISP to give extra features to your site. These will usually include a counter that shows how many visitors the site has had. If you are lucky you may also have a search facility. Each ISP uses different scripts and will be able to provide instructions on how to include them on your site.

Graphics

Use a graphics program to create and edit images for your site. You can use pictures to create buttons, photo albums, and even text banners. Use the GIF format to create images that don't need full colour and should therefore load quickly. Use JPEG for full-colour photos. If you are publishing lots of photos, you could use small, fast GIF files to show preview shots, and have visitors click on them to load the larger, more detailed JPEG files.

Browsers

Not every web browser shows pages in the same way. Test your site using as many different browsers as you can, and iron out the bugs before you publish the files.

USING YOUR WEB PAGES

Creating your own, basic website is relatively easy but you could devote all of your free time to messing around with the design and forget about the purpose of it! Once it's up and working, spend some time ironing out the bugs and design elements – but don't become obsessed. There will always be things to do, so draw the line early on. Below are a few sites that should help you do your final checks and keep on top of the world of HTML.

Once your website is up and running, use the articles at Webreview.com (www.webreview.com) to fine-tune its design and make sure everyone can use it, regardless of which browser they use.

For an excellent beginner's guide to HTML try the National Center for Supercomputing Applications (www.ncsa.uiuc.edu/Indices/Resources/html-resources.html). It also features more advanced articles to help you progress once you've mastered your first simple web page.

Keep up-to-date with all the issues surrounding the web, including its history and future, by visiting the World Wide Web Consortium site (www.w3c.org). There are also articles about mobile access, HTML, and style sheets within it.

Selling from your website can be as easy or complicated as you want to make it. You can list items along with pictures on normal, free, or low-cost web space or, at the other end of the scale, run an online store with credit-card handling facilities and order-tracking. The latter option is a library of books in itself and requires a substantial business investment. However, you can get halfway there using so-called "e-commerce hosting". Such services, including the likes of Intershop (www.intershop.com), provide an off-the-shelf online shop that you populate with your goods. An increasing number of ISPs are including such services for a fee with their standard home-user accounts. The more features you want (including storage space, search engines, and credit-card handling), the more expensive it will be. Ask your ISP about which e-commerce features they can provide or use one of the many directories, such as HostIndex.com (www.hostindex.com), to find an alternative supplier.

GENERAL INFORMATION SITES

This section lists the best general sites that offer services to people interested in antiques, art, and collectibles. For ease of use, the subject areas have been divided alphabetically here. Trade associations from around the world provide added confidence for buyers and often list member directories on their sites with hyperlinks so that you can contact them instantly. Many popular magazines and newspapers also have an online version, which allows easy access across the continents to articles and other resource material. Museum sites offer a cornucopia of history from Egypt to Korea, China to Greece, and Kenya to France, allowing a virtual world tour of the very best of decorative arts, antiques, and artefacts. Buying and selling are the cornerstones of the antiques trade and within this section you will find the top auction houses, antiques centres, and fairs all listed. This allows you to keep in touch with what is on offer across the globe. Many of these sites offer practical information on transport and accommodation to help you visit their physical site, as well as providing additional links to related areas. Use the site maps to get the most out of what is on offer. Here you will find sites that search every auction catalogue and site for a particular item, give insurance information, locate stolen items, and much more. Museums, auctions, and associations that are very specifically related to one area of the antiques world have been placed in "Specialist Sites" (see pages 127–275) so check out the relevant section there too.

ANTIQUES CENTRES

Alfies Antique Market

www.ealfies.co.uk

Situated in a former department store, Alfies is London's largest indoor antiques market, housing 150 dealers. Its website lists them all, giving potted histories of the dealers and showing samples of their stock. There is also visitor information as well as links to the sites of various dealers, the *Antiques Trade Gazette*, and the trade association LAPADA (see pages 117–22 for other trade associations).

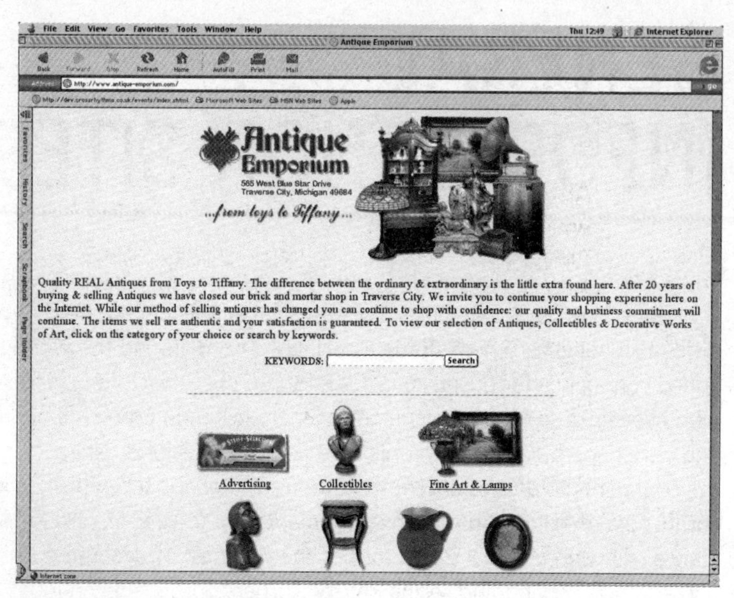

The Antique Emporium's shop is now closed but you can still buy a wealth of antiques online.

Antique Centre on the Web

www.antiquecenteronline.com

Stock on this online centre is monitored daily and regularly updated. Items for sale are listed by categories, which include some of the more esoteric collecting fields, such as pocket knives and chocolate moulds. There is a separate area for trade customers, for which registration and a password are required.

Antique Emporium

www.antique-emporium.com

This antique shop was based in Michigan, USA, but has now closed its physical doors and only does business online. The items on the site are categorized into antiques, collectibles, and decorative works of art and all you have to do is click on a category to get the listing of the available objects (which includes sporting goods, silver, textiles, and jewellery etc). Each of these is accompanied by an illustration and comprehensive description and if you buy from this site you will get a guarantee. The full name, email address, and telephone number of each dealer is provided on the site.

Antique Markets

www.marketantique.com

Three large antiques centres, all based in Massachusetts, USA, are represented on this large site, which covers a total of 225 dealers. Each centre has a map and/or directions, a phone number, and information about handicap accessibility for people who wish to visit in person. The site also provides a useful "wish list", where you can sign up and list what you are looking for; the individual dealers will contact you when they find the item. If you are an exhibiting dealer, you can access your sales using a password.

Antiques Associates at West Townsend

www.aaawt.com

This antiques centre's web page features a gallery that displays items within some unusual categories such as "Political/Historical" and "Western/Indian", as well as the more typical metalware, lighting, porcelain, and toys/dolls. The gallery items are displayed with their retail prices. The dealers rent space in the shop, based in West Townsend, Massachusetts, USA. You can telephone or email for further information on the items shown, which are covered by a guarantee for safe shopping.

Antiques Marketplace

www.antiquesmarketplace.com

This is the site of a large multi-dealer shop based in Putnam, Connecticut. The site contains pictures of the shop itself, but does not list specific merchandise for sale. However, there is a link to ebay for the auctions that the store runs there, as well as links to sites of the dealers that have stands in the shop, where these are available. The site also gives directions to the town and there is a map of local conveniences and restaurants.

Belper Antiques

www.belperantiques.ndirect.co.uk

This antiques centre in Tutbury in the East Midlands, UK, boasts 25 years' experience of retail experience in antiques and collectibles. It stocks a particularly good range of Denby pottery, among other antiques. The online Internet Gallery hosts a selection of the items in stock, from lorgnettes to commode seats. You can make purchases by email, phone, or fax, either by American Express or by posting a cheque.

Chappells and The Bakewell Antiques and Collectors Centre

www.chappells-antiques.co.uk

The site of this leading British antiques centre features lots of pictures of stock from its dealers. Quality furniture is much in evidence, but other stock, including silver, ceramics, and paintings, can also be seen. Descriptions are given, and include prices. If you want further information about any of the items, there is an online request form.

Circline

www.circline.com

Billed as "The First Global Gallery", Circline is effectively an online centre with an impressive tally of stock from more than a thousand of the world's top dealers. It concentrates on the high end of the market, and you can browse through a vast online selection that's definitely not for the bargain hunter. Prices are in US dollars, and many of these are in five figures. A sophisticated search engine helps you to narrow your search and all items have a "no quibble" guarantee. Anyone can take a look at the stock but you must register (free of charge) to buy, and payment is not accepted over the Internet (must be done via mail or fax).

Facets Antique and Collectibles Mall

www.facets.net

This antiques centre is based in Florida and its site includes 21 online shops (with dealers from various locations) that specialize in Depression-era glassware, porcelain, pottery, bedroom/bathroom accessories, jewellery, and other ephemera. Each vendor has their own ordering system but most accept credit cards and have an online order form. A link to the Contemporary Carnival Glass website provides many articles as well as listings of other manufacturers of glass from the 1950s through to today's glass. Over 250 links are categorized on this site, and it is worth a visit just for these.

The Ginnel and The Red House Antiques Centres

www.theginnel.co.uk

Not one, but two centres, both located in Yorkshire in the north of England, are featured on this site. The Ginnel and The Red House are home to approximately 50 and 60 dealers respectively, and these offer a rich mix of antiques. The site has pictures of the showrooms, but not of individual items of stock, and you cannot buy online. There is, however, a link to sales on ebay. The site also lists participating dealers and their specialities, and there's information on forthcoming lectures taking place at the centres.

The Internet Antique Store

www.tias.com

An online antiques centre claiming to have the Internet's largest catalogue of antiques and collectibles, this site offers you a choice of over 500,000 items, mostly with pictures. There are dealers in most collecting fields, and you can search for items by category, dealer, or keyword before buying directly online.

The Manhattan Art and Antiques Center

www.the-maac.com

This is the site of a large centre in Manhattan, USA, and it lists all the participating dealers alphabetically, providing links to their websites where these are available. Dealers are also listed by category, so that you can look up the subject area that you are particularly interested in and find out which dealers have relevant stock. Galleries feature items for sale from selected dealers – you cannot buy these directly from this site, but the pictures and descriptions are good. However, some of the dealers will have items for sale via their own website, others use the site to show a representation of their merchandise, while some have a link to their own sales on ebay. You can also download a video tour of the centre.

Marchés Serpette/Paul Bert

www.franceantiq.fr/serpette/uk.htm

A French antiques centre/market whose site offers a virtual tour through the stands and stock of its 400-plus dealers. Consult an alphabetical list of dealers, or click on an aisle to see whose stands are featured there, and what kind of stock they have. Most popular collecting fields are represented on this site.

Old Saybrook Antiques Center

www.oldsaybrookantiques.com

This centre is two miles from the Antiques Depot (see page 51). There are two other large antiques centres in the area as well, although neither has a website. This antique mall houses 125 dealers and the site shows examples of the furniture you can buy there, although you can't purchase online. There is also a room with showcases featuring "smalls" ranging from pewter and English pottery of the 18th and 19th centuries to American art glass and Oriental antiques. Prices are listed and payment may be made by cheque or credit card. There are links to sites that provide currency exchange, ebay, *Antiques and the Arts Weekly* (see specialist publications, page 112), and Antique Searcher (see resource and gateway sites, page 103).

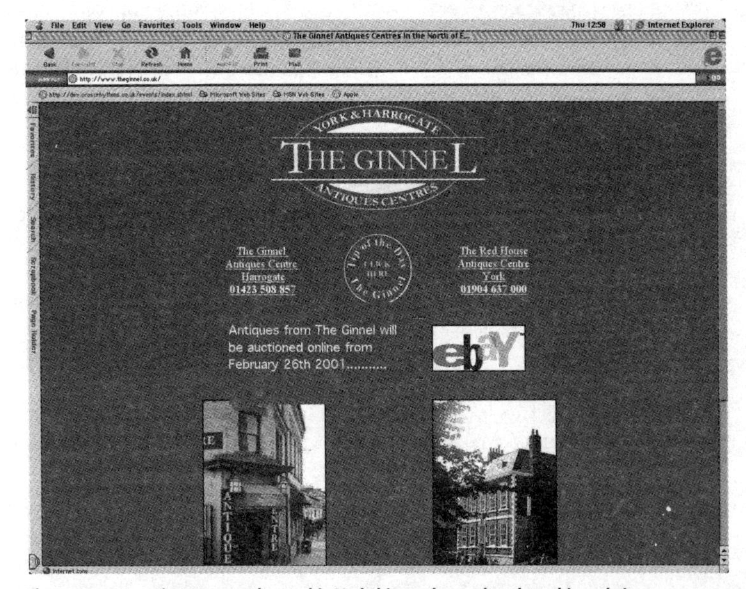

There are two antique centres located in Yorkshire to be explored on this website.

There are 60 shops to be found within this Tennessee centre, each with their own listing.

Palladio International Antique Market

www.palladioantiques.com

This is the online site of a market based in Memphis, Tennessee, USA. The market consists of more than 60 shops stocked by 45 dealers and each exhibitor has a listing with a picture of their shop online. There are items for sale at each shop and you can order via email or telephone. There are also links to some of the dealers' websites where available. A "Supply Shop" offers material to care for and display your antique purchases, such as plate holders, waxes, and polishes.

Regina Antiques

www.reginaantiques.com

Regina Antiques is based in western Canada, and houses 28 dealers offering antiques and collectibles of various kinds. Furniture, glassware, and ceramics are among the specialities, but other collecting fields represented include books and comics, clothing, and telephones. Online stock is arranged in the form of "classified ads", with descriptions and prices in Canadian dollars. You must send an email for further details or purchasing information.

Showcase Antique Center

www.showcaseantiques.com

This is the site of an antiques centre based in Old Sturbridge Village, Massachusetts, and it has items for sale in over 200 categories, which cover most areas of antiques and collectibles. Online purchases can be made using a credit card. This centre takes large ads each month in the *Maine Antique Digest* (see specialist publications, page 116), and all of the items from the ads are illustrated in colour and described in detail online. A nice feature is that updates for each sale category are dated, so that you can instantly tell how recent the listings are.

Slegers Antique Centre

www.slegers-antiques.com

There are more than 60 dealers at this trade-only Belgian centre, whose website shows a large selection of their stock. Online ordering is not an option, but you can send them an email requesting further details. Continental furniture is their particular speciality.

The Swan Antiques Centre

www.theswan.co.uk

This centre is set in the Cotswolds, in prime English antiques-hunting country. It is located in a former inn that dates back to the 15th century – a painted beam from that era, discovered during renovation work, is shown on the site. There is also an online catalogue with a small selection of current stock with prices, though you cannot buy online. The centre hosts regular talks by well-known speakers and you can find information on forthcoming events here. There is also a link to a celebrated Raymond Blanc restaurant for any gourmets thinking of visiting the area.

Sydney Antique Centre

www.sydantcent.com.au

Australia's oldest and largest centre, the Sydney Antique Centre is home to over 50 dealers. Its website keeps visitors up-to-date with changes, including any new dealers that join. The site shows a selection of stock accompanied by a thorough commentary on the type of items offered by specific dealers, rather than descriptions of individual pieces.

Tri-State Antique Center

www.tri-stateantiques.com

Even if you do not like vintage and mid-century modern antiques, this is a site worth visiting for the graphics and set-up alone. The introduction shows the shop's specialities tumbling and twirling about the screen in bright colours against a black background. You can also take a virtual tour of the shop, which is based in Pittsburgh, Pennsylvania. On the home page you can click on different areas to bring up available items in each category. The specialities of the centre are mid-century modern design furniture, accessories, vintage purses, and antique dolls. There are multiple listings for each category, and all prices include shipping. Purchases can be made online through a secure shopping cart service by credit card, by i-check (a secure online cheque service), or by fax (using your credit card). There are links to other antiques and collectibles sites, as well as a direct link to Barnes & Noble.

The Victory Theatre Antique Centre

www.bluemts.com.au/victory

The Victory Theatre Antique Centre is situated in Australia's Blue Mountains, to the west of Sydney. Consequently, the site promises stunning scenery as well as antiques to those who visit in person. But if you can't make the trip, then you can shop from an online store that includes jewellery, porcelain, books, silver, musical instruments, and "Australiana".

Windsor House Antiques Centre

www.windsorhouse.co.uk

The site of this UK antiques centre, which specializes in antique clocks, metalware, porcelain, paintings, and furniture, features information about the area where it is located (the Cotswolds) and includes photos of the centre and a map. There are good pictures of the showrooms, which give an indication of the quality of items to be found here. A gallery of stock has few accompanying details, but further information is available via email.

WORTH A LOOK

www.cvvm.com/Antiques/atiq.htm
The site of a Canadian centre in British Columbia.

www.paulallisonantiques.co.uk
The site of a sizeable antiques centre in the north of England.

www.otfordantiques.co.uk
An historic centre in southeast England.

www.rollermills.com
One of America's largest centres, boasting 400 dealers.

www.yorkantiquescentre.co.uk
Two centres from the north of England are featured online here.

AUCTIONS

AAAC

www.aaac.com.au

AAAC stands for Albion Antique Auction Centre, which is an online auction house based in Brisbane, Australia. Anyone can browse through the items on offer, but free online registration gives you the chance to consign or bid. Vendors pay a flat fee per item listed, plus a percentage of the final selling price.

Afinsa

www.afinsaportugal.com

Stamps and coins are among the specialities of this Portuguese auction house, which also offers a variety of art and antiques. Sale information is included on the site and also offers "fixed price" sales online – order via email.

Amazon

www.amazon.com
www.amazon.co.uk

Amazon are best known for their online book sales, but their site now offers much more, including antiques auctions and online shops. The addresses given here are for the main US site and its UK version, which are similar, but have slightly modified content – for example, the UK site might highlight sales of memorabilia relating to British sporting heroes. There is a search facility and you can pay by credit card, but must register (for free) to buy or sell through here.

Anderson and Garland

www.andersonandgarland.com

Based in the northeast of England, this auction house has been in business since 1840. The site has a news section, which shows off some recent saleroom successes, and you can view catalogues of forthcoming sales. Full terms and conditions are shown on the site, and there is an online form for any feedback.

Andrew Hartley Fine Arts

www.andrewhartleyfinearts.co.uk

Request an email condition report or digital images of lots coming up for sale on this UK auctioneer's website. You can subscribe to hard copies of the catalogues or browse through searchable online versions. An extensive list of FAQs should answer most queries, and there's an entertaining company history too.

Auction Consult

www.auctionconsult.com

This French site, available in English, offers access to the country's auctioneers through listings and links to their websites. Auction houses around the world are also listed. Information on the site includes recent sale prices, forthcoming sales calendars, and absentee bid forms. You can also search for items by date, subject, auctioneer, or artist.

Auction Guide

www.auctionguide.com

As its name suggests, this is a guide to auctions, both live and online. You can search for auctioneers specializing in any of a large number of categories such as militaria, stamps, or toys, and there's a directory of auctioneers on every continent. The directory gives a brief description of each auctioneer listed, and provides a link to their website, as well as an indication of whether they offer online buying and selling.

Auction Hammer

www.auctionhammer.co.uk

This site offers a listing of more than 2,500 auctions and salerooms in the UK. There is a search engine and the site also features a free listing section for collectors' clubs, as well as a listing of antique centres. Salerooms can be viewed online according to their geographic location.

Auction Hunter

www.auctionhunter.com

This site provides a search service for auctions in northeastern USA. Auctions are listed in categories covering antiques, jewellery, and collectibles, building material, real estate, stamps and coins, computers, etc. The site is updated weekly, and shows partial listings for each auction as well as website links where available. A form is available for auctioneers to place a listing on the site, and there is also information provided for advertisers.

Auction Port

www.auctionport.com

Registered users at this online auction site can receive email notification of chosen items as they come up for sale and can also obtain online valuations for a fee. Whether you are registered or not, you can also use the search engine that is provided to find items on offer, or, alternatively, just browse through the items that are for sale. Sellers at the auctions pay a commission on any sold items.

Auction Watch

www.auctionwatch.com

Search through hundreds of online auction sites at once with this site. Type in a keyword to find all items matching the description on a multitude of online sites. You can also register your account information here so you can launch, track, monitor, and manage all your online auction accounts from one place. This is a very useful site indeed.

BBR

www.bbrauctions.co.uk

This UK firm of auctioneers specializes in collectibles from Doulton figures to breweriana, pot lids, bottles, and kitchenalia. The site also features a full auction calendar and a selection of books for sale. You can also find out about the *BBR* magazine, but will need to email them if you wish to subscribe to it. Alternatively, just browse through a selection of classified ads online.

Bernaerts

www.auction-bernaerts.com

This Belgian auction house, whose site can be read in English, French, and Dutch, offers complete online illustrated catalogues as well as a news section, which analyses the results of recent sales. The auctioneers are especially strong on Old Masters, 19th- and 20th-century art, books, prints, and tribal art. Search the site, then email for further details of any items of interest .

Biddle & Webb

www.biddleandwebb.co.uk

This British auction house holds more than 40 specialist sales per year, and you will find full details of them on this website. Catalogues can be viewed online, or send an email to be sent hard copies. The site also has information on the company's various services, including house clearances and valuations.

Bonhams

www.bonhams.com

Now that this major London firm of auctioneers has merged with part of Phillips (see page 72), it is the third-largest auction house in the world. Its website offers an auction schedule for the next three months, recent sales results, the ability to download entire catalogues, and much more. You can leave a bid on lots in forthcoming auction sales, or take part in special online auctions. You must first register to be able to do either of these, but to do so is free of charge. You must also register if you wish to track the progress of specific lots of interest in a sale or to request condition reports on them.

Brightwells Auctioneers and Valuers

www.brightwells.com

This regional UK auctioneer holds specialist sales in such categories as militaria, antiquarian books, ceramics and glass, and musical instruments, as well as fine art and effects. Their website includes a calendar of forthcoming sales. You cannot actually bid online, but you can purchase their catalogues via email.

Bukowski

www.bukowski.fi

This major Scandinavian auction house offers an intriguing history of the company – it was established by a Polish nobleman – as well as details of

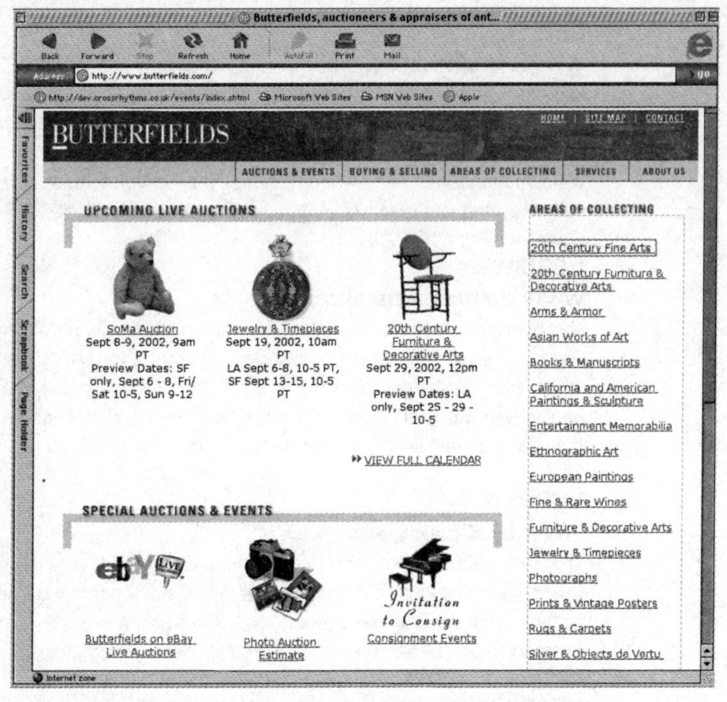

Butterfields' upcoming auctions are all detailed and illustrated on this site.

forthcoming sales. Sales results are included on the site and you can also browse through online catalogues, or order a hard copy. If you wish to buy anything, written bids can be submitted via email.

Butterfields

www.butterfields.com

This US site includes full and detailed descriptions of upcoming auctions, with illustrations. The auction company, which is actually owned by ebay, has links to ebay's collections (see page 63). There are good descriptions for beginners on how to bid at auction and what the terms used in auctions are. There are also links to fellow members of IA (International Auctioneers), which is a network of six international auction companies (see page 68).

Campo & Campo

www.come.to/campo

A virtual tour of the salerooms, featuring images of the auction galleries, is one of the features of the site of this Belgian auction house. You will also find a company history, details of forthcoming sales, and recent results. You can also order their catalogues via email.

Cannon & Cannon

www.cannons.co.za

This is the site of a South African auctioneer specializing in South African art and antique furniture and collectibles. You can download catalogues and submit email bids on any items of interest here. There's also a newsletter and you can fill in an online request form for further information, or to be kept informed of future auctions.

Charterhouse

www.charterhouse-auctions.co.uk

Illustrated online versions of sale catalogues and previews of forthcoming auction sales are the main features of this UK auctioneer's site. There's also news from the saleroom and a full list of the auctioneers' terms and conditions of sale, but you cannot bid online. The site also includes details of how to get to the salerooms, including local travel and accommodation information.

Cheffins

www.cheffins.co.uk

This website, of a firm of UK auctioneers based in Cambridge, offers searchable online catalogues and results of recent sales. Regular antiques and collectibles sales are featured at this saleroom, and some highlights of antique decorative items from these sales are included on the site. Another feature is the chance to obtain a valuation. Send your details via email, and a consultant will contact you to arrange an appointment to view your valuables.

Christie's

www.christies.com

A virtual tour of Christie's Paris premises, offering a 360° view of each room, is one of the features of the site of the world's second-largest auction house. You can also read articles from Christie's magazine, *Living with Art*, and find detailed information on forthcoming sales. There are special features on important items coming up for sale, and there's also a "lot finder" service that allows you to search by keyword for items coming up for sale at Christie's.

Corbitts

www.corbitts.com

Corbitts are specialist stamp, coin, and medal auctioneers based in the northeast of England. Their website features their forthcoming and most recent catalogues. Bids are accepted via email, and there is a bidding form provided on the site, but you will have to provide references if you are not already known to the firm.

Crayford Auctions UK

www.crayfordauctions.demon.co.uk

This site features an extensive gallery of items sold in previous auctions as well as items from forthcoming sales. Collectors can also register their interests by email to be notified of items as they come in, and to receive details of forthcoming sales. Crayford sell some items through online auctions such as ebay, and a link to their member's page on that particular site is provided.

Criterion Auctioneers

www.criterion-auctioneers.co.uk

This is the website of a London auction house that offers 500-lot sales every week. An online catalogue is hosted by icollector.com (see page 108) and you will find selected results of the sales, with pictures, on the Criterion site. The site features details of the firm's valuation services, and free informal valuations are available via email. There's full information on sale dates and viewing times for those who can visit the salerooms in person.

Cromwells

www.cromwells.com.au

This Australian auction house now incorporates the Wemyss auction firm and holds regular sales covering 40 different collecting categories, from animation cels (artwork for cartoons) and toys to model railways, books, clocks, and watches. Browse through their catalogues of recent and forthcoming sales, and find information on items for sale through online auctions. The site also offers online valuations – email a picture of your object and you will receive a "pre-sale estimate" by return of email and details of the next suitable sale in which to sell your item.

Cyr Auction Company

www.cyrauction.com

This US auctioneer from Gray, Maine, specializes in American antiques and folk art, and also has estate auctions. The schedule is posted online, and includes listings of the items – pictures accompany some of these. Catalogues from past auctions are also available, from £6/$10 each. A secure absentee bid form is available so that you can take part in their live auctions but there is also an online auction.

Dalia Stanley & Co

www.dalia-stanley.com.au

This Australian auctioneer's site features a selection of pictures and details of items recently sold at auction, as well as a full calendar of their forthcoming sales. These include regular monthly auctions of deceased estates, as well as specialist sales covering areas such as 19th-century English furniture, Australian art, and jewellery.

Dalkeith Auctions

www.dalkeith-auctions.co.uk

This is the site of an auctioneer who specializes in postcards, cigarette cards, ephemera, sports memorabilia, coins, autographs, and various other collectibles. Special, thousand-lot sales are held monthly, and complete catalogues are available on the site. You cannot bid online, but bids may be submitted by telephone, post, or fax.

Dominic Winter Book Auctions

www.dominic-winter.co.uk

Dominic Winter specialize in antiquarian and rare printed books, antique maps and prints, historical documents, manuscripts, autographs, pictures, graphics, and printed ephemera. Their website includes a full sales calendar, catalogues of forthcoming and recent sales, and an email form, which you can use to place a bid. There's also an online form for sending details of items you may wish to consign for a future sale.

Dorotheum

www.dorotheum.com

This Austrian auction house, founded by the Emperor Josef I in 1707, has a site written in both English and German. Old Master pictures and Art Nouveau are particular specialities of this auction house, although various other objects are also sold. The company's website features news from the saleroom, and catalogues can be viewed online. There are links to Dorotheum's fellow members of the IA, which is an alliance of auctioneers from various countries around the world (see page 68).

Dreweatt Neate

www.dreweatt-neate.co.uk

Download entire catalogues from the website of this auctioneer, or browse through selected lots online. You can search for specific lots and view results from entire past sales, going back more than three years. The site also features news and commentary from the auctioneer.

E-Auction Room

www.eauctionroom.com

This French site, which also has an English version, offers live Internet coverage of auctions around the world. View catalogues online and see a video clip about the sales and the salerooms. You must register if you want to bid, and then you can either leave a bid via email, or bid live through the Internet as an auction actually takes place.

ebay

www.ebay.com

www.ebay.co.uk

This well-known online auction site boasts millions of listings and more than 42 million registered users. You must register before you can bid or sell items – registration is free, but you will be asked for credit card details for verification purposes if using an anonymous email account such as hotmail or yahoo etc. Even if you are not registered, you can still browse through items for sale, which are arranged into a large number of different categories. The site encourages questions and discussion, and so a discussion board is included on the site for users. The site has both US and UK versions, which are very similar, except that there might be a different emphasis on highlighted items. Much of ebay's business comes from the many companies and individuals who regularly sell through the site.

Edgar Horns Auctioneers

www.edgarhorns.co.uk

This auction house is based on the south coast of England and it holds general sales every two weeks, plus six fine art and antique sales per year. Its website includes advice on valuations and their importance for tax purposes, plus online catalogues, hosted by external sites, and dates of forthcoming sales here.

Eldred's Auctioneers and Appraisers

www.eldreds.com

This is the site of the Cape Cod, Massachusetts-based auction house. The site includes listings of future auctions, and pictures accompany a lot of the items. Highlights from past auctions can be found by date, and these consist of thumbnail images of items, descriptions, and selling prices. Complete directions and information on accommodation in the area is given so that you can visit

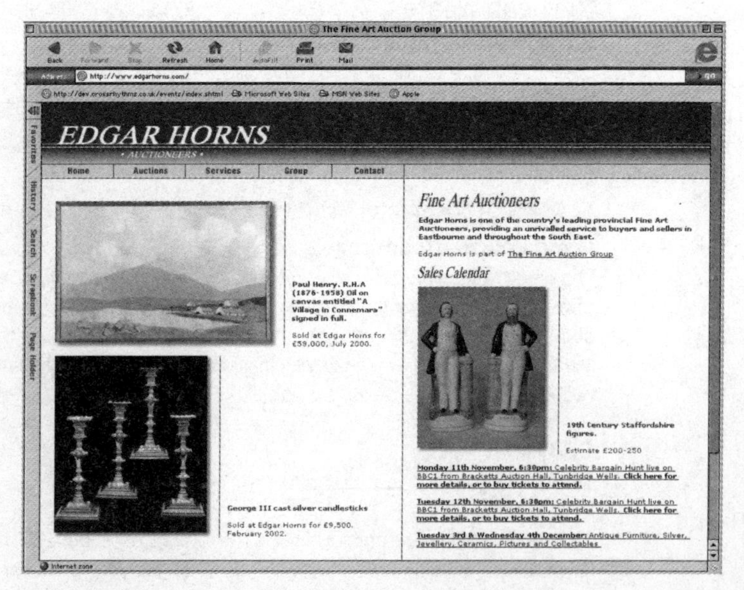

Full details of Edgar Horns' specialist fine art sales can be found online.

the auction house in person. The site has links to the Cape and Islands Visitor and Information Network Service, the local Chamber of Commerce, and several gateway antiques sites (see pages 101–11 for resource and gateway sites).

Empire Auctions

www.empireauctions.com

This is the site of a Canadian auction house that offers traditional and online auctions. Their traditional auctions are held in Montreal, Toronto, and Ottawa, and fully illustrated catalogues for these can be found on the website. You can browse through the items for sale in the online auctions, but you must register in order to take part. This site also features articles on antiques and collecting.

Etude Tajan

www.tajan.com

The website of France's leading auction house, includes illustrated online catalogues, which can be downloaded in their entirety for perusal offline. Hard copies can also be ordered online. There is also a full sales calendar, and you will find that Tajan offer sales in all of the major collecting categories. This site is available in English.

Ewbank Fine Art and General Auctioneers & Valuers

www.ewbankauctions.co.uk

Reviews of past sales can be found on the site of this British regional auctioneer. Archives of their past sales go back for two years, while the sale calendar runs for several months ahead. There is also a detailed map of how to find Ewbanks, plus an interesting news page.

Falkkloos

www.falkkloos.se

Download catalogues from the website of this leading Swedish auctioneer or order hard copies of them if you prefer. Online valuations are also available through this site, which is available in English, and you can register your "wants" and you will be notified if a desired item should appear in future auctions. The auction house specializes in Scandinavian and international paintings, prints, sculpture, and modern glass.

Fellows & Sons

www.fellows.co.uk

Browse through a searchable catalogue, which can be downloaded and printed from the website of this UK auctioneer, and register to be notified by email as soon as new catalogues are available. Established in 1876, Fellows lies at the heart of Britain's largest jewellery-making district, so jewellery is an important feature of auctions here. Regular auctions do, however, offer everything from furniture and silver to clocks and porcelain – you will find a full auction calendar giving you the details on the site.

FS Auctions

www.fsauctions.co.uk

This online auction site allows you to browse through a wide range of items, including antiques and collectibles. Free registration will also allow you to buy and sell – items on the site are offered by dealers as well as private individuals, and, usefully, you can see the ratings that other users have given to the vendors. Some items are also sold at fixed prices.

GE Sworder

www.sworder.co.uk

This regional UK firm of auctioneers lists details of forthcoming auctions and viewing times on its website and you can also search the catalogues to find specific items. Most lots are illustrated, and, if you like what you see, you can also bid via email. The site also includes a brief history of the company, which dates back to the 18th century.

Gilding's

www.gildings.co.uk

Sales of Victoriana and Edwardian furnishings are among the attractions of this UK auction house, which lists full details of what is available on its website. Specialist sales in subjects ranging from model engines to books are held, and you can read about past sales, browse through online catalogues, and submit an email bid. Feedback about the site and the sales is positively welcomed – users are invited to submit their comments via email.

Glerum Auctioneers

www.glerum.nl

This Dutch auctioneer holds sales both in the Netherlands and in Indonesia. The website, which is in Dutch only, contains details of the sales schedule, online catalogues and pictures, and prices realized at recent auctions. You will also find information on the educational courses organized by the auction house.

Gorringes Auction Galleries

www.gorringes.co.uk

Anyone can browse through or download entire catalogues and view the results of, and commentaries on, recent sales of this UK auctioneer. If you are a member (joining is free via an online form) you can also place bids online and receive automatic notification of the latest sale catalogues.

Hampel Auctions

www.hampel-auctions.com

Hampel is one of Germany's leading auction houses and its site (available in English) includes video clips of recent auctions. Browse through online catalogues or use the search facility to locate desired objects on the site. You can also place bids on lots coming up for sale, once you have registered.

Hamptons International

www.hamptons.co.uk

This is the website of one of the UK's best-known regional auctioneers. On the site you will find full details of services offered by the company, while catalogues, as well as pre- and post-sale reports, can also be viewed. Hamptons cover most popular fields of collecting, and there's an online form to email details if you would like an opinion on something that you might wish to sell. You must register to use parts of this site, but registration can be done online and is free.

Harvey Clars Auction Gallery

www.harveyclar.com

This California-based house conducts a two-day auction every four weeks and their schedule is posted online, alongside an illustrated catalogue. There is an online bid form, which can be submitted to the online auction if you wish to purchase something. You can also download complete copies of the catalogues, or you can request hard copies to be sent to you.

Hauswedell & Nolte

www.hauswedell-nolte.de

Fine art and rare books are the specialities of this German auction house, whose site includes illustrated online catalogues of forthcoming and recent sales. Hard copies can be ordered via email, or you can send an email requesting notification of future auctions as soon as the information is available. Recent sales results are also included on the site.

Henry Aldridge

www.henry-aldridge.co.uk

Artefacts and memorabilia from the golden age of travel are the specialist interests of this UK firm of auctioneers. Items relating to the great ocean liners of the past are discussed in some depth on this informative site. The auctioneers hold periodic specialist sales devoted to the most famous liner of all, the *Titanic*, but there are no online auctions. Visitors to the site are invited to email any details of objects relating to the liner. The site also includes a full auction calendar of sales of a more general nature.

Horta Auctioneers

www.horta.be

Based in Brussels, Horta is one of Europe's best-known auction houses. Its website offers online catalogues of forthcoming auction sales, and the prices are available in various currencies. The site, available in English, also contains an auction calendar and a search facility that allows you to search the catalogues by artist, type of object, or auction estimate. Hard copies of the catalogues can also be ordered through the site. There's also a virtual tour, which offers you a 360° view of the salerooms.

International Auctioneers

www.internationalauctioneers.com

International Auctioneers (IA) is an umbrella organization that represents nine independent auction houses in the United States, France, Switzerland, Germany, Sweden, Austria, Spain, and Italy. The auctioneers collaborate with each other in major sales and the website allows you to find out more about past and forthcoming sales. There's a searchable database of lots and you can register your interests (free of charge) to be kept informed about forthcoming sales and lots that you may be interested in.

Internet Auction List

www.internetauctionlist.com

This site lists auctions both live and online, and has links to each of the relevant sites. The search engine provided will find the items in your chosen category from all of the online auctions and then give them to you in one listing – it also has a separate entry just for ebay. There is also a section on the site covering forthcoming auction news and an image-hosting area to help list your items. A list of auctioneers is done by category and you can also search for auctions by date, location, or content. There are also lists of auction schools, where you can learn to become an auctioneer. Auction software for use by both live auction houses and those wishing to post items for sale on online auctions is available on this website too.

Jones & Llewelyn

www.jonesllewelyn.freeserve.co.uk

Catalogues featuring more than a thousand lots are displayed on this Welsh auctioneer's site, accompanied by a small selection of images from their sales. You cannot bid through the site, but you can send an email request to be put on the catalogue mailing list. The range of items offered is wide, ranging from small ceramic pieces to vintage motorcycles.

Kunsthaus Lempertz

www.lempertz.com

This auction house is based in Cologne and handles Old Masters, sculptures, silver, jewellery, and decorative art – especially modern and contemporary. Download catalogues from the site (which is available in English), and browse through items from recent and forthcoming sales, or order hard copies which will be sent to you.

Lacy Scott & Knight

www.lsk.co.uk

The site of this British regional auctioneer shows highlights of recent sales, and also gives a full description of services offered. A list of sale dates is included, with viewing times, and you can browse through catalogues online, although you cannot bid. Themed sales range from Victoriana to model steam engines.

Lawson-Menzies

www.lawsonmenzies.com.au

The website of Australia's oldest auction house includes a complete history of the firm as well as a full sales calendar. There's advice for those thinking of buying or selling through Lawsons, and you can also order copies of catalogues through the site. If you would like to place a bid on lots in forthcoming live auctions then you must print out a form and fax or post it to the auctioneers. You can, however, also now take part in online "timed bid" auctions.

Leonard Joel

www.ljoel.com.au

Leonard Joel is the largest Australian-owned auction house based in that country. Its site allows keyword searches of its catalogues and you can also view pictures of selected lots from forthcoming sales. Many of these are in a large format, allowing close scrutiny. If you choose to register online, you can place bids through the site on lots coming up for sale.

Lloyds International Auction Galleries

www.lloyds-auction.co.uk

Catalogues of future sales can be viewed or downloaded from the site of this London firm of auctioneers. You can also use a search facility to look for specific items from these catalogues. There's a profile of the company on the site too, and an archive of highlights from previous sales. You cannot bid

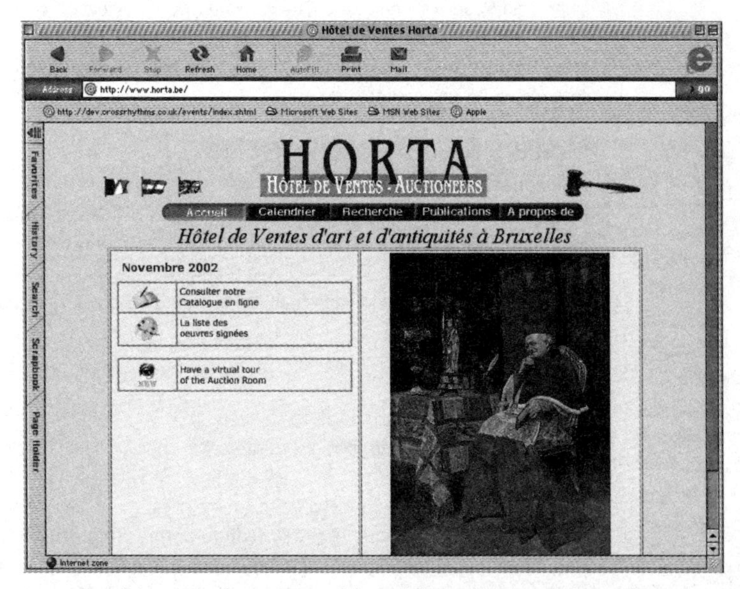

Horta, the Belgian auction house, is one of the best-known in Europe (see page 67).

online, as it is the policy of the auctioneers that no lots should be sold unless the purchaser has had a chance to inspect them in person first.

Lots Road Galleries, Chelsea

www.lotsroad.com

A company history is included on the website of these auctioneers. Former Christie's employees founded the firm in the 1970s. There is a detailed list of services available. You will also find the latest auction catalogue online, as well as a sales calendar, auction reports, and results. You can print out a bidding form to fax to the auctioneers.

Lyon and Turnbull

www.lyonandturnbull.com

The website of this Edinburgh-based auction house features catalogues for forthcoming sales and an archive of past catalogues – you can search through both for specific items. There is also an archive of past newsletters. Sale results are displayed on the site, and you can choose your preferred currency for these. The home page also features a "lot of the month", highlighting an important item from a forthcoming sale.

Martin Spencer-Thomas

www.martinspencerthomas.co.uk

This firm of auctioneers is based in the west of England and holds regular sales of Georgian, Victorian, Edwardian, and later furniture and effects as well as porcelain, books, china, etc. The website offers a selection of images of items recently sold at auction, and online catalogues for forthcoming sales. The auctioneers do not accept trade goods for sale, so everything shown has come from private sources.

McTears & Co (Auctioneers) Ltd

www.mctears.co.uk

The site of this major Glasgow auctioneer features online catalogues of the lots on offer. While there are no illustrations online, they can often be emailed on request to those who would like to see them. There is also an online email form for questions, or you can email the auction house specialists direct.

Michael Zeller

www.zeller.de

The site of this German firm of auctioneers gives you the chance to subscribe to catalogues online, and to register interest in specific items that might come up for auction in the future. You can also find out what happened at recent auctions, and what will be included in future sales, as well as place a bid on lots in the online catalogue. Another feature of this site is a "permanent sale" area, which has goods for sale at fixed prices. A few items are shown as examples – send an email for full details of what is on offer.

Midwest Auction Galleries

www.midwestauctiongalleries.com

This American business describes itself as "pioneers in online auctions of fine art, antiques and books". There is a section on past auctions, including toys, dolls, and Oriental books, which illustrates items in colour and shows the prices they realized. You can join an email mailing list, and you can also register to bid (and pay by credit card) online.

Mill House Auctions Ltd

www.mill-house-auctions.co.uk

This Cornwall-based, family-run auctioneer's site offers full details of its range of services, which includes property clearance. There are pictures of the salerooms, an online auction calendar, and copies of the latest catalogues can be emailed on request. Typical catalogues cover a broad spectrum of collecting interests, from furniture to sports memorabilia.

Monsantic

www.monsantic.com

This is the site of a Belgian auction house (available in English), and it features a full sales calendar and details of viewing times. There is also a catalogue of the next sale, which can be downloaded and printed from the site. Photos can be seen on a separate page within the site, and you can email your bid. A links page includes other Belgian auction and resource sites.

Morphets

www.morphets.co.uk

This is the website of an auction house based in Harrogate, in the north of England. The site features fully illustrated reports on recent sales, an auction calendar, and an email bidding facility. You can also send an email to request a report on the condition of any item of interest. There's also a page of questions and answers dealing with the procedures and advantages of selling at auction and, specifically, through this auction house.

Noel Wheatcroft & Son

www.wheatcroft-noel.co.uk

A history of the company, complete with old photographs from the 1920s, is one of the features of this UK family firm's site. You will also find an auction calendar for the year and a catalogue for the next auction online with photographs of selected lots – telephone if you wish to make a bid. There are also links to UK trade publications (see pages 112–17 for specialist publications).

Peter Wilson

www.peterwilson.co.uk

This British auctioneer's site features online versions of past catalogues, complete with results, as well as catalogues of forthcoming sales. You can request further information on any of the lots shown on the site via an email form, but the site contains full details of the auction process at Peter Wilson. You can also join an email list to receive news from the saleroom.

Phillips Auctioneers

www.phillips-auctions.com

Phillips auctioneers have a history going back more than 200 years. In 2001, Phillips split into two, as part of the firm merged with Bonhams (see page 59). This is the site of the other part, known as Phillips de Pury & Luxembourg, which has salerooms as far afield as New York, Sydney, and Zurich, as well as offices in Paris and London. Their website offers a worldwide sales schedule, plus online catalogues. You will have to register in order to browse the online catalogues, however, but this is free of charge.

Pottery Auction

www.potteryauction.com

This special auction site for ceramics enthusiasts not only offers a range of auctions, but also provides a chat room for pottery lovers. The site is particularly strong on American Art Pottery, but also includes Staffordshire, Belleek, Chintz, and much more. Browsers are welcome, but you must register (which is free) to use the site. There are also links to various pottery and glass sites.

Quittenbaum

www.quittenbaum.de

This Munich auction house is strong on Art Nouveau and Art Deco, modern design, and 19th- and 20th-century art. Its site, available in English, includes online catalogues and information on recent and forthcoming sales. You can also order hard copies of the catalogues through the site, and bid online.

QXL.com

www.qxl.com

This European online auction site has versions for several different countries in their respective languages. It offers online sales of various items, including art and collectibles. Individuals as well as dealers buy and sell through this site, and you can browse through categories or use the search engine to find specific items quickly. You must register to take part in auctions, and the vendor pays a commission. You can also sign up, free of charge, to an email newsletter that notifies users of bargains from various categories on offer.

Ribble Reclamation

www.ribble-reclamation.com

This specialist architectural antiques firm holds auctions twice a year of items ranging "from a roofing slate to an entire church". There is a catalogue online, and you can also request a hard copy by email. Ribble Reclamation are also dealers, and a selection of photos of typical stock is also included on the site.

Riddetts

www.riddetts.co.uk

Based on the south coast of England, these auctioneers offer a photographic and video service, recording details of valuables for insurance purposes. Full details of this and the company's other services are available on the site, along with a company history and auction calendar. Catalogues of forthcoming sales can be viewed via a link to the external Auction Hammer site (see page 58).

Ritchie's

www.ritchies.com

The website of this Canadian auction house, which is based in Toronto, offers online catalogues of forthcoming sales with pictures, full descriptions, and estimates of the items. These auctioneers have special sales dedicated to fashion, jewellery, and accessories as well as furniture, silver, porcelain, and works of art.

Sandford Aldefer Company

www.alderfercompany.com

This is a straightforward auction site, giving upcoming auction dates, the location of the auction house in Hatfield, Pennsylvania, USA, the company policy, auction results, and showing limited pictures of items in upcoming auctions. There is a weekly auction of personal property, antiques, art, coins, and guns, etc on a Thursday as well as catalogue auctions that are held throughout the year with special merchandise as well as personal property. There is an appraisal service too on the site – this is done using the photographs and information that you provide them with.

Semley Auctioneers

www.semleyauctioneers.com

The site of this British firm of auctioneers features sales catalogues via links to the external icollector and Invaluable sites (see pages 108 and 124). There's a calendar of dates of forthcoming sales, and a map of the area where they are based to help you find the salerooms. You can also register to be notified by email of any news, new catalogues, or items of particular interest to you.

Sharon Boccelli & Company

www.sbauctioneers.com

This is a no-nonsense website showing the American company's current auction listings (only available to buy in person, not online), plus a record of recent auctions with illustrations and prices realized. Almost everything is illustrated, and the items are described and listed with estimates – there is furniture, art, clocks, and much, much more here. Information about the company's appraisals is given, and buying or consigning for auction is described. The site is also good at providing information about the artists whose work is being sold at auction as well as describing the items themselves.

Simmons and Sons

www.simmonsandsons.com

The website of this British regional auction house features online catalogues, subdivided into sections (such as silver, ceramics, etc) for ease of navigation. Several lots are illustrated online, and there's a special form for requesting further information on any of the items shown. You cannot bid through the site, but you can order copies of catalogues via email.

Skinner

www.skinnerinc.com

This is North America's fourth-largest auction house and it has 60 auctions per year. The site has details of upcoming and recent auctions, with online illustrated catalogues. There are directions on how to bid by telephone and fax, or, alternatively, an absentee bid form can be used online. Tips on how to preview an auction, how to bid, and how to sell at auction are all given. The section "Insider Tips" gives advice on a variety of subjects: how to get an appraisal, furniture refinishing, the importance of provenance, and how to protect your prints and watercolours, as well as general tips on restoration.

Sold.com.au

www.sold.com.au

This Australian online auction site includes a helpful online tutorial. You don't need to register to browse through items for sale, but you must if you wish to buy or sell, and there is a commission paid by vendors on successful sales. There is a useful search function for finding items on the site more quickly too. You will also find a listing of collectors' events taking place across Australia.

Sotheby's

www.sothebys.com

The site of the world's largest auction house offers a series of helpful collectors' guides to all kinds of antiques and collectibles as well as full information on Sotheby's own auctions. There's also an online bookshop, and current and past catalogues are for sale too. The site offers special online auctions, for which you must register with your credit card details. Sotheby's can, however, only accept registration for bidders in selected countries – there are 15 of these at the moment, including the UK, USA, Canada, Australia, and Germany – a full list of countries is available on the site.

Spink

www.spinkandson.com

Spink was founded in 1666, the same year as the Great Fire of London (the first premises were destroyed in the fire), and is world famous as an auctioneer and dealer in coins, banknotes, medals, stamps, and Asian Art. Today, Christie's owns the firm. The site features monthly newsletters by specialists in medals and coins. There's also a calendar of forthcoming sales and other events. You

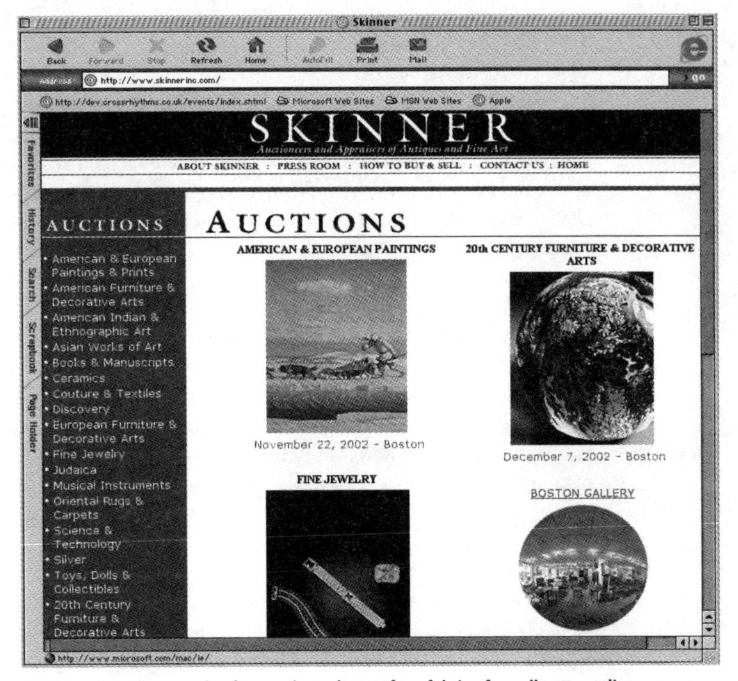

This large American auction house gives plenty of useful tips for collectors online.

cannot bid online, but you can purchase catalogues and register your interests to be kept informed of consignments by email.

Stockholms Auktionsverk

www.auktionsverket.se

The website of this Swedish auction house, which has an English-language option, offers news and full reports of recent sales as well as an auction calendar and lists of results. The site also features direct email contact information for the experts in various departments, and advice on buying and selling through the auctioneers. You can leave a bid via the Internet, but must register first to be able to do so.

Teletrade Auctions

www.teletrade.com

This online auction house specializes in the sale of collectibles such as coins, sports cards, memorabilia, stamps, and film posters. Each collectible has its own home page where you can view and search weekly auction catalogues, watch a real-time auction in progress, and obtain lists of prices realized. You must register to take part, and there is a fee charged to vendors as well as to buyers on the final hammer price.

Tennants Auctioneers

www.tennants.co.uk

The website of this leading British regional auction house includes a catalogue archive, allowing the user to browse through items from previous, as well as forthcoming, sales. Not all of the lots are illustrated, but they are described in detail. Digital images of lots not illustrated on the site can be emailed, free of charge, on request. The site also includes full reports of past sales and the latest news from the salerooms.

Thomas Watson

www.thomaswatson.com

Based in the north of England, Thomas Watson has been in business since 1840. The website introduces current saleroom staff and explains buying and selling procedures at the auction house. The site also features results from recent sales and selected lots from forthcoming sales are shown on the site. You may place a bid by email, or fax them via a printable form available from the site.

Thos Wm Gaze & Son

www.twgaze.com

This is the website of a leading UK regional auctioneer, which was founded in 1857. The site includes searchable sale catalogues that are updated on a weekly basis, and there's a telephone number to request verbal condition reports on lots featured. You can also place a bid via email.

Trade Me

www.trademe.co.nz

This New Zealand-based online auction site features a selection of antiques and collectibles listings. Unusual items, such as a 1930s barber's chair, have appeared on this site but, more typically, you will find popular items from Staffordshire pottery to kitchenalia. Joining the site is free, and it also costs nothing to list items for auction, unless you find a buyer, in which case the vendor pays a percentage of the price.

Tring Market Auctions

www.tringmarketautions.co.uk

This is the site of one of Britain's older regional auction houses – the firm was established back in 1832. Their online presence offers details of their popular "Saturday sales", which generally include items such as agricultural equipment as well as antiques and collectibles. You will also find past and forthcoming catalogues for the firm's special Fine Art Sales, which include furniture, glassware, clocks, and ceramics as well as paintings.

U Bid

www.ubid.com

This vast online auction site offers a huge range of items, from computers through to exercise bikes. There is, however, also a selection of collectibles, which is strong on sporting items – particularly those with an American flavour. Modern collectibles and limited-edition pieces are also well represented.

Van Ham Fine Art Auctions

www.van-ham.com

This is the website of a German auction house that was founded by art historian Carola Van Ham in 1959. The site (available in English) includes a full company history as well as details of forthcoming sales and sale results. There's an online form to fill in should you require any further information about anything. The specialities of this auction house include Old Master paintings, sculptures, furniture, porcelain, silver, and tapestries.

Waddington's

www.waddingtonsauctions.com

The site of this leading Canadian auction house includes articles about particular artists or objects from recent or forthcoming sales. You can view their catalogues online, order hard copies, or see lists of prices realized at recent sales. Email addresses of various inhouse specialists are also given so that you can contact them directly with any queries that you may have. The site also makes good use of animation and features audio clips relevant to the auctions.

Walker, Barnett & Hill

www.walker-barnett-hill.co.uk

On this regional British auctioneer's site there are links to other useful sites, including one on porcelain marks and another on hallmarking. Complete online catalogues of forthcoming sales are also available here, and these have been subdivided into categories for the user's ease of navigation. The site also has a very useful search engine that allows individual items to be located much more quickly.

Wallis and Wallis

www.wallisandwallis.co.uk

This leading specialist auctioneer offers regular sales of militaria and toys. Based on the south coast of England, the firm has been sending out catalogues worldwide for many years – now you can see them on the web. You can also register for an account and bid online. Their militaria auctions are strong on uniforms and regalia, but include weapons as well, while their toy auctions focus on die-cast cars and toys.

Weller and Dufty Ltd

www.welleranddufty.co.uk

Established in 1835, Birmingham-based Weller and Dufty rank among the UK's oldest provincial auction houses. The firm is particularly well known for arms and armour, and you will find online catalogues that include photographs and detailed descriptions of the items in specialist sales. Details of their fine arts sales are also included here. You can request hard copy catalogues via email.

Whyte's

www.whytes.ie

The website of this Dublin-based auction house features numerous pictures of items coming up in future sales. Whyte's are particularly strong on Irish art and artefacts as well as coins, stamps, militaria, medals, maps, prints, and toys. Read sales catalogues online and then place your bid by email. The site also includes a useful selection of links to antiques resource sites, sites of Irish interest, and antique coin sites.

Wiener Kunst Auktionen

www.palais-kinsky.com

This is the website (available in English) of a leading Austrian auction house that specializes in paintings, contemporary art, and Art Nouveau, as well as in general antiques. You will find an auction calendar, sale results, and searchable online catalogues here. Hard copies of their catalogues can be ordered online – payment is made by bank transfer. You can also place bids online for the lots that are on offer in the regular auctions.

Wilkinsons Auctioneers

www.wilkinsons-auctioneers.co.uk

Browse through an online catalogue of items from forthcoming sales on this UK auctioneer's site, or dip into a recent catalogue that can be found in the online archive. Their online catalogues include full descriptions and pictures of many of the lots. If you are suitably impressed, you can then place a bid via a form that is available online.

Wilson's Auctions

www.wilsonsauctions.com

Established in Northern Ireland over 60 years ago, Wilson's are Ireland's largest auctioneers and are also one of the largest in the whole of the UK. This company sells classic cars, boats, and other related items, as well as fine art and antiques. Their website gives details of the kind of lots that are regularly included in their auctions, such as Irish art, and there's also information on forthcoming sales. Send them an email request and you will be kept fully informed of the latest consignments.

Windibank

www.windibank.co.uk

This British regional auction house, based in Surrey, offers advice on buying and selling at auction. Send an email to request notification of new catalogues as they appear, and you can submit bids via email. Details of the firm's valuation service appear on the site, but you must contact the auctioneers to arrange a visit.

Woolley and Wallis

www.woolleyandwallis.co.uk

Saleroom news, including recent staff appointments, can be found on the site of this UK regional auction house, as well as information on the 50-plus sales held annually. This well-illustrated site has a friendly, chatty style and discusses some highlights of past sales from the various specialist departments. You can contact them for a free verbal valuation, or send an email with attached photo. Searchable catalogues of forthcoming sales are also available online, and there is a printable form to order catalogues by post.

Yahoo! Auctions

auctions.yahoo.com
auctions.yahoo.co.uk

This large auction site has both a US and a UK (and Ireland) version. They are similar in content except that they have highlighted items and features that might be of more interest to the target audience, and prices are listed in the appropriate currency. A vast selection of goods is on offer with collectibles from jewellery and watches to coins and stamps, as well as antiques and art. Registration for buyers and sellers is free, and, as well as the regular auctions, you can also bid in charity sales.

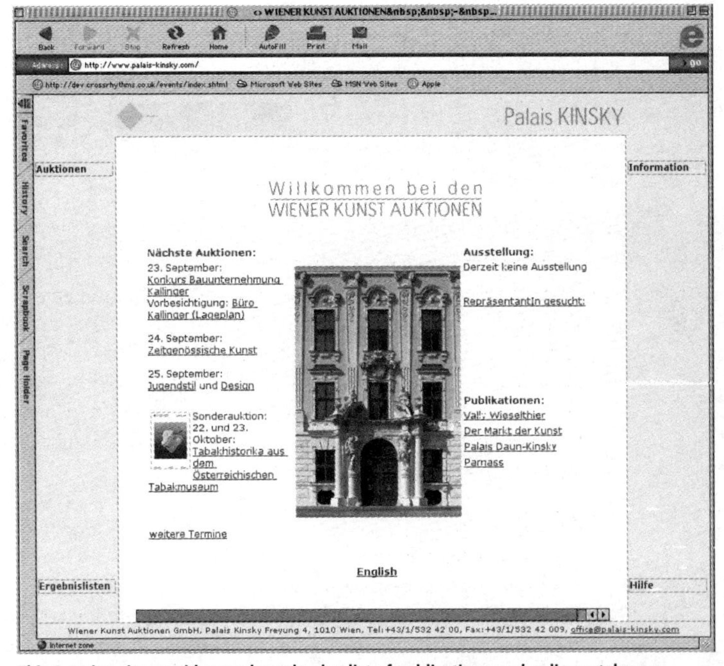

This Austrian site provides a sales calender, list of publications, and online catalogues.

WORTH A LOOK

www.anaf.com
French auction house.

www.antiquesuk.net
Online auction site

www.aucland.com
Online auction site in French and Spanish.

www.bidbonanza.com
General online auction site with a selection of antiques and collectibles.

www.clausenauction.com
Canadian auction house.

www.duran-subastas.es
Spanish auction site.

www.internetartauctions.com
Artists offer work for online auction and fixed price purchase.

www.thesaurus.co.uk/hyduke&son
Leading UK regional auction house.

www.users.skynet.be/anselmo
Belgian auction house, which is based in Antwerp.

FAIRS

Adams Antiques Fairs

www.adams-antiques-fairs.co.uk

London's longest-running monthly Sunday fairs are represented on this website, which features a calendar of events. As well as the London fairs, the organizers also run a show at Newbury in Berkshire. There's booking information for would-be exhibitors, links to the BBC's antiques website, and even a demonstration of restoration work.

America's Piccadilly Promotions

www.piccadillypromos.com

These fair organizers promote 21 antique and collectible events in Palm Beach and Sarasota, Florida. The fairs have between 100 and 2,000 dealers, and include antiques and collectibles. The site gives details of locations, dates, and information to vendors about booth charges.

Amsterdam Arts and Design Fair

www.aadf.nl

The best of art and design during 1880–1980 is featured at this Dutch fair, and its website shows off a selection of the items from its recent fairs. There are also views of the stands that give an impression of the style of the fair, as well as an online shop that offers a selection of goods including lamps, clocks, Murano vases, postcards, and catalogues.

Ann Zierold Fairs

www.ann-zierold-fairs.co.uk

This UK organizer specializes in Art Deco fairs, and there's a full listing of their events here (mostly in the north of England). Many are held in attractive venues and there are pictures of these online. There are links to the sites of Art Deco dealers, and one to a specialist in collectible pens. There's also advice on, and details of, the tests that some venues now insist upon before electrical items, such as lamps, can be put up for sale.

Armacost Antiques Shows

www.armacostantiquesshows.com

This fair organizer began in 1985 and now runs charity antiques fairs in seven states (Florida, Maryland, Missouri, Ohio, Oklahoma, Pennsylvania, and Virginia). The site lists the dealers represented, giving website links where available. Dealers can fill out an online form if they wish to participate in one of the fairs. A detailed list of services offered to committees outlines Armacost's credentials, so if you're looking for someone to run a fair for you, check out this section. There are also listings of fairs (some with pictures from previous years), previews for upcoming fairs, and links to some individual fairs' websites.

Artexis: The Art of Exhibitors

www.artexis.com

Major fairs in Belgium and the Netherlands are featured on the site of Artexis who run, among other events, the Eurantica Antwerp and Eurantica Brussels events. The site is in English, Dutch, and French, and features a full calendar of events as well as the latest news.

Artizania and Art Fairs

www.artizania.co.uk

Browse through a selection of vintage costume, shoes, lace, and other items on the site of this specialist costume and textile fair organizer. You can place orders online by email and you can pay by credit card, cheque, or international money order in US dollars or pounds sterling. There is a full calendar of events, details of textile-related events worldwide, and information on special "fair tours", which involve group visits to fairs with a guide who will show you round. There is also a special section for "bargains".

The Art on Paper Fair

www.artonpaper.co.uk

Selected examples from the stock of some 50 dealers are pictured on the site of this London art fair, complete with contact details for the organizers. Dealers specialize in everything from 16th-century woodcuts to 20th-century lithographs by artists such as Matisse.

BADA Antiques and Fine Art Fair

www.bada-antiques-fair.co.uk

The website of the annual fair of the prestigious British Antique Dealers' Association includes information on stock and exhibiting dealers, and has links to individual dealers' websites (see page 118 for further information about the association's site). There are also pages on the numerous ancillary events that accompany this fair, which include talks on history and interior design.

Bailey Fairs

www.baileyfairs.co.uk

An annual antiques fair at the top London hotel Claridge's is among the highlights of the calendar of this UK organizer. Details of the firm's various regional fairs are also included on the site. If you are a dealer you can find details of the reward scheme, which offers a cash incentive to introduce new exhibitors to the fairs. If you are just planning to visit, you may find information on the "Connoisseur Club" of interest – membership allows discounted admission and gets you into special previews of the fairs.

Bowman Antiques Fairs

www.antiquesfairs.com

Bowman's have been organizing quality antiques fairs in England and Scotland

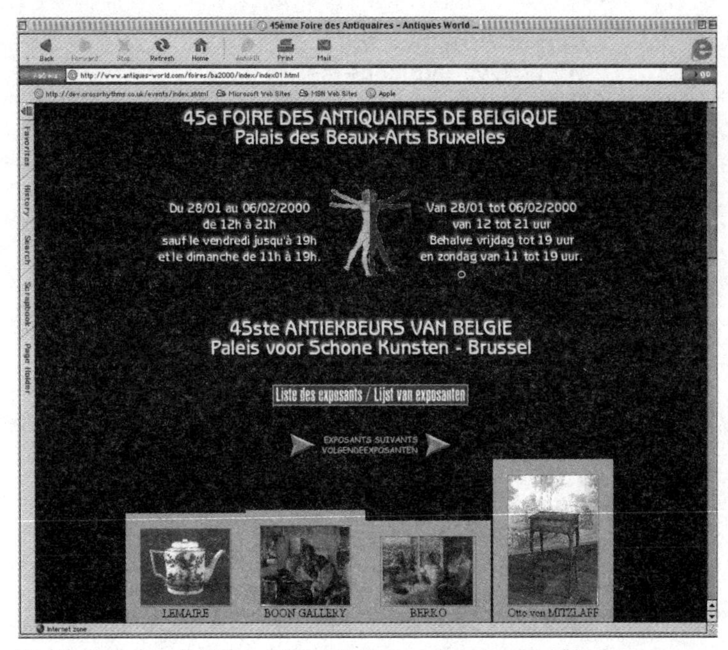

The site of the Brussels Antiques Fair includes images of a huge range of stock.

since 1973. Everything you need to get you to Bowman's regular fairs at Bingley Hall, Stafford, UK, can be found on this site. There's travel and accommodation information, including railway timetables, and pictures of the fairs' stands so that you can see what they are like before setting out.

British Antiques Fairs

www.antiques-for-everyone.co.uk

The website of Britain's largest vetted antiques fairs has regularly updated information on several prestigious events. This includes fair previews and exhibitor information as well as details of the venues where the fairs are held. The organizers are based at the National Exhibition Centre in Birmingham, where they have been running fairs at the huge exhibition complex for many years. However, they now also run antiques fairs in London, Glasgow, and Manchester.

Brussels Antiques Fair

www.antiques-world.com/foires/BA2000/HOME/home.html

The image-rich site of Belgium's premier fair includes a large selection of representative stock. Most collecting fields are represented here, and the stock is all described in detail. There are also links to dealer websites where available, as well as contact information given.

Classic Antiques Fairs

www.classic-antiques-fairs.co.uk

This British fairs organizer holds regular events in Warwickshire's Shakespeare Country. The venue for the fairs is a motor museum, itself a major local tourist attraction. There are pictures of some of the classic cars you can see if you visit, and a sample of the kind of antiques you will find on the stands. There's also a full calendar of events, and links to the sites of local tourist organizations and selected fairs organizers and dealers.

CMO Antiques

www.cmo-antiques.com

Images abound on the website of this French organizer, who is responsible for some major Parisian events. Exhibitors, organizers, and stock are pictured, and you can search exhibitor lists alphabetically or by category. Visitors are invited to submit questions directly to the organizers via email.

Cord Shows Ltd

www.cordshows.com

Cord Shows have been organizing fairs for over 30 years. Their site lists their 14 annual fairs in New York State and western Connecticut and gives details of location, merchandise (rather than exhibitor list), admission, directions, and special events. They also run four arts and crafts fairs and the site gives a lot of details about these fairs too. "Interesting links" will take you to websites about crafts, antiques and collectibles, publications, and collectors' organizations.

Cultura

www.cultura-fair.ch

Cultura, an antiques fair held in Basel, Switzerland, bills itself as the World Art and Antiques Fair, and it is particularly strong on antiquities. Its site is unusual in that it contains full details of its vetting procedures and what will and will not be accepted at the fair and why. There is also general information on the fair, including contact details for tourist information.

DMG Antiques Fairs

www.dmgantiquefairs.com

The website of one of Britain's major fairs organizers includes all the dates of the year's fairs and information on facilities and opening times. DMG events include the Newark Fair, which is Europe's largest antiques fair. Travel and accommodation information is included and there's also information on the Overseas Buyers' Club, which offers special deals for visitors from outside the UK.

The European Fine Art Foundation

www.tefaf.com

This foundation runs leading European fairs, most notably the event at Maastricht in the Netherlands. This annual event attracts as many as 60,000 visitors, and its animated and musical website includes a floor plan and exhibitor information. You can also take a virtual tour of the exhibition complex where the fair is held – this includes 360° views of the halls.

The Fine Art and Antiques Fairs

www.olympia-antiques.co.uk

The Fine Art and Antiques Fairs take place at Olympia in London each year. The site of the organizers includes full details and dates of all the events, and you can send an email requesting travel and accommodation information too. Catalogues and tickets can be ordered online.

Flamingo Promotions

www.nyflamingo.com

This organizer promotes fairs throughout Long Island (New York) and across the northeastern United States. The site contains a complete listing of all the fairs they run, giving directions, admission fees, and opening times. There is a $1-off-admission coupon to print out and take to any of the fairs too.

Gadsden Promotions Limited

www.antiqueshowscanada.com

Experienced Canadian fairs organizers Gadsden Promotions have events of various types and sizes on their calendar. You will find more than just listings of the events and dates on their site: there are also full details of the type of stock, the venues, and instructions on how to get to each fair. There are also links to the sites of the exhibitors, who come from both sides of the Atlantic.

Galloway Antiques Fairs

www.gallowayfairs.co.uk

Stately home settings are popular with Galloway Antiques Fairs, who organize events around Britain. The venues are pictured on the site, and there is a full calendar of events. The site is rich in graphics and animation, so you may have to be patient when viewing it if you have a slow machine.

Grosvenor House Art and Antiques Fair

www.grosvenor-fair.co.uk

The Grosvenor House Fair is London's longest-running fair and is one of the finest in the world. The site includes examples of stock from exhibitors, accompanied by full and informative descriptions, and there is contact information so that you can get in touch with them. You can also order your ticket and catalogue online.

International Fine Art and Antiques Fairs

www.haughton.com

This is the website of Brian and Anna Haughton, who organize major events in both the UK and USA. There are full details of each of the fairs, which include

London's International Ceramics Fair and Seminar and New York's International Asian Art Fair. A selection of the typical stock is shown too and there are full lists of exhibitors.

Kunst Messe Koln

www.kunstmesse-koeln.de

The Cologne Fair is one of Germany's finest, and attracts dealers from around the world. Its website is available in English, and offers tourist information on the city of Cologne as well as travel and accommodation information and news of other major art and antiques fairs in the city.

Lomax Antiques Fairs

www.lomaxantiquesfairs.co.uk

A potted history of the fairs of this UK organizer is included on this site as well as a history of the venues, some of which are quite historic. There are detailed directions for those wishing to go to one of the fairs and an email will get you complimentary tickets.

The Maven Co. Inc. and The Young Management Co.

www.mavencompany.com

This is the site of fair promoters in New England and Westchester County, New York, who run antiques and collectibles fairs; vintage clothing, jewellery, and textile fairs; and doll, toy, and teddy bear fairs. There is detailed information about each fair online giving opening hours, directions, dealer lists, and bus transportation schedules from New York City. There are also links to other antiques and collectibles sites, as well as to several relevant publications.

Mercanteinfiera & Bagarre

www.fiere.parma.it/index.htm

The major Italian fairs, Mercanteinfiera and Bagarre, which are held in Parma, can be found on this site, as well as detailed information on the art, food, and culture of the city itself. The site has versions in various languages and visitors can search for exhibitors by geographical area – full contact information for each of them is included.

New England Antique Shows

www.neantiqueshows.com

A slideshow of goods featured at these New England shows is the main feature of this site. The merchandise is mostly country. There's news of forthcoming events, and you can subscribe to an email mailing list for the latest updates.

Penman Fairs

www.penman-fairs.co.uk

Penman Fairs have been established for around 30 years and run both art and antiques fairs. Their website offers details and complimentary tickets to all

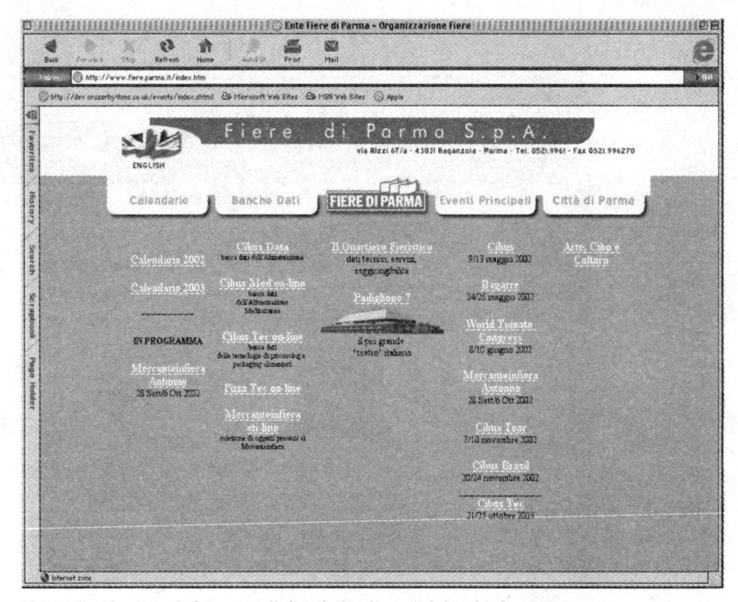

This Italian company's fairs are all detailed online, with local information on Parma.

Penman fairs. Exhibitors have their own web pages, with details of other fairs at which they stand, and there are also various links to trade association and dealer websites.

Professional Show Managers Association, Inc.

www.psmashows.org

This is a group of American fair managers/organizers who are dedicated to advancing the professional standards of the antiques fair business. A "Code of Ethics" encourages honest representation with dealers and the public, and high ethical and business standards. A "Calendar" lists all associated fairs by month or state and there is a separate listing of weekly markets. The website also provides information on how to become a member.

Renningers Antique & Farmers' Markets

www.renningers.com

This manager owns three large antiques and farmer's markets, which are open on weekends. Two are in Pennsylvania (Kutztown and Adamstown) and one is in Florida (Mt Dora). In addition, each of these markets hosts two or three "extravaganzas" each year, which are large fairs (with over 1,000 dealers). They also run two major fairs, one outside Boston and the other outside Philadelphia, each with over 500 dealers. The site provides directions to, and opening hours for, each event, as well as giving information to any vendors who wish to participate.

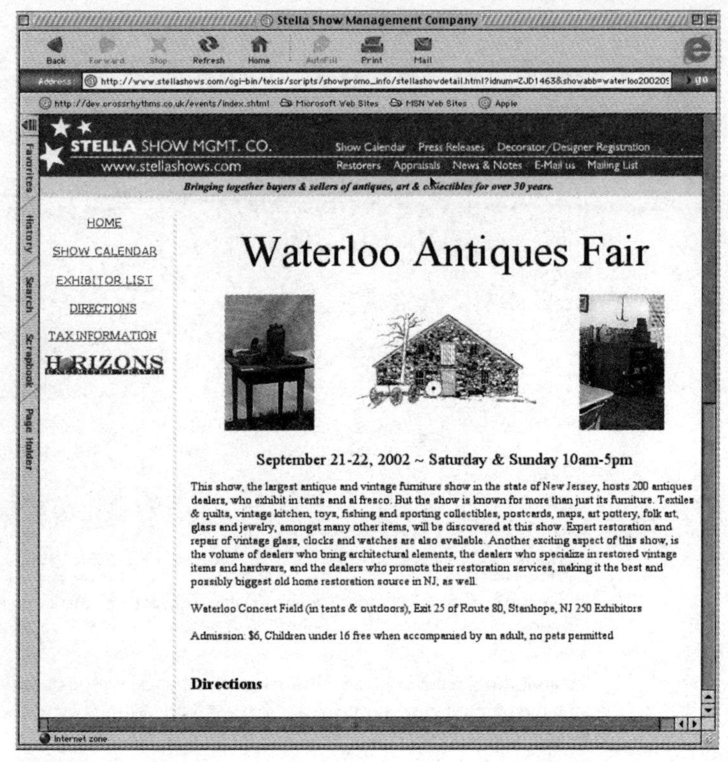

All 22 events run by the Stella Show Management Company are described here.

Robert C Lawler

www.antiquemarkets.com

This fair organizer is based in mid-western USA, and manages 18 events per year. Each event is listed online, and the details that are given include maps and accommodation information as well as descriptions. Several of the monthly markets have online dealer application forms available too.

Sha-Dor/Pappabello

www.shador.com

This is an experienced American organizer's site, which includes a calendar of forthcoming shows with links to advertisements for these. You can register online for show updates, and there is a separate registration form for dealers. Full contact details are also included.

SRP Toy Fairs

www.srptoyfairs.com

Toy cars, trains, and beanies are all found at SRP's specialist events, which are mainly held in the south of England. Their website includes prices charged for space at these events, and, if you are a dealer, you can actually book space at the fairs directly online. The site also has a calendar, listing all the year's events.

Stella Show Management Company

www.stellashows.com

This US organizer runs 22 fairs, mostly in New York City and New Jersey, as well as the Chicago Botanic Garden Antiques and Garden Fair in Glencoe, Illinois. This company has put the term "triple pier" into the antiques vocabulary, taking over three passenger piers in New York to fill them with antiques, folk art, and collectibles. Pier 88 has 20th-century collectibles, Pier 90 contains decorative arts and Americana, and Pier 92 houses classical antiques. The fairs vary from having 60 exhibitors to 600 and each individual fair has an icon online to click on, which gives the location, dates and opening times, admission fees, and a partial dealer list. There is also a useful listing of appraisers and restorers.

20/21 British Art Fair

www.britishartfair.co.uk

British art of the last and new century is included at this fair and on its Internet site. There is a floor plan online and list of exhibitors with links to websites where they are available. Also included are details of the fair's informative lecture programme.

Wakefield Ceramics Fairs

www.wcf.ukdealers.com

Wakefield Ceramics Fairs have been organizing events around Britain for over 20 years. Their website includes a full calendar of events, and there are pictures of typical stock, linked to the site of the dealer who supplied them. Fairs listed typically feature between 20 and 50 dealers, offering porcelain, pottery, and glass dating from 1600 to 1940.

The Watercolours and Drawings Fair

www.watercoloursfair.com

Browse through the searchable catalogue of this top London art fair, and book your tickets to the fair online. You can also contact the exhibitors (there is an excellent page of links to business details for these), and read about the special charity previews that are held.

World Wide Antiques Shows

www.wwantiqueshows.com

This organization has been running for 40-plus years and holds three large fairs each year in Denver, USA, with over 190 exhibitors in each fair. Pictures of some of the booths are on their website. It also provides directions on how to get to each one and there is an online application form for would-be exhibitors.

WORTH A LOOK

www.antiquesireland.com
Irish dealers' site, which includes information on fairs.

www.caskeylees.com
Leading American organizer offers information on its shows that are held in various states.

www.pigandwhistlepromotions.com
The website of London's largest fair, the Alexandra Palace Fair – popularly known as "the Ally Pally".

www.sonic.net/~rtnc/fm.html
Useful site which gives details about flea markets and antiques fairs in Northern California.

MUSEUMS

The Antiquarian & Landmarks Society

www.hartnet.org/als

Despite its rather spartan appearance, this American website contains a lot of useful information. The Society, founded in 1936, has 12 historic homes open to the public. There are listings of future events, membership details, and each of the society's properties are shown and discussed. For example, the Butler-McCook House has an unusual collection of Japanese armour, American paintings, antiques, and a collection of Victorian toys. There are also details of the heritage tours in the Connecticut area run by the society, and an outreach program made up of travelling lectures. There is even a small online gallery, and information on how you can rent one of the homes to hold your own function.

Birmingham Museums and Art Gallery

www.bmag.org.uk

The main city museum in Birmingham is acknowledged as one of Britain's finest and its website offers a searchable online database, with pictures, of the many and varied items in its collections. Of particular interest is the gallery's world-class collection of pre-Raphaelite paintings. Also featured is treen, in the form of the unique Pinto Collection of some 6,000 wooden objects, ranging from gingerbread moulds and tea caddies to children's toys. There is an impressive "Virtual Reality" tour, in which you click on the room which you wish to visit, and also locate its position within the museum. This site also covers various other museums and sites of historical interest in the city, including Sarehole Mill, which inspired *Lord of the Rings* creator JRR Tolkien – fans can trace their hero's steps in the "Tolkien Trail".

The British Museum

www.thebritishmuseum.ac.uk

Items from one of the world's largest collections of antiquities are displayed on this site, but its main attraction lies in the informative online essays about various aspects of ancient life and customs, and the interactive "online learning" section. The cultural significance of all the objects featured is fully explained. There's an online shop, and information on educational events and tours that are run by the museum to some of the archaeological sites where artefacts on show were unearthed.

Colonial Williamsburg

www.colonialwilliamsburg.org

The Colonial Williamsburg site is a complete synopsis of the facilities to be found at this institution. The "Almanack" is a place where you can experience colonial life through various means: exploring trades and politics, seeing various sites, looking at the colonial dateline (covering 1750–83), as well as providing a variety of teacher resources, a historical glossary, and navigational aids for the site. Information is provided for those wishing to visit the physical site in America. In one section, archaeological works of the past are detailed, as well as places to visit to watch such work is in progress now. There is also a section on archaeology for kids, with games and puzzles. An online exhibit features 12 "treasures" illustrating the history and culture of the colonial Chesapeake, and there is a search engine for the online library catalogue.

Danish Museum of Decorative Art

www.kunstindustrimuseet.dk

Copenhagen porcelain is an expected highlight of this website (available in English), but the museum also houses Danish and international glass, textiles, furniture, bookbindings, metalwork, and jewellery. The collections also contain Chinese and Japanese works of art. Click on a floor plan to view selected items with descriptions. Industrial design and electrical appliances are also represented. There are links to other Danish museums and cultural institutions.

Discovering the Museums of Great Britain

www.cornucopia.org.uk

This site is a gateway to the collections of the United Kingdom. There are links to the sites of the country's most important museums, as well as information on their holdings. Search for museums in different areas of the country, or look for specific items and discover which collections house them. The site now features a comprehensive searchable database of all the UK collections.

The Egyptian Museum

www.emuseum.gov.eg

The treasures of Ancient Egypt are illustrated on the website of Egypt's national museum. The museum was originally set up to gather objects in one place, where they would be safe from treasure hunters. On the site there are objects ranging from jewellery and statues to furniture, including the thrones of the Pharaohs, not to mention the odd mummy. There are also online games to enjoy, including one based on hieroglyphics.

Finnish National Gallery

www.fng.fi

Silver, icons, drawings, and miniatures are all well represented at Finland's National Gallery and many items from the collection can be viewed online (the site is available in English). The miniature collection is particularly impressive and, while Scandinavian art accounts for the majority of the collections, art from many other countries can also be found here. A searchable database is included on the site.

German Historical Museum

www.dhm.de

The website of this Berlin Museum is rich in social history, poster art, and militaria, especially uniforms. English and German language versions are available, and the site includes "potted histories" of various nations. Graphic arts dating from the 15th century are strongly represented, and a highlight is a collection of political posters. This collection was once confiscated by the Nazis, but is now available for all to see on the web.

Henan Museum

www.chnmus.net

Fossilized dinosaur eggs, millions of years old, can be viewed on the website of this 70-year-old museum. China is rich in these artefacts, but you will also find many of the bronzes, jades, and porcelain for which that country is also famous here. Images are accompanied by thorough and informative explanations (available in English), which set the objects in their historical and cultural context. There is also a "gallery-by-gallery" tour of the museum, and descriptions of forthcoming exhibitions.

Henry Ford Museum and Greenfield Village

www.hfmgv.org

This museum has exhibits of transportation, manufacturing, home life, entertainment, and technology, which contain everything from railroads to agriculture, as well as clockwork, jewellery, aviation, and racing cars. The village itself comprises over 50 buildings, including inventor's studios and workshops. Online exhibits include automobiles, stories of inventors, and a catalogue of images for commercial or research purposes. There is an extensive section on how to care for and preserve historical items, which also provides a relevant bibliography. There is a gift shop catalogue online as well, but you must contact them by telephone, mail, or fax if you wish to order anything – there is an order form that can be downloaded from the site and then printed out.

Historic Deerfield

www.historic-deerfield.org

This is the site of a museum in northwestern Massachusetts that consists of 14 museum houses plus the new (1998) Flynt Center of Early New England Life and Library. The emphasis is on early New England history, decorative and fine arts, architecture, and material culture. Information about the hours, directions for those wishing to visit the museum in person, and membership details are all available online. There are lists of the summer programmes for college students, details of educational and group tours, and pictures of new acquisitions, as well as images of objects in the museum that, with a click of your mouse, can be turned around for a 3-dimensional view. The online museum shop includes books about Deerfield and you can also request a complete museum store catalogue using an email form from the site.

Ho-Am Art Museum

www.hoammuseum.org

The Ho-Am Art Museum is Korea's largest private art museum. Its online collection includes a fine offering of Buddhist art. Its real strength lies, naturally enough, in Korean artefacts, and the site contains a rich selection of images and information on metalwork, ceramics, paintings, and religious objects dating back thousands of years. Images can be enlarged on screen for closer examination. An English version of the site is available. There are extensive links to the sites of the Samsung Museum of Culture and the Samsung Museum of Modern Art.

Israel Museum, Jerusalem

www.imj.org.il

As you might expect, the collections of Israel's premier museum are especially strong on Jewish culture and artefacts. However, the collections are international in scope, encompassing everything from Dutch Old Masters to pre-Colombian art – and even modern art. Their detailed website, available in English, includes a searchable database which will prove invaluable to researchers, a list of exhibitions past, present and upcoming, resources available, and all the information you could need as a visitor. The online shop is especially rich in Judaica, books, videos, and posters.

The J Paul Getty Museum

www.getty.edu/museum

The Getty Museum collections are made up of seven areas of art: Greek and Roman antiquities, decorative arts, drawings, medieval manuscripts, paintings, photographs, and sculpture. Selected objects from each of these are displayed on the website. The site also contains listings and introductory information on current exhibitions, together with related events, as well as providing you with exhaustive information to help you plan your visit. There is also information on the services offered by the J Paul Getty Trust.

The Hamburg Museum site offers impressive panoramic "virtual tours".

Musée du Louvre

www.louvre.fr

A virtual tour is one of the features of this site, which seems as vast as the famous museum itself. There's also a history of the museum and a detailed and illustrated guide to the collections, in a choice of languages (French, English, Spanish, and Japanese). Finally, there's the online shop, which even offers gift suggestions for different people and occasions.

Museum of Hamburg

www.hamburgmuseum.de

The site of the Museum of Hamburg consists almost entirely of QuickTime virtual reality views of the museum. A 360° panoramic view from the museum roof is just one example of these, and you can pay similar visits to each of the many galleries, which house a wide range of artefacts. An English version of the site is available. The museum café is on the itinerary, as is the workshop where conservators carry out their work.

Museum of Domestic Design and Architecture

www.moda.mdx.ac.uk

The Museum of Domestic Design and Architecture, part of Middlesex University, UK, houses one of the world's most comprehensive collections of 19th- and 20th-century decorative arts for the home. Its website offers information on current and forthcoming exhibitions, but its most useful feature is a searchable database of the museum's store. This allows users to search for items not normally on show, and searches can be made by designer, date, type of object, or even by decorative motif – such as animals or flowers. Not all of the search results will be illustrated, but a search will yield plenty of information to satisfy even the keenest design scholar.

Museum of London

www.museum-london.org.uk

The Museum of London claims to be the largest and most comprehensive city museum in the world. It tells the story of the city through a range of objects, and it's one of the few places where you can see medieval costume alongside the creations of Vivienne Westwood. Online artefacts illustrate different aspects of life in the capital, from childhood through to transportation. The site can be viewed in German, Spanish, and French, as well as English.

Museum of National Antiquities, Stockholm

www.historiska.se

Sweden's most important historical artefacts from the Stone Age to the 17th century are stored in this museum, and many of these objects can be seen online, with accompanying information in Swedish or English. Viking and medieval artefacts are especially prominent, and the majority of the collections consist of archaeological finds and ecclesiastical objects. A virtual tour of the galleries using QuickTime is available.

Museums of the World

www.musee-online.org

An extensive list of links to museum sites all over the world can be found on this useful website, which is run by an American charitable foundation. The site offers brief descriptions and information on the facilities of each museum listed, which will help you to decide whether it might be worth clicking your mouse to make that link.

Museums online: South Africa

www.museums.org.za

This is the web page of South Africa's premier museums. Pay a virtual visit to Robben Island, where Nelson Mandela was held prisoner, or browse through collections that include the paintings, ceramics, and furniture of the William Fehr Collection, which dates from the 17th century.

National Archaeological Museum of Athens

www.culture.gr/2/21/214/21405m/e21405m1.html

The most important archaeological museum in Greece has a website that includes images and text on a representative selection from its extensive holdings. Greek art and sculpture from Hellenic cultures are predominant and there are links to archaeological sites and institutions across Greece.

National Gallery of Australia

www.nga.gov.au

While it's particularly strong in Australian and Asian art, Australia's national gallery has a collection that is truly international in scope. Its website allows you to search the collections for artefacts by culture, keyword, or artist. Online educational resources are linked to the exhibitions programme, and you can subscribe to a free email newsletter. An online shop offers gifts from jigsaws and jewellery through to books and postcards.

National Gallery of Canada

national.gallery.ca

The "Cybermuse", a virtual addition to the gallery space, is one of the main features of this site. It offers an online guided tour of the galleries and more than 5,000 images of works in the collections, many of which are not normally on display. The online collections naturally have Canadian, including Inuit, as well as European, American, and Asian art, dating from the Middle Ages to the present day. There is also a collection of photographs – the museum was one of the first in the world to recognize photography as an art form.

National Gallery of Ireland

www.nationalgallery.ie

Ireland's national collections are online at this site. The gallery's holdings include paintings by Caravaggio, Poussin, and Fragonard, as well as Irish sculpture (predominantly portrait busts), furniture, lace, and silver. A small selection can be seen on the site, which also includes links to other major museums and institutions, a news section, calendar, and an excellent e-shop.

National Historical Museum of Brazil

www.visualnet.com.br/mhn

This museum is one of South America's premier cultural institutions, and it displays a good selection of objects online (the site is available in English). The museum boasts the largest numismatic collection in Latin America, and a small number of examples are shown on the site. Also featured are clocks and watches, including a fine array of pocket watches. Objects in the main collections range from sculptures and carriages to historical documents.

National Museum in Warsaw

www.ddg.com.pl/nm

Polish and Eastern European art, applied and decorative arts, and artefacts from several centuries dominate this site, but works by artists such as Botticelli and the Dutch Old Masters can also be viewed here. Of particular interest is the Faras Gallery, which contains some excellent examples of medieval Christian art from Africa – several of these pieces can be seen on the museum's website, which is available in English. There is an informative section giving a history of the museum.

National Museums of Kenya

www.museums.or.ke

African art and ethnography are features of the website of Kenya's national institutions. Online images include a collection of botanical paintings by Joy Adamson, of *Born Free* fame. The country's big museums and tourist attractions are linked to this site, and there are details of the work of the research departments.

National Museum of New Zealand

www.tepapa.govt.nz

This museum, opened in 1998 and also known as Te Papa, has a large collection of European artefacts dating from the time of the first settlers, and Maori items dating back much further. A good selection of 19th- and 20th-century pictures and Maori costume can be seen online, and you can email the experts with a question, or contact the image library for details of an unrivalled stock of pictures relating to the country. There is a two-minute video about the museum, which can be downloaded from the site.

National Museum of Decorative Arts, Norway

www.nkim.museum.no

Choose your language (Norwegian or English), then enter the site of this Trondheim-based museum, which offers a look at life in the past. Room settings and furniture by various designers are illustrated, which should give ideas to today's interior designers. Pictures and information on a manor house dating back to the Viking period, and on Trondheim's Royal residence, are also included.

National Museums of Scotland

www.nms.ac.uk

A web cam, with a view from the roof of the Museum of Scotland in Edinburgh, is one of the more unusual features of this site, which brings Scotland's national treasures to the web. The collections of several museums can be seen here – they are wide ranging and international in scope, but Scottish items are naturally prominent.

National Museum of Slovenia

www.narmuz-lj.si

The National Museum of Slovenia dates back to the 1820s. Its online version is available in English and features a selection of objects dating from the medieval period to the 20th century. These include antique weaponry, ceramic objects, religious artefacts, archaeological finds, coins, and much more. There is also information on the work of the museum's restorers and conservators.

National Palace Museum, Taiwan

www.npm.gov.tw

Taiwan's major museum has artefacts from 7,000 years of Chinese history. Its site, which is in both English and Chinese, includes informative essays on various topics supporting the current exhibition programme. Examples of bronzes, jades, lacquer ware, paintings, and ceramics from the permanent collections can also be viewed online. Any admirer of Oriental art will truly love this site.

Prado Museum

museoprado.mcu.es

The website of Spain's most famous national institution includes an online "quick tour", which shows 49 of the most important exhibits in the museum. These include many superb Old Master paintings, images of which can be bought online in the form of telephone cards. The links on the site take you to various other museums and institutions around the world.

Rijksmuseum

www.rijksmuseum.nl

You'd expect to find Dutch Old Masters at Amsterdam's world-famous museum, but there's so much more to see here. A realistic virtual visit using QuickTime is a highlight of the site, and you can also take a tour of more than 150 rooms featuring a staggering array of art and artefacts. However, the site warns that some rooms may have been rearranged, so the online tour may not be an exact representation of the museum. All the relevant information about the collections can be found here, and the online shop has an appropriate selection of gifts, including books on art and reproduction glass and Delft.

Royal Museum of Ontario

www.rom.on.ca

A QuickTime virtual reality tour of two of the galleries is a key feature of the site of this Toronto museum. Pan round the gallery and zoom in on whatever interests you. Detailed information on the museum's library and each of the research resources is available, as well as on past, present, and future exhibitions, and there's also an online shop.

Shelburne Museum

www.shelburnemuseum.org

This is the website of a museum in Shelburne, Vermont, which has 37 buildings housing collections reflecting New England history. Buildings include a 1950s house, an apothecary, a blacksmith's shop, a one-room schoolhouse, a lighthouse, and even a jail. The site gives a detailed background on each building, and outlines the collection as a whole. The 1950s house is of particular interest to collectors as it is in fact a replica of the founders' New York City apartment, with the furnishings and French Impressionist paintings in situ. The museum boasts great collections of decoys, quilts, band boxes, sculptural folk art, and dipped wares – its collection of mocha ware is the largest public collection in the world. The various physical tours that are

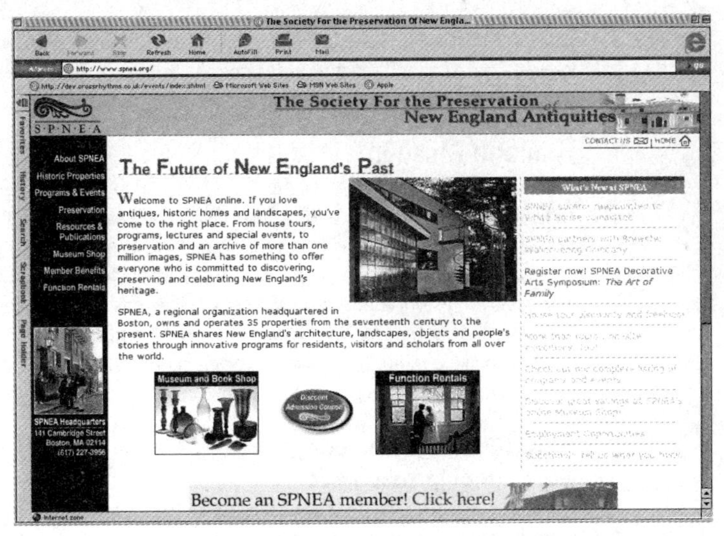

This society's website details all its events and also has an online museum shop.

available are described on the site, including those that are appropriate for children. Current special activities are also listed, as well as directions for visitors and membership information. There is an online gift shop that you can buy directly from too.

Society for the Preservation of New England Antiquities

www.spnea.org

Founded in 1910 to protect the cultural identity of the New England area, SPNEA is a cultural museum that owns and operates 35 historic properties in five different states as well as having an extensive library and image archive. This well-illustrated site contains listings of all the society's activities and places to visit. There is also an online museum shop where you can buy SPNEA merchandise, books, and videos as well as reproduction glass, jewellery, and rugs. The site also gives details of competitions, as well as information about the organization and its important preservation work. There is a telephone number for the SPNEA's useful Old House Resource Line, which homeowners can call for advice and information on dating, maintaining, and preserving their own old houses.

State Hermitage Museum, St Petersburg

www.hermitage.ru

St Petersburg's finest museum, the Hermitage, boasts a collection of three million objects dating from the Stone Age to the present day. It's hard to know where to begin, but the site helps out with a virtual tour of the galleries, and it's available in English. Browse through the arms and armour collection and visit the Michelangelo and Leonardo rooms, as well as the Winter Palace of Peter I. The "Digital Collection" also permits browsing through a much wider selection of the museum's holdings.

Thailand Museum

www.thailandmuseum.com

Thailand's major museums and cultural institutions are listed on this site, though only four have their own web pages – which have links here. However, they do offer an impressive array of online artefacts from this unique culture, as well as an historical background to the collections and their formation. The King of Thailand, for example, opened the Bangkok National Museum, in 1874, while a monk who collected artefacts from the surrounding area founded the collection at Chaiya.

Tokugawa Art Museum

www.cjn.or.jp/tokugawa

The Tokugawa Art Museum was founded in 1935 and it is one of the oldest privately endowed museums in Japan. A room-by-room virtual tour of the museum is offered on its website. The site is in Japanese, but it also has an English-language version. Details of important artefacts and cultural phenomena that can be seen in this museum, such as the Tea Ceremony, are also included here.

24 Hour Museum

www.24hourmuseum.org.uk

The 24 Hour Museum provides links to a huge selection of museums and similar institutions all over the United Kingdom, as well as supplying news from the British museum world. Search for a specific museum, or browse through listings for details. The site includes valuable resources for teachers, and also has advice on how to start your own museum in the classroom or at home.

Victoria and Albert Museum

www.vam.ac.uk

The world's largest museum of decorative arts has 145 galleries, including several of Britain's national collections. Its website is elaborate, and includes various online activities and displays. You can browse through 2,000 images from the collections and search by country or historical period. Full details of all of the current exhibitions are given, and a large selection of gifts can also be ordered online.

Western Australian Museum

www.museum.wa.gov.au

The Western Australian Museum largely focuses on anthropology and natural history. However, it is also concerned with social history and, more especially, maritime history. There's information on shipwrecks on its website and you can also search through a database of 25,000 items for shipwreck finds – which include ceramic bowls right through to anchors.

Winterthur Museum, Garden & Library

www.winterthur.org

This is the website of a museum near Wilmington, Delaware, USA, which was the country estate of Henry Francis du Pont – an avid collector of decorative arts. The museum is filled with his American collection from the 1640–1860 period. A 60-acre garden is open all year, and there is an extensive research library covering all aspects of American art and material culture. An online "Period Rooms Tour" takes you through the history of the house and the development of the collection, pointing out highlights along the way, such as a set of silver tankards by Paul Revere. Extensive information about current exhibitions, scheduling an appointment for a specialized tour, opening hours, details on membership, and the gift shop are all available online. Shopping from a varied catalogue is also offered in a secure setting online.

See fine art, pages 177–187, for listings of art galleries and museums.

WORTH A LOOK

www.beamish.org.uk
Open air museum in the north of England.

www.fitzmuseum.cam.ac.uk
The Fitzwilliam Museum, part of Cambridge University, houses a collection that includes antiquities, fine art and a variety of other interesting items from Europe and elsewhere.

www.icom.org/vlmp/galleries.html
A listing of museums and galleries worldwide.

www.khonkaen.com/english/attractions/museum.htm
Thai museum with online artefacts and links to local attractions.

www.tmag.tas.gov.au
Tasmania's museum and art gallery.

RESOURCE AND GATEWAY SITES

Antiqnet.com

www.antiqnet.com

This site will put you in touch with, and link you to, the websites of insurance firms, restorers, shippers, educational resources, publications, and various other services. However, that is not all – you will also find fair organizers, online auctions, and a shopping mall, which has various items for sale by dealers at fixed prices that you can buy directly online. There's an online demonstration of the buying and selling process to help you get started.

Antique Alley

www.antiquealley.com

This site has a large "classified" section, which lists objects for sale from both dealers and non-dealers. There are no pictures, except for a small selection of highlights, but the relevant dealer's email is given so that you can contact them directly for further details. A "Notes and Queries" section allows you to ask questions about items you own – and anyone can respond to your queries.

Antique Hot Spots

www.antiquehotspots.com

This site lists many Internet antiques and collectibles sites and has international links as well as American ones. Free classified ads are available for anyone to use, and show collectibles for sale. A question board allows people to post questions about items they own (which anyone can answer), and occasionally those items are up for sale – a "wanted" board allows you to post up your wish list. A search will produce lists of sites that mention the specific words you entered and the site is updated every 24 hours.

Antique Mall

www.antiquemall.co.za

This is a gateway to antiques in South Africa and includes dealers, auctioneers, restorers, and miscellaneous events. A particularly useful feature of the site is its list of international links. Click on a flag to find listings of dealers, auctioneers, and antiques-related sites and information in the relevant country.

The Antiques Directory

www.theantiquesdirectory.co.uk

This site is a little confusing because clicking on a button will take you to a page that looks much like the one you just left. But if you scroll down the page, the information you want will appear. That aside, this site does contain an extensive listing of auctions and fairs, publications, shops, books about antiques, and even videos on the subject of antiques and collecting. In a few cases, you can even watch a clip from the video online.

Antique Searcher

www.antiquesearcher.com

This US site has a huge amount of listings to help you find antique centres, dealers, auctions, collectibles, directories, fairs and shows, publications, reproductions, resources, and services. An "ask the experts" section is an open forum where you can send in your related questions to be answered. You can choose to be taken to a "random link" if you are feeling adventurous, and a "what's new" page lists the latest links and additions to the site.

Antiques and Art Australia

www.antique-art.com.au

As its name suggests, this website offers a gateway to antiques and art Down Under. You can choose from more than 1,500 items that are for sale in the virtual gallery, and also follow the links to the top dealers' associations of Australia and New Zealand, as well as to the *Australian Antique Collector* magazine. You can also use the search engine to carry out a keyword search for items that particularly interest you.

The Antiques and Collectibles Guide

www.acguide.com

This useful US site is the web page of the guidebook of the same name and it contains over 3,000 businesses, organizations, and events, as well as related products and services – it has been online since 1994. There are three main sections to the site: a shops index, specialities index, and an events calendar. A nice feature is the "clickable map" of the USA, which provides lists of shops and dealers state by state, and includes links to their websites. The month-by-month list of events has many, but not all, major and minor shows across the USA as well as a few listings from the UK and Europe.

Antiques Atlas

www.antiques-atlas.com

This site gives a geographical guide to antiques in the United Kingdom and Ireland. Click on an area of the map to find a breakdown of shops, auction houses, centres, fairs, museums, and other places to see and/or buy antiques and art. Full listings of places are given, including their opening hours. You can also search a database of items for sale from around the world and get in touch with a vendor. No transactions take place through the site – any deals are directly between you and the seller.

Antiques Listings on the Internet

www.antiques-internet.com

Listings of antiques dealers, shops, malls, fairs, and auction houses throughout the USA, Canada, and Mexico can be found on this site. Links include other general antiques sites and recommended software sites and there's also advice on preparing web pages. There is a patent date chart for the US from 1836–1965, which can be printed out and used as a useful reference. Dealers are listed by their specialities and there are links to their websites from here.

Antiques UK

www.antiques-uk.co.uk

A free listing for collectors to register their wants online for all to see is one of

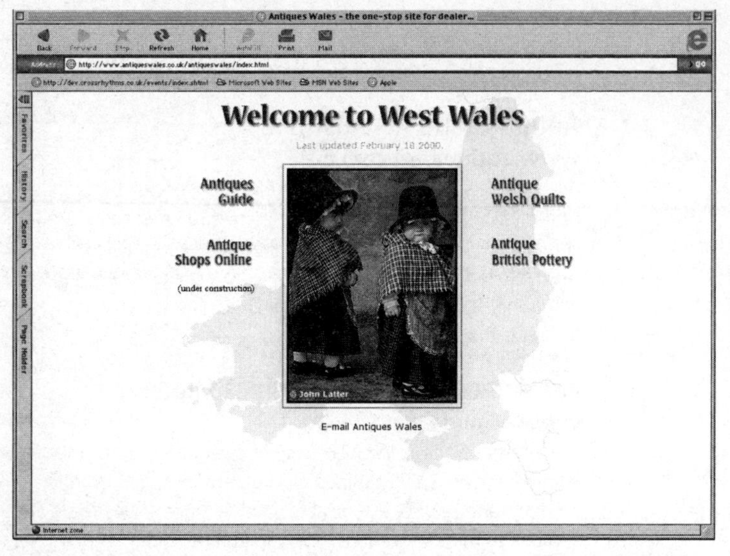

An introduction to antiques in Wales, this site has a particularly good guide to Welsh quilts.

the most useful features of this website, which is dedicated to the British trade. The site features items from the catalogues of numerous antique dealers, and you can send an email enquiry for further information on any of the items that interest you and/or follow a link to their website. There is also an online directory of dealers, shippers, trade associations, and fairs.

Antiques of Wales

www.antiqueswales.co.uk

This site offers a guide to antiques in Wales, including a list of dealers with their specialities and contact information. A selection of stock on offer by some of the dealers is also featured, and there are links to their individual websites if you wish to ask for further information before buying a particular item.

Antiquesweb

www.antiquesweb.co.uk

A section of items for sale, a listing of antiques dealers, an auction guide, and a fairs guide are among the many facets of this site. There's a free email newsletter for updates on new features and information and you can use the "wanted" section to post up details of your own object of desire or to email other users if you can provide what they are looking for.

Antiques World

www.antiquesworld.com

This US site sells items from most collectible categories but it is not an auction site, as the prices are set. There is an extensive bookstore with listings by category – once you click on one you will be linked to amazon.com to purchase it. There is also an online antiques shop link to The Princeton Antique Shop, with an inventory of items that are available for sale. The extensive "antiques marketplace" allows you to post your own articles up for sale, or list what it is that you are looking to buy. The site also contains many informative articles for the beginner such as "What are antiques?", "What is meant by collectibles?", and "Getting started". There is a useful glossary of words pertaining to antique jewellery and a guide to weights and measures for gold, silver, and gemstones.

Antiques World Belgium

www.antiques-world.com

This site offers links to antique dealers in the Benelux countries as well as auctioneers (complete with an auction calendar), trade associations, and much, much more. Fairs, markets, and exhibitions are also featured on the site, as is stolen art. You will find news from the world of antiques, a classified ads section, and can even get advice on planning your business trips to this part of the world – and it's all available in English.

Antiques World UK

www.antiquesworld.co.uk

This site is a directory of information for anyone with an interest in art, antiques, and collectibles. It includes features by experts, book reviews, and links to organizations such as collectors' clubs. You will also find information on fairs, markets, exhibitions, antiques tours, study courses, and much more. There is also a guide to regional museums and art galleries (see pages 90–101 for specific museum sites).

Belgium Antiques

www.belgiumantiques.com

A vast and comprehensive introduction to the antiques world in Belgium and the Netherlands, this site (available in English) offers a guide to dealers, auctioneers, trade associations, fairs, and markets – and there's even shipping information. You will also find details of educational courses and stolen items, as well as an online guide to styles and periods. An interactive map of the two countries helps you to find the location of specific dealers, and there's travel information, should you decide to visit.

Clougherty Jeans

www.cjeans.com

This New England site does not have any items to buy directly from it, but has links to many dealers, as well as to the MADA (Maine Antique Dealers Association) and NHADA (New Hampshire Antique Dealers Association) – see trade associations on pages 117–22 for further details of these sites. There is also an extensive listing of New England auctions and fairs as well as links to publications, including *Maine Antique Digest* and *Antiques and the Arts Weekly* (see specialist publications on pages 112–17). The site also contains classified ads for both buying and selling as well as a listing of restorers, who are given alphabetically by state.

Collector Cafe

www.collectorcafe.com

This is a non-commercial web portal that caters for the needs of the collector, providing information, articles, a bulletin board, and collecting resources. Ninety different collecting fields are catered for here, and there is also a listing of various specialist dealers as well as classified ads. Go to your area of interest, read an article, then see a list of relevant dealers and other websites, with instant links to them.

Collector Network

www.collectornetwork.com

This site is dominated by coins, banknotes, and stamps, but it is also expanding into other collecting fields. It features an online shopping mall, a news stand with links to the sites of collecting publications, and bulletin boards for you to contact and have debates with other users. Perhaps its most useful feature is, however, its web directory, which features links to almost 10,000 sites, from general antique sites to specialist sites devoted to topics ranging from advertising to sporting collectibles.

Collector Online

www.collectoronline.com

This US site is essentially an online antique mall but it offers much more than just that. It provides the Inventory Management System free of charge, which helps dealers manage all aspects of their online selling. It also allows dealers to sell items on multiple auction sites as well as in a "booth" within its own online mall. You can search this mall using a category system and there is also a request form that you can use to get them to do a thorough search for a particular item for you. The site also includes informative articles on collectibles, covering everything from action figures to trade cards. The "Resource" section includes lists of dealers, centres, publications, other online sources, and collectors' clubs. This is a site that is truly worth visiting, whether you are a dealer or a collector.

Collectors Universe

www.collectors-universe.com

This site is aimed at collectors of autographs, coins, currency, records, sports memorabilia, records and music memorabilia, and stamps, and each of these subjects has a separate area within the site. There are online price guides for each, and an extensive library of articles on collecting these items. Useful definitions of collecting terminology are also included. The Collectors Universe experts are all pictured, with short biographies. You will also find specialist online auctions and online shopping malls here as well as links to lots of dealers and resource sites.

Curioscape

www.curioscape.com

On this American site, you can search approximately 13,000 independently owned shops for that coveted item, be it a Chinese snuff bottle or a lunchbox. Browse through a feast of items illustrated in colour, and click on the picture of your choice to make your purchase online (prices are given in US dollars). You can also register to post your own items online. The latest arrivals to the site are listed on the main page, so you can keep up-to-date on what is new. There is also an online bulletin board for each category, enabling you to contact other enthusiasts in your field.

Directory of UK Antiques and Collectors' Fairs

www.antiques-web.co.uk/fairs.html

As its title suggests, this is a thorough and extensive listing of antiques fairs taking place in the United Kingdom, including specialist fairs such as Art Deco events. Contact details are given, as well as links to the pages of individual organizers and their websites where applicable.

Finelot

www.finelot.com

Billed as the place "where you'll find the extra, not the ordinary", Finelot offers both online galleries and auctions with quality objects for sale by top dealers. You can shop online at the auctions, or buy fixed-price items. Participating dealers pay a commission on items sold through the site, but there is no commission for the buyer. There are also online forums and details of offline educational courses based in the UK. Finelot also provides many useful links to the sites of dealers and online showrooms. (See pages 57–80 for details of other auction sites.)

Gospark

www.gospark.com

This Italian gateway site offers online shopping in a mall that has over 40,000 items for sale, which are all on a searchable database. Full contact details of the dealers are given, including websites where possible. The site also offers a listing of exhibitions and auctions in various countries, and there's an archive of articles on art and antiques.

icollector

www.icollector.com

This site offers the chance to buy antiques through online auctions and via links to dealer sites, with live, real-time bidding in selected auction sales. Icollector was founded in 1994 and today represents more than 300 auction houses and 650 galleries and dealers. Offline auctioneers also display their catalogues on the site. There's a dealer directory here and auction news, and you can sign up to receive regular email updates on items that may be of interest. You will also find a "Community" section, which offers the chance to exchange views with fellow collectors via bulletin boards – you must register (it is free) to take part or to bid in the auctions, but you can browse without joining.

The International Arts, Antiques, and Collectibles Forum

www.the-forum.com

This commercial service provides information on the arts, antiques, and collectibles. You can also buy online – there are items in each of these categories available and every one of them is illustrated. A "price guide" lists objects that have sold on the site previously, with their prices to give you an idea of how much things go for. The "buyers guide" contains a wanted list, which is placed by individual advertisers. There is also a bookstore with a huge

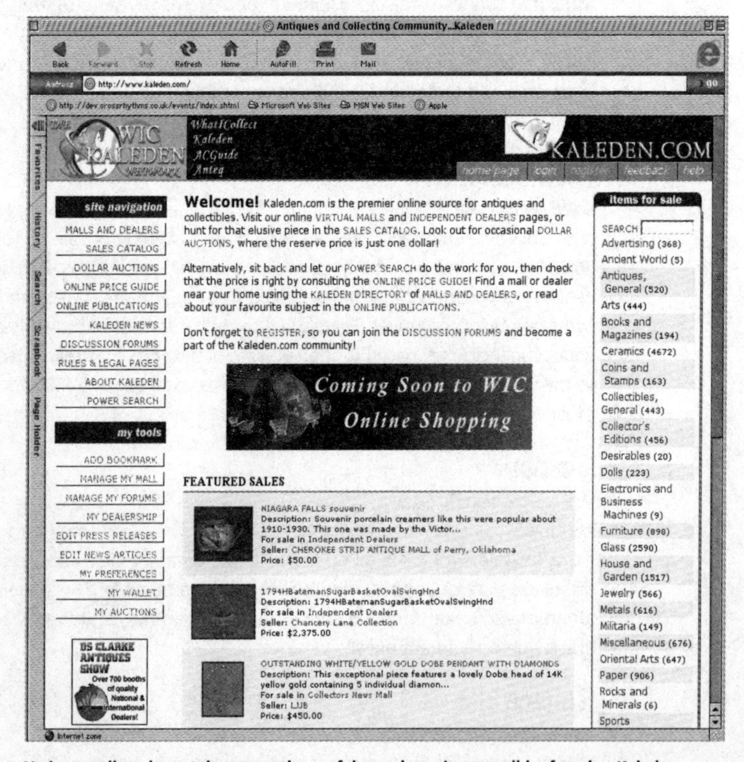

Various malls, sales catalogues, and a useful search engine can all be found at Kaleden.

listing of books on collectibles – this provides details of any new titles as well as stocking out-of-print and rare books. You can order via email, telephone, or post. The site also lists US museums by state, and there is a brief introduction to each museum, including hours, collections, and location.

Kaleden USA

www.kaleden.com

This site consists of a list of 16 virtual malls with live inventories, and another list of malls that are coming soon. There are also listings of offline antique malls across the United States. It has links to 12 publications too, with articles on almost every relevant subject and you can exchange views with fellow collectors via an online forum. There are 44 dealers with online stock listed on the site, each with a categorized inventory that is largely made up of collectibles. A general links page will hook you up with publications, dealers, price guides, a bookstore, and other informative sources.

New England Antiquing

www.antiquing.com

This site covers the world of antiques in all five New England states. Antiques shops and centres are listed by state, or you can search for what is available in a particular town or city. Some antiques are for sale online and there is also a list of dealers who have online inventories, as well as a list of auctioneers. A holiday-planning section includes lists of historic inns and B&Bs, historic restaurants, historic homes open to the public, villages worth visiting, antique-related and maritime museums, and fairs and events so if you are planning a visit to this area, look at this site to find out what to do when you are there.

Ruby Lane

www.rubylane.com

This American site is a great place for finding, buying, and selling antiques, collectibles, and fine art. A "Global Search" produces items from many online auctions and private sellers and most of these are accompanied by pictures. Online shops are divided into categories such as antiques, collectibles, and fine art shops. Items offered in the antiques section must be pre-World War II, and those offered as collectibles must be at least 20 years old. There are links to Ruby Lane's own shops, which allow you to go into each one and see their catalogue, as well as online auctions and over 40 other sites. The area called "Courtyard" has e-postcards, chat boards, surveys, articles, and web links. There are also fun reproductions of old postcards to send online and a selection of articles to read. Press articles that mention the site and press releases put out by the site are also available online.

SalvoWEB

www.salvo.co.uk

A gateway to information on anything to do with architectural antiques, garden statuary, and salvage, this site provides links to a multitude of dealers in this field. It also provides a listing of forthcoming UK auctions featuring these objects, warnings of stolen items in circulation, and information on publications. There's also a list of buildings that are due for demolition, and a link to an American site that offers similar useful information in the United States.

Search for Antiques

www.search-for-antiques.co.uk

A user-friendly site, written in a chatty style, this offers a directory of nearly 700 antiques dealers, trading both on- and offline. The directory is divided into subject categories so you can easily identify specialists, and there are also links to online auction sites. Some of the linked auction sites are for charity antique and collectible sales, such as Oxfam. You can also search the dealer listings by region for UK-based dealers, which is a great service for those wishing to plan an antiques-hunting holiday.

Secondhand Savvy

www.secondhandsavvy.com

An e-zine featuring news and views from the world of antiques hunting is one of the main features of this Canadian site. It acts as a guide not only to shops and auctions, but also to flea markets and even garage sales. There are also some "tricks of the trade" and articles on related fields such as interior design. Much of the content is Canadian, but there are contributions from around the world – most notably in the classified ads section.

SimplyAntiques.com

www.simplyantiques.com

This site offers a showroom with access to items for sale from architectural antiques through to wine-related antiques. Dealers and individuals can register to sell items through the site, for which the vendor pays an 8 per cent commission on items sold – there are no up-front fees. Buyers must also register, but they pay no commission. A useful section with typical buyers' and sellers' questions should clear any uncertainties.

UK Antiques

www.antiques.co.uk

An online mall is the main feature of this site; you must register if you wish to buy, and all items for sale are vetted by experts prior to inclusion. The site also offers an advanced search facility, enabling you to search for antiques by category, period, country of origin, price band, and keyword. The site also features articles on a range of subjects relating to art and antiques including exhibition reviews. If you can't find exactly what you are looking for, the "Wanted Items" facility allows you to send a request with a few details and the specialists will do the rest – and notify you by email when they find it.

World Collectors Net

www.worldcollectorsnet.com

Run "by collectors, for collectors", this site offers an online magazine, a price guide, message boards, and a shopping arcade. There's also a news section, which gives the latest on limited-edition products, location filming for antiques TV programmes, and much more. The online shops are especially strong on limited-edition pieces, and you can buy online from many of them. Links galore can be found on this site, and they are subdivided into specialist areas for the user's convenience.

WORTH A LOOK

www.antique-dealers-directory.com
A directory of dealers and services that offers free listings.

www.antiques-directory.co.uk
Database of more than 17,000 antiques-related businesses.

www.antiques-finder.co.uk
Online antiques directory.

www.antiques-web.co.uk
UK site listing fairs, dealers, centres, and more.

SPECIALIST PUBLICATIONS

American Antiquities

www.americanantiquities.com

This quarterly publication includes many of its articles online, as well as an events calendar. There are antiques maps of the states that are covered by the journal (12 states east of Illinois and Tennessee). If you click on the map of the state you are interested in, it will bring up the names of all the cities there. You can then go into a city or town to find its antiques dealers. Each entry has a short description with address, telephone, and email address where available.

Antique Collectors' Club

www.antique-acc.com

The Antique Collectors' Club is well known as a major publisher of antiques-related books, as well as the club's magazine. Subscribe to the magazine online, or consult the extensive list of books published by the club to date, which are on a vast range of collecting topics.

Antique Dealer and Collectors' Guide

www.antiquecollectorsguide.co.uk

This monthly UK magazine is devoted to producing wide-ranging and informative articles on every aspect of antiques and the decorative arts. The website shows material from the magazine including a fairs calendar, saleroom reports, news, and articles on furniture, clocks, porcelain, and glass, etc. You can request subscription information via email, and there are links to trade association websites, as well as to the Birmingham NEC antiques fairs.

Antiques and Art Around Florida

www.aarf.com

This publication comes out twice a year and its online version contains a list of advertisers, as well as a search facility for dealers by location or category. There is also a list of merchandise for sale by category, and separate sections for Florida's most popular shopping areas, Dania and West Palm Beach, with a link to each one's own web page. There is also a complete list of fairs and auctions in the state with links wherever these are available. A list of articles is also given, with special markings for articles that relate directly to Florida. Other topics range from Canton China to antique fishing lures. Other links include collectors' sites in various categories.

Antiques and the Arts Online

www.antiquesandthearts.com

This is the online home of *Antiques and the Arts Weekly*. It contains various articles, including arts news as well as fair and auction reviews. A book section has reviews of books on antiques and arts, with a link to the online bookshop amazon.com. The site also provides a search facility, which you can use to search for a particular item and it will bring up the names of any auctions that have it mentioned in their listings. The "Calendar" lists auctions and fairs for that month taking place in the USA and you can click on any given day to bring up a detailed list. There are also various links that will connect you to almost every site on the web involved with antiques and the arts – this is an extremely useful site.

Antiques Info

www.antiques-info.co.uk

The *Antiques Info* magazine is published six times per year, and features information on the UK antiques scene. Online, you can read articles from recent publications, such as letters from readers and replies to their antiques queries. The site also features a price guide and fairs and auction listings, although you will have to subscribe and pay a fee to be able to see some of this information.

Antiques Magazine

www.antiquesmagazine.com

This is the online home of a UK-based weekly magazine that covers all aspects of art and antiques. The website, which is updated weekly, features searchable auctions and fairs calendars, and lists thousands of events and dates around the UK and overseas. You can search the calendars by date, name of the auctioneer/fair you are interested in, or area. You will also find material from recent issues, including reports of auction sales, articles on fakes and forgeries, and much, much more. Some features of the site are only available to subscribers – you can take out a subscription online.

Antiques Trade Gazette

www.antiquestradegazette.com

This is the online version of a weekly UK newspaper for the antiques trade. The site includes news from the antiques trade and calendars listing all the major international fine art and antiques fairs and auction sales. There's an Internet directory, featuring links to art- and antiques-related sites, and you can also request a free sample copy of the paper. There is also an "online price guide", though you must register to use this part of the site.

AntiqueWeek Online

www.antiqueweek.com

The site includes informative articles from this paper, which typically include topics ranging from starting a collection, fiesta ware, and whether auctioneers or their staff should bid at their own auctions, to how to define fakes, revivals, and reproductions. It also provides a listing of fairs, auctions, and flea markets taking place in America in the current month. There are also classified ads on the site, as well as a section of book ads – these are for older books, mostly of historical interest, with some first editions. The site also provides various links to online auctions, online malls, informational sites, media and related sites, and fair links.

Art & Antiques

www.artantiquesmag.com

The award-winning American *Art & Antiques* magazine is aimed at high-end, affluent collectors, and says its aim is "to capture the passion and elegance of the diverse world of art and antiques". Its website not only offers a preview of the current issue and subscription information, but also gives an events listing for exhibitions all over the USA, online antiques advertising, comments on up-and-coming artists, and news on recent thefts and crimes within the art world around the globe.

Art & Australia

www.artaustralia.com

This quarterly magazine features articles on art, new and old, by leading Australian and overseas writers. You can read a selection of articles on the website, which also features a gallery directory. This lists galleries all over Australia and New Zealand, and also features some from the United States. There are links to other magazines, art schools, and web resources too.

The Art Newspaper

www.theartnewspaper.com

Old and new art, decorative art, and the art of the commercial and non-commercial worlds are covered by this UK-based publication. On its site, there are news stories from the art world, reviews of exhibitions, and reports on the art market and conservation issues. There are also interviews with artists.

Arts of Asia

www.artsofasianet.com

A Hong Kong-based publication with the largest circulation of any Asian arts magazine, *Arts of Asia* is currently distributed to 80 countries. Its online home lets you browse through features from its past issues, and you can also order copies of back issues online. You can also search the site for articles on a specific subject. There are links to auction houses, galleries, fairs, and art societies, too.

BBC Homes and Antiques Magazine

www.beeb.com/homesandantiques

The website of the BBC *Homes and Antiques* magazine gives you the chance to submit pictures and information on your home for a possible feature in the magazine. Online reader offers range from the chance to cruise the Caribbean with experts to the chance to buy limited-edition Steiff teddy bears. There's an online bookstore and you can also subscribe to the magazine online.

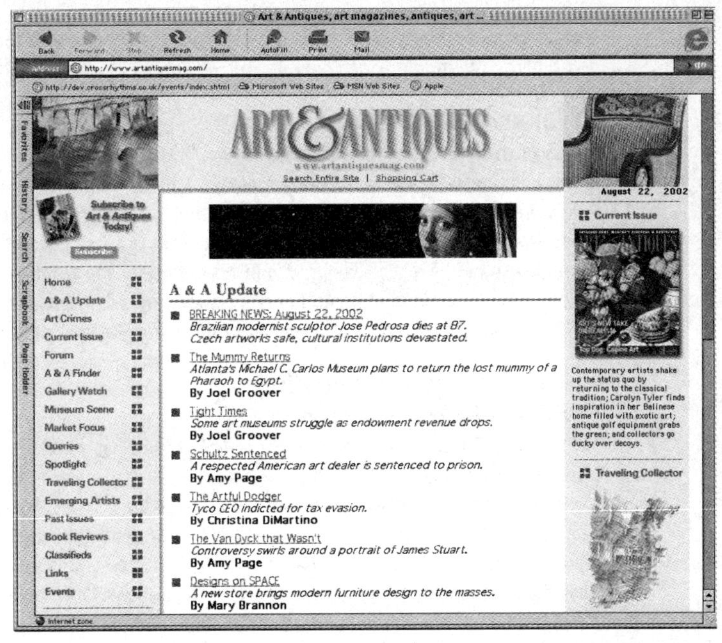

The *Art & Antiques* magazine site does much more than just preview its current issue.

The Burlington Magazine

www.burlington.org.uk

The Burlington Magazine was founded in 1903 by a group of scholars and its aim is to further the serious study of art. Its online home offers details of the contents of recent issues, and the opportunity to subscribe. The philosophy behind the magazine is explained, and there are notes for would-be contributors.

Collecting Consciousness

www.shecollects.com

This online publication provides information about various aspects of collecting and the resources that are available, both online and through other media. It also welcomes outside contributions of articles, if you fancy yourself as a writer. The site provides a list of recommended reading on collecting as well as giving you plenty of reading material in the form of articles on a huge variety of subjects. There are many links, arranged into categories including online auctions and auction tips, storage and preservation, and kids and collecting.

The Fine Arts Trader

www.fineartstrader.com

This is a monthly American publication for the fine arts market. The online version has a series of articles from past issues, which mostly consist of biographies of various artists. It also has listings of museum exhibitions, auctions, and fairs. The site has a direct link to Barnes and Noble's arts and antiques books.

Maine Antique Digest

www.maineantiquedigest.com

This is the web supplement to the monthly American newspaper. The site is very well-organized: on the left are advertisers, on the right are auction and fair ads arranged by date, and in the centre you can click on the latest articles from the newspaper, a dealer directory, a prices database, site search, over 1,100 book reviews, a list of stolen art and antiques, and subscription information. There are also useful details of computer programs for dealers and collectors.

New England Antiques Journal

www.antiquesjournal.com

This is a monthly publication and the online version has some interesting features: "Around the Block" provides auction news from around the USA, with illustrations of interesting items or things that sold for surprising amounts of money. "Stock Market" is a text-only listing of items for sale from the journal's advertisers, while "Whatsit?" is a monthly column showing a puzzling item – the first person to email with the correct answer wins a year's subscription to the printed version of the journal. A showroom section offers various items for sale. Features cover everything from Flow Blue ceramics to Madame Alexander dolls. The site also has links to the sites of companies that advertise in the journal.

Southeastern Antiquing and Collecting Magazine

www.go-star.com/antiquing

Southeastern Antiquing and Collecting Magazine covers the antiques scene across several states in the southeastern United States. The site offers news and views, a directory of dealers and a "Collectors' Clubhouse", which provides news of society meetings. There are selected articles from the printed version of the magazine, and you can subscribe to an email newsletter. A links page includes some sites connected with specialist collecting fields.

Teddy Bear Times

www.teddybeartimes.com

Teddy Bear Times is a leading UK-based publication for teddy enthusiasts. Its website offers the chance to subscribe online and tempts the visitor with news of teddy bear fairs, makers, patterns, videos, and much more. The site also features an online shop, where you can buy bears, materials, and accessories. There are also numerous links to teddy bear sites on the Internet.

The World of Antiques and Art

www.antiquesandart.com.au

The website of this leading Australian publication offers online articles from the current issue, as well as a diary of events, exhibitions, and fairs around the world. Articles cover a wide range of subjects, and contributors include noted academics. There's also a directory of dealers, auction houses, and institutions in Australia and various other countries to be found here.

World of Interiors
www.worldofinteriors.co.uk

The website of this leading interior design magazine includes information on the content of the latest issue and also gives you a chance to subscribe online. The website also includes a searchable catalogue of leading names in British interior design, and this listing contains details of antiques dealers in various disciplines.

WORTH A LOOK

www.gazette-drouot.com
French antiques publication.

www.ubr.com/clocks/journ/clkmag/clkmag.html
Specialist magazine for those with an interest in all aspects of horology.

TRADE ASSOCIATIONS

American National Association of Collectors (NAC)
www.collectors.org

The official NAC site provides a whole host of information and advice, such as how to care for, display, and insure a collection. An "Appraisers" section describes what to look for in a personal property appraiser (as well as what to watch out for), and there are also links to appraisers' organizations. The site also has classified ads, and display ads link to dealers, online malls, and auctions. An extensive listings section gives details of seminars and workshops, museum exhibits, speciality auctions, and flea markets. There is also an alphabetical listing of auctioneers, which gives links to their websites where available. A calendar lists fairs by state and the "Industry News" has short articles from various publications and collectors' clubs. There is also a useful listing of theft reports.

Antiques Dealers' Association of America (ADA)
www.adadealers.com

This organization was formed to provide education and make the business of buying and selling antiques more professional. Members must practise ethical and honest conduct, and must guarantee all the items that they sell. The site also has links to member sites.

The Antiques Council

www.antiquescouncil.com

This council is made up of a group of top North American dealers who run fairs, promote education, and offer a guarantee on all items at their fairs. The council now has some 80 members in more than 20 states. There are links to the members' websites or email addresses as well as details about the fairs.

Australian Antique Dealers' Association

www.aada.org.au

Dates of Australia's fairs, educational workshops and seminars, and services offered by the members of Australia's leading trade organization can all be found on this site. The association's code of practice is also included, together with a list of members, and there is also a society that the public can join.

The Bath and Bradford on Avon Antiques Dealers' Association (BABAADA)

www.babaada.com

The Bath and Bradford on Avon Antique Dealers' Association represents 80 dealers in the west of England, and you will find information on all of them here – there are even detailed maps showing you where each dealer is located. There's a searchable directory that not only allows searches by specialist category or location, but also by size of centre. There is also a directory of services that includes information on shippers, courier services, and hotels.

British Antique Dealers' Association (BADA)

www.bada.org

"Art has no enemy but ignorance" is the motto of Britain's oldest dealers' association. The website enlightens us with information on its educational activities, annual fair, "friends" organization, and a list of its members. Dealers are listed by category or by location. (See page 82 for further details of its fair.)

CINOA

www.cinoa.org

The Confédération Internationale des Négotiants en Oeuvres d'Art is the global association of the antiques and art trade. Membership comprises the leading associations of many countries. Its website, which is available in several languages, sets out its aims and has links to the websites of member associations, or gives lists of individual members where these are not available.

Cotswold Antique Dealers' Association

www.cotswolds-antiques-art.com

The Cotswolds is one of the best-known areas for antiques shops in the UK. Its

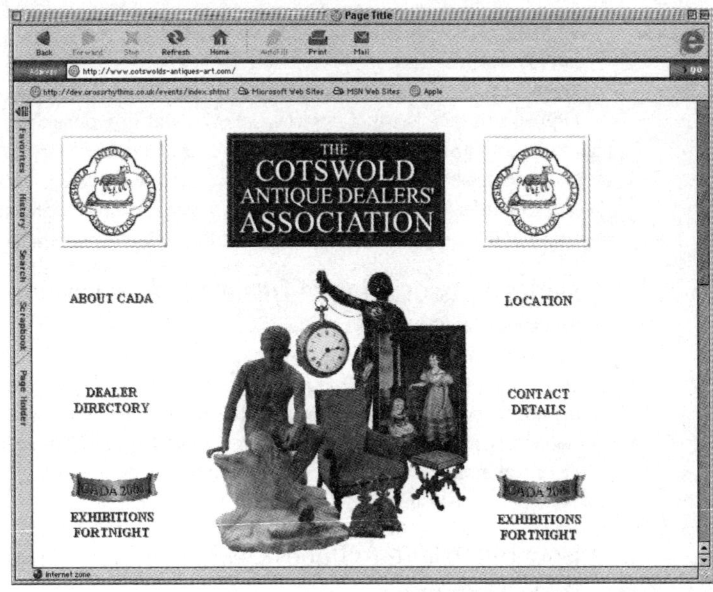

A full dealer directory and details of its annual festival appear on this association's site.

leading dealers are represented by this association, whose site includes a full dealer directory as well as local maps and information on hotels in the area. The site also offers information on the "Exhibitions Fortnight", an antiques festival that takes place every autumn. Members bring out their best stock and put on a fine show for this event, which has become the highlight of the association's year.

Harrogate Antique Dealers' Association

www.harrogateantiques.com

There are two sections to the website of the Harrogate Antique Dealers' Association: the first features information on visiting this attractive spa town in the north of England, while the second has items for sale. You cannot buy online in the latter section, but you can enquire about items and arrange to see them in person. Shops and dealers are listed, as are local hotels and restaurants. The directory of local antiques dealers includes full details of their opening hours and links to their websites where available.

LAPADA

www.lapada.co.uk

LAPADA has over 700 members throughout the UK. Its site has a membership directory and a search engine enabling you to find the members that sell what you want, using a keyword. It also includes advice on the care of antiques, importing and exporting, and security, with links to various websites including that of The Art Loss Register, which is a database of stolen art (see page 122).

Maine Antiques Dealers Association

www.maineada.com

This US trade association aims to keep the standards of ethics and service high. It runs two fairs that attract a national audience, one in July and the other in August/September. The website gives full information on both as well as listing dealer members, along with links to their websites where available. You can order a printed directory online, which describes all the members, giving addresses and telephone numbers for each of them.

National Association of Dealers in Antiques Inc

www.nadaweb.org

This American organization was formed in 1961, and its goal is to promote ethical business practices, integrity, honesty, and provide education for both members and the public. The appraisal division of the organization is the National Association of Personal Property appraisers (NAPPA), which also carries a code of ethics. There are links to all members' websites and these members can also post classified ads that anyone can buy from.

New Hampshire Antiques Dealers Association (NHADA)

www.nhada.org

This is a 360-member organization of dealers from New Hampshire and other states. It runs one of August's most popular antiques fairs. A directory of members is listed by town or speciality on the website and there is a list of links to members' websites. Information about the annual fairs is given, along with maps of New Hampshire that point out the dealers' locations.

The Online Auction Users Association

www.auctionusers.org

This non-profit-making organization aims to provide a collective voice for the buyers and sellers who use online auctions. Topics covered on the site include education, tools and training, how to secure benefits and group deals, and lobbying to promote laws and regulations to benefit the community. A list of sponsors shows companies that provide assistance to online auction users, helping either with posting items or tracking auctions. All of these useful sites have banner ads with direct links. To become a member of the association, just provide proof of identification – benefits include access to online educational pages, discounts on products and services, mentoring, and participation in online discussions. All of the major online auction sites are listed, with links. There are also links to buyer and seller resources, payment systems, image hosting, HTML help, pricing and item identification, software, bidding guides, escrow, software and tools for buyers, as well as hints on dealing with fraud.

Petworth Art and Antique Dealers' Association

www.paada.com

Petworth is an English market town with a high concentration of quality antiques dealers. The local trade association's website will tell you all about the town and its history, as well as the dealers who trade there. The dealer list includes links to individual websites where possible, and there are other links to trade publications, associations, and antiques web resources.

Portobello Antique Dealers' Association

www.portobelloroad.co.uk

Portobello Road is London's largest antiques market, and this special dealers association exists both to promote the area and to encourage fair trading. There are lots of pictures of the market crowds and stalls, and you can even hear an audio recording of the bustle of market life. There are lists of dealers by category. Interestingly, Portobello Road actually boasts the largest group of textile dealers in the UK. You will also find a map of the surrounding area and suggestions for nearby places to eat.

South African Antique Dealers' Association

www.saada.co.za

South Africa's premier dealers can all be found on this site, listed alphabetically and by region. The listings are all fairly detailed, giving a reasonable indication of the kind of stock on offer from each of them. There is also information on the association's fair.

Syndicat Nationale des Antiquaires

www.franceantiq.fr

The extensive site of this French association is available in English and features a dealer directory, subdivided by category for ease of use, and there is also a map of Paris. You will find information on exhibitions and fairs as well as links to dealers in various other countries. This association was founded in 1901 and boasts around 400 members.

Thames Valley Antique Dealers' Association

www.tvada.co.uk

The Thames Valley Antique Dealers' Association (TVADA) represents 250 quality antiques dealers from a region of England that is rich in such businesses. Members are listed by name and by location, and there's a map to help you find them. An events directory includes information on the association's two fairs, which are held in spring and autumn.

World of Art and Antiques

www.worldartantiques.com/phonebookindex.htm

This "phone book" section of an American site is a rich source of information on art and antiques associations from around the world. It lists trade associations from different countries, and has links to the websites of each where available. It also lists museums (see pages 90–101 for other museum sites), book dealers (see pages 142–5 for specific book-dealer sites), etc.

WORTH A LOOK

www.antiqueandcollectible.com
Listing of associations plus trade news.

www.antiques-london.com
The site of the Kensington Church Street Antique Dealers' Association, with listings and a map of this high-quality London antiques district.

www.wkada.co.uk
Association representing dealers in West Kent, in the southeast of England.

USEFUL SITES

Antique Restorers

www.antiquerestorers.com

This is an online community of restorers and on their site they share ideas and provide information and advice about the proper restoration and care of antiques. There are extensive discussion boards and archives about many categories of restoration here. There is also a recommended antique restoration book list, which discounts most titles and gives direct links to the online bookshop amazon.com. There are over 640 articles on restoration, which cover all aspects of the subject: furniture, porcelain, silver, textiles, and general subjects. The list of antique restorers covers the USA, UK, and many other international locations.

Artinsure.com

www.artinsure.com

Art insurance underwritten by Lloyds of London is available through this site, although you may not be eligible to purchase cover if you are outside the UK. The site also includes useful definitions of insurance terms, and has links to security organizations as well as antiques dealers and fairs.

The Art Loss Register

www.artloss.com

The Art Loss Register maintains a database of stolen art from around the world. The register co-operates with international law enforcement agencies and has helped in the recovery of art worth more than £50 million since 1991. Its regularly updated website has news of recent thefts, and victims are invited to register losses free of charge for any insured items. Those involved in buying and selling art can check suspicious items against the register for a fee.

Asheford Institute of Antiques

www.tias.com/stores/asheford/

This US website describes the institute's courses on antiques. It also provides informative articles written by its founder, Peter Green, on silver, hardware, and other aspects of antiques as well as featuring an essay by a student each month. The courses cover all aspects of antiques in most categories, including using the Internet, buying and selling, and how to determine if a piece is real or actually a reproduction.

Classic Web Design

www.classicwebdesign.com

Jill Probst is the creator of many websites for top American antiques dealers. This website includes details on the costs of creating and maintaining a site, the services provided, and options involved for the individual site. Many technical questions are also answered here. An extensive list of sites designed by Probst is available for viewing, and these include both antiques dealers' and other commercial sites from central Virginia (her home). She will, however, take on work from any location.

Collectors Worldwide

www.collectorsworldwide.co.uk

This free service puts collectors in touch with whatever they are looking for. Just register your requirements online and they will do their best to fulfil them for you. The site holds a database of requirements that is constantly being updated. Collectors are advised by email when an item is found, and payment for it is then made to Collectors Worldwide. The site includes a selection of recent successes.

D'Antiques Ltd

www.dantiques.com

This site is a home business featuring eclectic collectibles. Categories of items for sale cover ceramics, items from fraternal organizations, science, railwayana, militaria, electronics, games, Disney, etc. The site also has many resources including a list of patent dates, a currency converter, and links to sites covering almost everything in the world of antiques and collectibles: automobilia, ephemera, photographica, tobaccoiana, tools, and toys, to name just a few.

Go Value It

www.govalueit.com

Millions of valuations compiled by collectors, auction houses, and museum valuers from the USA and Europe are featured on this site. Toys, annuals, and popular culture collectibles are a strong feature. You must register, which costs just £10/$14 per year, to use the service, but registration enables you to request as many valuations as you like. Submit as many details as possible about your item and you will receive a valuation by email.

The Grove Dictionary of Art

www.groveart.com

The Grove Dictionary of Art is the result of 15 years of work by more than 6,800 leading scholars. It contains 45,000 articles on every aspect of the visual arts from pre-history to the present day. Its online version allows access to limited content free of charge, featuring excerpts from some of the articles in the dictionary. You can also register for a fee to gain access to the entire database. If you are not certain about wanting to do this, then read the testimonials on site, or register for a free 24-hour trial first.

Invaluable

www.invaluable.com

This is a large site that was originally set up as a service to help bidders find objects coming up for sale worldwide. The facility to search through the catalogues of a multitude of international auctioneers at once is still a key feature, but the site also includes general articles and news from the antiques world. Users can also register details of possessions so that, in the event of theft, they can be added to a stolen items' database that is checked against lots that are coming up for sale.

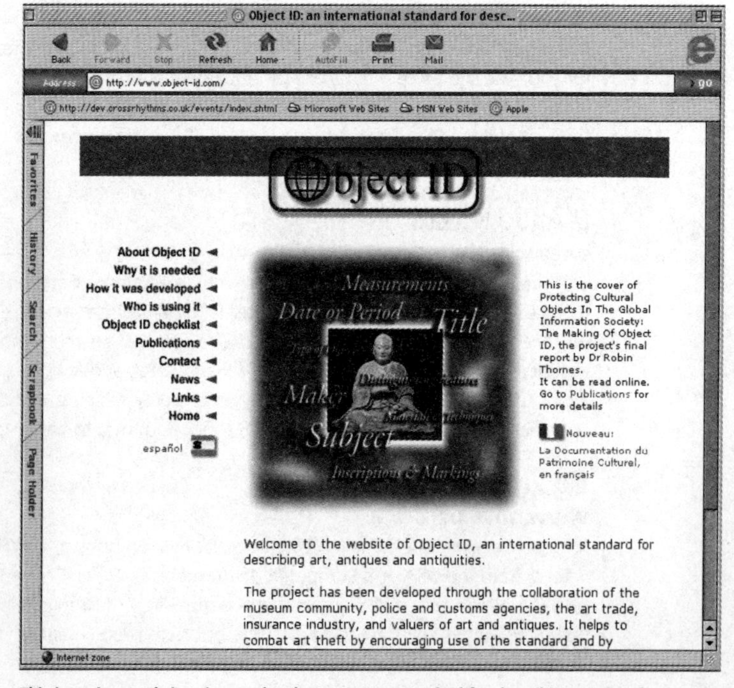

This ingenious website aims to develop a common method for describing works of art.

Kovels Online

www.kovels.com

This site is an American antiques and collectibles reference point, giving information on prices and marks, fakes, an analysis of the marketplace, and answering collectors' questions. Information from five of their published price guides has been compiled to establish values, and you can search the list for a specific item to know how much it should go for. The online articles include titles such as "What didn't sell on ebay", "Steiff animals", "Watch out for reproduction phonographs", etc. There is an online bookstore, and leaflets and videos are also for sale. An extensive links page will put you in touch with a wealth of auction sites, dealers, etc.

Miller's Publications

www.millers.uk.com

The Miller's website is designed both as a showcase for the many Miller's antiques and collectibles titles, and as a resource for antiques and collectibles enthusiasts. There is a discussion forum for lively debate on all aspects of antiques and you will also find details of the free Miller's Club, which offers information on forthcoming titles, and a chance to have your questions on antiques answered by the experts. The site includes a copy of the Newsletter, and a list of useful links to other antiques sites, as well as news of the annual British Antiques and Collectables Awards. There is also a complete catalogue of Miller's books – over 75 titles on a wide variety of subject categories – and a facility to purchase these online.

Object ID

www.object-id.com

Whether or not a stolen item is recovered often depends on an accurate and consistent description from the owner. This site is part of a project that aims to develop a common, internationally understood method of describing works of art to facilitate their recovery in the event of theft. There's a checklist for use in preparing your own inventory and links to many organizations. There is also a list of related publications to buy or read online, a news page, and a checklist which will be of invaluable help when documenting your possessions.

Prices for Antiques

www.p4a.com

This is a subscription service, which provides a database of items sold at auction throughout North America. There is a listing of all the auctions that have been covered, as well as those that will be covered in the future. Items are listed by category and these are split into further subcategories; for example, under furniture there are categories for corner cupboards, hanging cupboards, wall cupboards, sideboards, stools, etc. There are over 23,000 items in the database. There is also a list of US auctions with dates, which is handy if you are looking for a specific item from a particular auction.

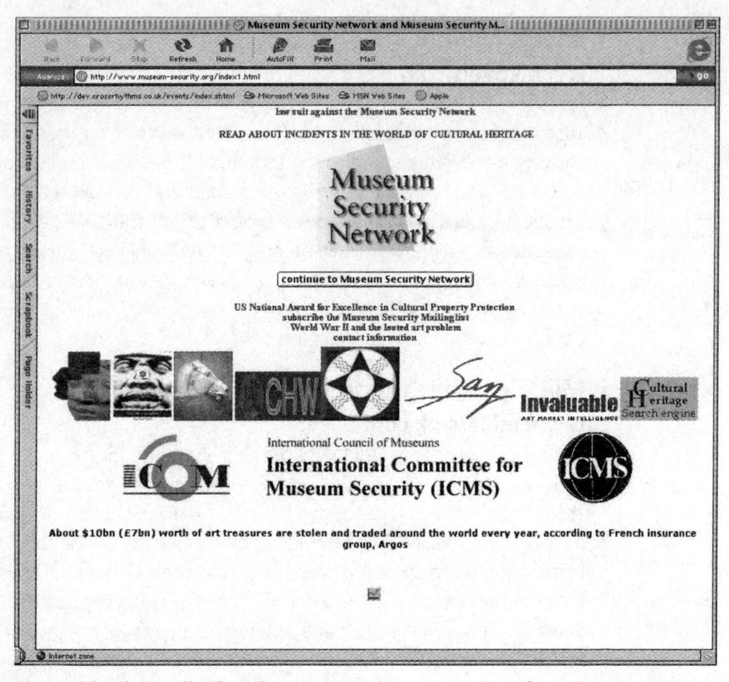

This useful website will tell you how to protect your own antiques from all eventualities.

Protecting Art and Antiques

www.museum-security.org

While this site is aimed at museum professionals, much of the advice given could apply to anyone who owns works of art. It is all about protecting art and antiques not only from thieves, but also from other threats, such as fire. There are informative articles on disasters such as the Windsor Castle fire in England, and links to relevant sites, including those of security organizations.

WORTH A LOOK

wwar.com

Resource site with links to museums, galleries, art history sites, and more.

www.findstolenart.com

An online register of stolen works of art.

SPECIALIST SITES

The following websites have been grouped into 58 specialist subjects and then the sites are listed alphabetically within them. Here you will find a wide range of sites, from the academic through to the plainly bizarre! Some will open up valuable resources for identifying and finding out more about your collection, while others will provide opportunities for buying and selling within your own collecting area. Specialist auctions, clubs, museums, and associations have been included too, but it is also worth looking at the more general sites in the previous section (see pages 49–126). Many sites also offer further links to other dealers, collectors, museums, and much more, so a spot of surfing could turn up exactly what you are looking for. Use the site maps provided to navigate your way round easily and review the FAQs for useful information, particularly if you are buying or selling online. If you decide to purchase online you should always follow the recommended guidelines to ensure that you are protected (see pages 23–30). And don't forget that the best organizations will update their sites on a regular basis so you should visit them regularly. If you can't find what you are looking for here, then check the index on page 279.

ADVERTISING AND PACKAGING

Antique Advertising Collecting

www2.charleston.net/heiland

This is the site of a collector whose own collection is displayed on the site – there is nothing to buy here. Items shown range from cocoa tins to signs advertising syrup and cigarettes. There are plenty of full-colour pictures of a wide range of advertising memorabilia, which in some cases dates back to the Victorian era. There is also a small selection of links to other advertising collectibles sites.

Awsum Advertising

www.tias.com/stores/awsumadv

Advertising signs, badges, tins, and other ephemera can all be found on this site, which is run by an American dealer based in New Jersey. Stock is subdivided into themes including aviation, food, distilleries, Coca-Cola, utility companies, and oil companies. For each of the different themes there are

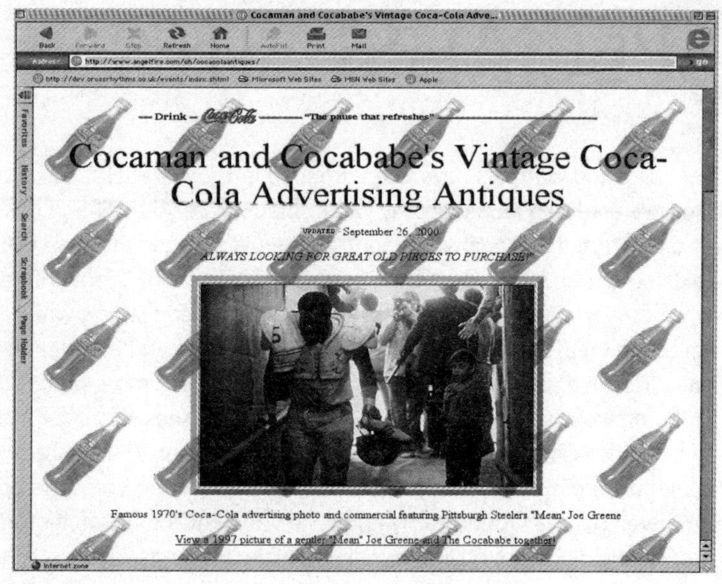

Coca-Cola collectibles galore can be found on this American website.

pictures, full descriptions, and prices, and you can also buy online. There is an email form if you have any questions for the owner. Awsum Advertising's site also includes a selection of Disneyana and other collectibles (see pages 166–7 for Disneyana sites).

Bennett Family Tins

www.ds.dial.pipex.com/bennett.family

This is the site of a family whose collection includes Bluebird toffee, Colman's mustard, Weetabix, and Cadbury's chocolate tins. Many examples can be seen online, and there's also information on the history of these companies and their packaging. Nothing is for sale here, as it is a personal collection. The site also features a history of the Trocadero restaurant in London, and some Victorian menus of that era that are in the family collection.

Cocaman and Cocababe's Vintage Coca-Cola Advertising Antiques

www.angelfire.com/oh/cocacolaantiques

This American site has a multitude of Coca-Cola collectibles for sale. These range from rare commemorative bottles to advertising signs, packaging, promotional items, and much more. You will find a history of Coca-Cola advertising on this site, plus links to Coca-Cola memorabilia sites. Items for sale are priced, but you have to send an email for further information if you wish to buy something.

Harvey's Antique Advertising

www.antiqueadvertising.com

A musical introduction greets the visitor to this site, which features pictures of old tins and advertising items, especially smoking collectibles. These are from a private collection, and most are not for sale. However, part of the site is devoted to items for sale – prices are given, but you must send an email for further details concerning ordering and payment etc. There is also a "most wanted" page featuring lists of items the collector would like to buy. You will also find links to various advertising collectibles and web resource sites.

WORTH A LOOK

www.americancola.com
Coca-Cola collectibles.

www.pepsistore.net
Pepsi-Cola advertising ware and memorabilia.

www.toymuseum.com
An American museum dedicated to advertising icons such as the Jolly Green Giant.

ANTIQUITIES

Ancient and Oriental

www.antiquities.co.uk

Shop online for artefacts from many ancient cultures on this British dealer's website. There are numerous pictures of items for sale, with prices and descriptions, and stock is subdivided into Egyptian, Roman, and so on, with a separate section of coins (see pages 156–9 for other coin sites).

Baidun

www.baidun.com

Israel is the only country in the Middle East where it is legal to trade in antiquities, and this Jerusalem-based dealer has been licensed to do so for many years. The site includes Roman, Greek, Byzantine, Persian, and Islamic items. Send an email enquiry if you like what you see.

Bridgeview Galleries

www.bridgeview.com.au

This Australian site offers a vast array of objects from numerous ancient cultures. Stock also includes medieval and tribal artefacts, and you can order via a secure online form. Prices are given in Australian dollars, but there is a currency converter for those from outside Australia.

Fragments of Time

www.antiquities.net

Ancient art of museum quality can be seen and bought on the site of this American dealer whose speciality lies with the Mediterranean cultures. Browse the online galleries and read through historical background information. There is a search facility, and you can order a free copy of the firm's catalogue.

Guy Clark

www.ancient-art.com

This informative site is dominated by ancient coins, but it does also have many other artefacts including jewellery and assorted everyday items. Ancient Rome and Egypt are represented as is the medieval period, and orders can be placed online. An extensive links page includes clubs and societies, commercial sites, and history sites.

Helios Gallery Antiquities

www.heliosgallery.com

Greek, Roman, Egyptian, and Oriental artefacts are displayed on this dealer's site, which includes a special section of lower-priced objects. A description and price tag accompany pictures, and you can order by telephone or fax if you would like to buy anything.

Ken Mannion

www.kenmannion.btinternet.co.uk

Some of the oldest antiques in existence are included on the site of this dealer, who offers fossils and meteorites as well as ancient artefacts. There is an illustrated online catalogue (an email will get you purchasing information) and a page devoted to unusual recent sales. You will also find a selection of tools for mounting and displaying items for sale, and details of the firm's own mounting and presentation service.

Malter Galleries

www.maltergalleries.com

Coins and artefacts from the Greek, Roman, Byzantine, and Pre-Columbian civilizations, among others, can be found on this site. Malter Galleries offer a wide selection of items for online purchase, and also runs Internet auctions. Tribal art from Africa to Papua New Guinea is also featured, and you can buy books to tell you more about these and other artefacts.

Sands of Time

www.sandsoftimeantiquities.com

Ancient weapons are particularly in evidence on this site, but you will find all kinds of other objects here. A variety of Greek, Roman, and Egyptian artefacts are offered for sale through the site, and the cultures of the Middle East and Central Asia are also represented. Objects are illustrated and there is a useful guide to the items' condition. The site offers a selection of links, mainly to academic and reference sites, and you can register with any special interests online (if you register, you will also receive a half-yearly catalogue).

Traces from the Past

www.traces.nu

This Dutch dealer's site, available in English, offers ancient artefacts, coins, and other collectibles – including a large selection of Romano-Celtic bronzes and jewellery. Neolithic and medieval artefacts are also well represented here. Stock can be viewed and ordered online and a selection of links includes ancient history resource sites and numismatic sites.

Vikings and Saxons

www.vikingsandsaxons.com

Tangible reminders of English history from AD 450 to 1066 can be purchased through this site, which only sells items that come from that period. All of the items offered were unearthed in England, and these include brooches, axe heads, shield bosses, and bracelets, as well as coins. Items are pictured and described in full on the site but if you are not happy with your purchase, there is a money-back guarantee too. There are also links to resource and Anglo-Saxon history sites.

WORTH A LOOK

www.fordham.edu/halsall/ancient/asbook.html
An ancient history resource.

www.julen.net/ancient
Web resource with links to sites on the ancient world.

ARMS AND ARMOUR

Bonehill

www.bonehill3.freeserve.co.uk

This militaria dealer has a vast selection of stock that can be viewed online and ordered via email. Many related services are offered on this site, which is updated weekly; these include military genealogy for tracing service records and medal entitlements. The site also features details of the proprietor's career as a champion swordsman, stunt double, and adviser to Hollywood productions!

Bosley's

www.bosleys.co.uk

This is the site of a leading militaria auctioneers, which has a particular interest in military badges. These are sold via regular postal auctions as well as in the salerooms – details are available on the site. A typical auction at Bosley's might have a thousand lots and you will find them all listed on the site, though photographs are scarce. Highlights of forthcoming sales are discussed on the site as well; send an email if you have any further queries or would like to obtain a catalogue.

Buying Militaria in the UK

www.arms-and-armour.co.uk

This site is an extensive guide to buying arms and armour in the UK. There are full details of militaria fairs, markets, auctions, and shops as well as links to dealers' sites where available. Information covers everything from Japanese swords to military vehicles and there are hints and tips for collectors. There are also reviews of shops, fairs, etc so you will know what to expect if you decide to visit in person.

Eureka Militaria

www.1earth.com.au/militaria

This is an Australian militaria site that, while specializing in Australian items, covers everything from weapons of the American Civil War to German police cap-badges. It has a particularly large selection of military history books, and the site is being constantly updated to include new stock.

Knighthood, Chivalry, and Tournaments Resource Library

www.chronique.com

This well-illustrated site is aimed at anyone with an interest in medieval weaponry and battle tactics. It includes a comprehensive and extremely useful glossary of terms relating to arms and armour, which also explodes many myths. One such myth is about the "fuller", which is a groove running along the length of a sword. This is often described as the "blood groove", as it

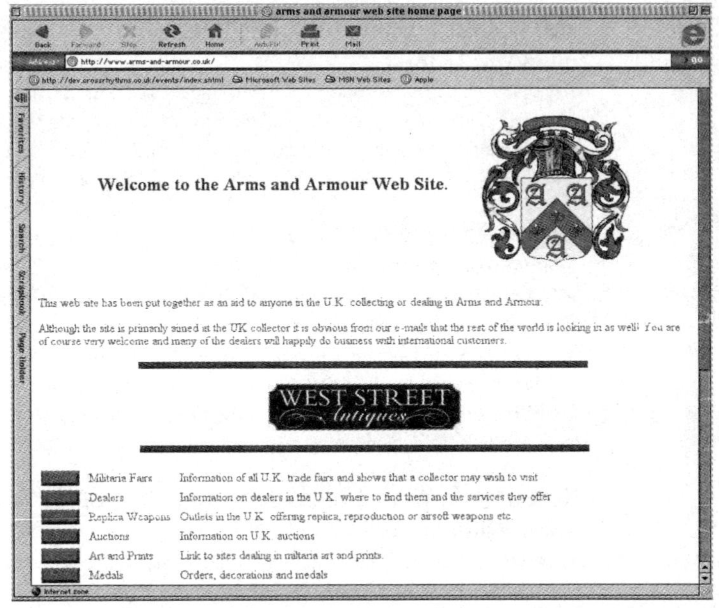

Let this site guide you if you are interested in buying arms and armour in the UK.

supposedly channels the blood from an enemy! The site explains its real purpose – to make the blade a little lighter. There are also reviews of books on the subject, and a calendar of re-enactment events, which are mostly held in the USA and Canada.

Michael D Long Ltd

www.michaeldlong.net

This is the website of one of the largest militaria dealers around, and it provides music while you browse. More than 4,000 items "from a machine gun to an African spear" are in stock and on the site at any one time. There is an extensive catalogue from which you can purchase online using your credit card. This is divided into categories such as edged weapons, deactivated firearms, Japanese items, and so on. There are also online auctions.

Michael German Antiques

www.antiqueweapons.com

The site of this London dealer features antique walking canes as well as militaria. The arms and armour section of the site offers many items for sale, with pictures, full descriptions, and prices in US dollars and pounds sterling. Take a "virtual tour" of the showrooms, and, if you like what you see, you can order by telephone, fax, or email. There's a recommended books list for further reading, and videos on this branch of collecting are also available.

The Militaria Collectors' Exchange

www.tmcx.com

This site is a vast web resource for the militaria collector and has a "What is Militaria" guide for the novice. Topics covered range from the American Civil War to aviation art, and you can buy and sell online. Books for further reading are reviewed, and a multitude of links take you to other sites around the world.

Online Antique Militaria

www.antiqueguns.com

This American online auction site is dedicated to collectors of antique firearms, swords, and related collectibles. The American Civil War period is a favourite, but most popular fields, including World War I and II items, are also covered. Vendors pay a flat fee to list items for sale, and users must register (which is free) to use the site. Also included on the site are resources for collectors, including links to dealers and a classified ads section.

Resource Site for Collectors and Historians

www.militaria.com

For militaria collectors and military historians, militaria.com has a huge selection of links to publications, books, re-enactment societies, dealers, and replica manufacturers, not to mention the website of the US 8th Infantry division. There are reviews of books and bulletin boards where collectors of British, US, and German militaria can discuss their hobby.

Treasure Bunker

www.treasurebunker.com

More than 1,000 items of militaria, from Waterloo to World War II and including everything from de-activated weapons to foreign medals, are for sale from the site of this militaria dealer, who is based in Glasgow, Scotland. Many of the items are illustrated, and you can order online with your credit card. All items sold come with a no-quibble, money-back guarantee, and there is a special link to a currency converter so that overseas customers can compare prices without confusion.

WORTH A LOOK

www.deadlynostalgia.com
An American site offering 19th-century weapons plus restoration services.

www.fineantiquearms.com
A specialist dealer with a large online weapons catalogue, plus books and links.

www.militaryantiques.com
Resource site with information on antique swords and guns as well as classified ads.

ART DECO

Altamira

www.altamiradeco.co.uk

Ceramics, glass, furniture, bronzes, paintings, and "curiosities" await the visitor to the site of this Art Deco dealer, who is based on the south coast of England. Only original pieces are stocked, and these typically range from cinema lighting to table centrepieces. Telephone or send an email for further information on any of the stock shown on the site.

Art Deco Napier

www.hb.co.nz/artdeco

This is an online guide to the Art Deco city of Napier, New Zealand, which was totally rebuilt following an earthquake in 1931. Its unrivalled Art Deco architecture is pictured, and there's tourist information and details of the city's annual Art Deco festival. There is an online Art Deco shop and a range of books and other souvenirs can be bought online.

Art Deco Society of New York

www.artdeco.org

This is the site of an American, non-profit-making organization that is devoted to the study, preservation, and promotion of the Art Deco style. It includes a gallery of posters that can be ordered online and back issues of the society's newsletter are also available.

Deco Dog's Ephemera and Popular Collectibles

www.decodog.com

This American site has an array of generally inexpensive Art Deco and Art Deco-style items for sale online. These include kitchenalia, lighting, and ephemera, and there are even Christmas decorations from the 1920s and 1930s.

Detroit Area Deco Society

www.daads.org

This is the site of the American collectors' and enthusiasts' society devoted to promoting all aspects of Art Deco. There's an online newsletter featuring the latest news on building-preservation campaigns as well as a variety of links.

Directory of UK Dealers

www.decodealers.co.uk

Decodealers is a directory of Art Deco dealers in the UK. Amusing illustrations and animations guide the visitor through the maze of dealer listings and online shops, links to clubs and societies, Art Deco news and views, and a fairs calendar. There's also an online arcade where goods can be bought and sold.

Lattimore's Global Art Deco Directory

www.lattimore.co.uk/deco

This site has a wealth of links to Art Deco dealers, mostly in the UK but with many international sites too. Also included on the site are links to collectors' clubs and Art Deco sales and "wants". If you are a dealer and would like to be included then you can take advantage of the following free of charge: listings in the dealer directory, email links from your listing, and links to your website.

Learn About Art Deco

www.arts.ilstu.edu/exhibits/pcfare/deco.html

This educational site looks at all aspects of the Art Deco era. There are shots of Art Deco interiors with a commentary on their designers, a section on Art Deco architecture, and even information on music and film. You can also play short recorded clips of music by Gershwin and Ella Fitzgerald.

Modernism Gallery

www.modernism.com

French and American Art Deco is plentiful on this site, which offers furniture, lighting, and accessories by all the best-known designers. Stock is described in detail, and you can zoom in on pictures for a better look. The site also features informative articles on designers and design houses.

Muir Hewitt

www.muirhewitt.com

Three-dimensional images of selected stock are featured on the musical site of this Art Deco specialist based in the north of England – and you don't need to download any special software to see them. Take a 3D tour of the shop and browse through a selection of Art Deco goodies that is strong on Clarice Cliff, but also includes general Art Deco ceramics, furniture, posters, lamps, and much more. You can then order online.

WORTH A LOOK

www.artdeco-shop.com
A Dutch online shop, available in English, with a varied selection for Art Deco lovers.

www.c20fires.co.uk
Specialists in fireplaces from the Art Deco era, plus Art Nouveau and Edwardian examples.

www.deco-echoes.com
An Art Deco and modern design magazine online.

www.serial-design.com
Design site with a good Art Deco section, including designer biographies.

ART NOUVEAU

Anne's Antiques

www.annesantiques.com

Art Nouveau silver, jewellery, and ceramics are particularly well represented on this dealer's site. You can use the search engine to look for specific items that you can order online, or just browse through the catalogue. Pictures are accompanied by thorough descriptions.

Art Nouveau World Wide Server

art-nouveau.kubos.org

This site has comprehensive information on Art Nouveau around the world. There's a list of FAQs, details of Art Nouveau exhibitions and museums, and even a selection of Art Nouveau doors. The site also includes virtual tours of Art Nouveau cities like Barcelona, and the illustrated biographies of several influential artists including Gaudí and Gallé.

Collectics Virtual Museum

www.collectics.com/museum.html

This online museum has an emphasis on Art Nouveau and Art Deco items. A wide range of objects can be seen here accompanied by detailed commentary, which includes biographical information on those responsible for the works of art. The site also contains informative articles on various aspects of antiques.

Gaudí Central

www.come.to/gaudi

This site is devoted to the celebrated Spanish Art Nouveau designer Antoni Gaudí. There are pictures of his works, biographical information, and a list of places to visit in Barcelona, as well as links to other Gaudí and general Art Nouveau sites. Books and videos about Gaudí are available to buy online.

Gordon Inglis Antiques

www.inglisantiques.com

Ceramics circa 1900 are on offer via the site of this specialist dealer, which also houses Scottish pottery and glass. You can order online via a secure server and, while other collectibles – from TV memorabilia and kitchenalia – also feature, Art Nouveau is very well represented. There are also links to other dealer sites and web resources.

Lillian Nassau

www.lilliannassau.com

This is the website of a leading American dealer in Art Nouveau, which deals particularly with the glass, pottery, and sculpture of the period, although the

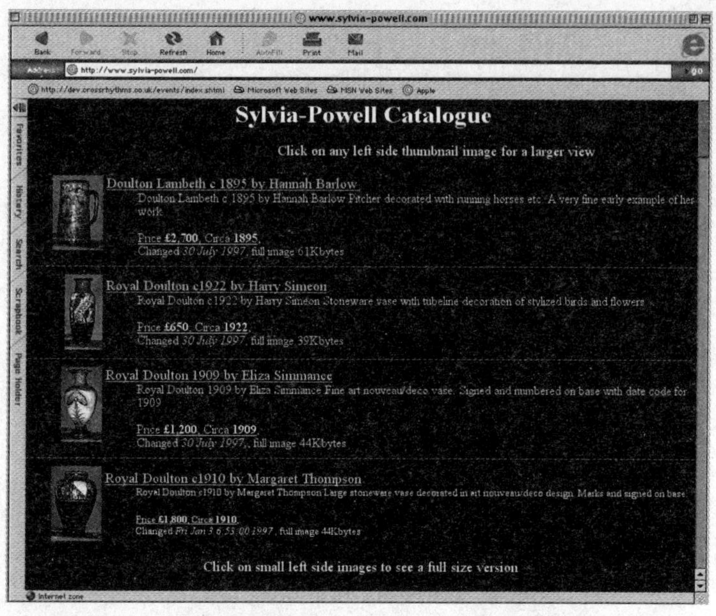

Sylvia Powell has an extensive range of Art Pottery that can be viewed online.

stock also includes Tiffany lamps. The site provides background information on the makers, and there's a very useful Art Nouveau bibliography as well.

Mucha Museum
www.mucha.cz

The world-famous Prague museum devoted to this celebrated Czech doyen of Art Nouveau, Alphonse Mucha, shows few of the artist's works online. However, the site, available in English, is useful for researchers, with a definitive chronology and biographical information, as well as email contact details.

Sylvia Powell Decorative Arts
www.sylvia-powell.com

Art Pottery is the speciality of this London dealer, and a wide selection can be viewed online. All the best-known makers of the late 19th/early 20th century are represented here, particularly Royal Doulton and Martinware. The online catalogue is well illustrated and informative, and you can send an email for purchasing details if you want to buy something.

20th-Century Decorative Arts
www.20thcentury-decorative-arts.co.uk

Art Nouveau and Art Deco are featured on the site of this UK dealer, which shows ceramics, glass, metalwares, lighting, and furniture for online purchase.

A miscellaneous section includes items such as Art Nouveau photo frames, and you can email or telephone for further details. There are also links to Art Nouveau, Art Deco, and interior design sites.

What is Art Nouveau?

www.tile-collector.co.uk/art-noo.htm

This specialist tile collector's site includes a useful section on Art Nouveau, which acts as something of a "style guide". There is a gallery of decorative tiles with typical Art Nouveau features pointed out by an informative commentary. There is also information on famous factories such as Minton and lesser-known ones such as Gibbons Hinton, with examples of their Art Nouveau designs.

See pages 135–6 for Art Deco sites.

WORTH A LOOK

www.ecole-de-nancy.com

French Art Nouveau site devoted to its leading exponents in France. Available in French only.

www.museocasalis.org

Spanish Art Nouveau and Art Deco museum site, available in English.

www.nymuseum.com/mucha.htm

The Alphonse Mucha Galleries, held at a major American dealer/showroom, online.

ARTS AND CRAFTS

Art Furniture

www.artfurniture.co.uk

Original English and Scottish Arts and Crafts period furniture, lighting, prints, and metalwork can be enjoyed on the site of this London dealer. Illustrated stock is accompanied by a "Who's who" of designers and manufacturers. Prices are given, but you will need to contact the gallery before purchasing.

Arts and Crafts Society

www.arts-crafts.com

This is the online home of the Arts and Crafts community. An archive section has all you need to know about the movement, its philosophy, and the places and people associated with it. There's a forum for exchanging views, a bookshop, and links to dealers and other sources of Arts and Crafts artefacts.

Cheltenham Art Gallery and Museum

www.artsandcraftsmuseum.org.uk

Cheltenham Museum and Art Gallery, in the west of England, has an important collection relating to the Arts and Crafts Movement in Britain. On its website there is background information on the movement, an A–Z of designers, and a look at materials, techniques, and decoration favoured by the designers.

Craftsman Farms

www.parsippany.net/craftsmanfarms.html

The New Jersey home of Gustav Stickley is now a museum, and this is its website. There's information on Stickley and his place in the Arts and Crafts Movement, including quotes from the man himself that illustrate his philosophy of building in harmony with the environment. The site includes an illustrated history of the house and there are details of how you can support the charity that maintains it.

The Dome Art and Antiques

www.dome-art.freeserve.co.uk

"Puritan values" are promised at the site of these British Arts and Crafts dealers. The site includes pictures of the stunning Art Deco building in which they are based, as well as a large and comprehensive selection of pictures of Arts and Crafts items in stock. These include everything from clocks to dressing tables and decorative pottery. There is also a research service; for a fee, you can email details of your possessions for assessment by an expert.

Founders of the Arts and Crafts Movement

www.burrows.com/found.html

This is an online anthology of articles on various aspects of the Arts and Crafts Movement. Authors of the articles include William Morris and W R Lethaby, and you can even read the transcript of a speech given by Oscar Wilde on "Art and the Handicraftsman".

John Alexander Furniture & Decorative Arts

www.johnalexanderltd.com

Museum-quality furniture and decorative arts from the 1860–1920 era can be seen on this US dealer's site. Typical stock includes Ruskin pottery, glass by James Powell and Son, and furniture attributed to Collinson and Lock. Items are clearly illustrated, and close-ups of individual pieces can also be viewed. Send an email enquiry if you are interested in buying any of the stock shown.

The Mackintosh House

www.hunterian.gla.ac.uk/mackintosh/mackintosh_index.html

Take a virtual tour of a reconstruction of the former home of Charles Rennie Mackintosh, courtesy of Glasgow University. The tour uses QuickTime and full

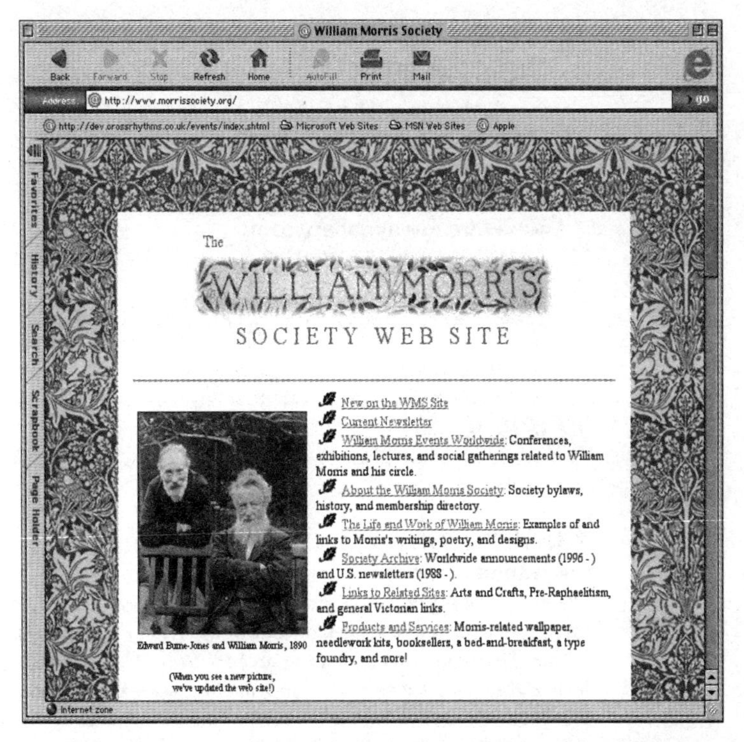

The official William Morris website is packed with information and examples of his work.

commentaries on the rooms are also included. You can email or write to the university for an appointment to see the real thing.

Marbles in Your Head Antiques

users.erinet.com/39160

Marbles in Your Head Antiques is the quirky name of an American dealer offering Arts and Crafts pottery, metalware, and a miscellany of other items. Send an email for further information on the illustrated stock. The site also has a summary of the Arts and Crafts movement and links to relevant auctioneers and web resources.

William Morris Home Page

www.morrissociety.org

The William Morris Society's large website includes extensive articles on the man and his wide-reaching influence, details of forthcoming Morris-related events worldwide, and much, much more. There's a biography, newsletter, back issues of the society's journals, pictures of many of Morris' designs, and links to related sites as well.

WORTH A LOOK

www.designsintile.com
Useful for its Arts and Crafts links.

www.franklloydwright.org
Informative site dedicated to the great designer Frank Lloyd Wright.

www.treadwaygallery.com
US auction house specializing in Arts and Crafts, Art Nouveau, and Art Deco.

BOOKS

A Gerits & Son

www.nvva.nl/gerits

The site of this major Dutch book dealer includes a copy of the firm's latest catalogue, which contains descriptions of the volumes on offer. An email will get you further information on the books shown. Register with the site, and future catalogues will be sent to you free of charge. You can also take a virtual tour of the bookshop, with 360° views of the showrooms.

Advanced Book Exchange

www.abebooks.com

Used, second-hand, rare, and out-of-print books from more than 9,000 independent dealers are available through this site. Here you can search through a database of stock from around the world and buy online. A number of articles are posted online and different booksellers are profiled each month. There is a collector's corner offering access to a panel of experts, who will answer your queries on maps and prints as well as books (see pages 207–10 for map sites).

Antiquarian Book Review

www.abmr.co.uk

The Antiquarian Book Review is a leading monthly magazine for bibliophiles. Its website offers content from the current issue as well as previews of relevant exhibitions and events, book reviews, and a listing of book fairs and auctions. A large selection of links will take you to the sites of dealers, associations etc.

Beckham Books

www.beckhambooks.co.uk

Bibles and books on theological subjects are the specialities of this book dealer. The site includes a fairs calendar, as well as a search engine that allows searches by title, author, and price range. You can also specify that you are looking for first editions, or books that are signed/inscribed.

Bernard J Shapero

www.shapero.com

Travel guides, such as the famous Baedekers, are among the specialities of this London dealer. Shapero's searchable online catalogue also features first editions of English and European literature, and many other rare and unusual books. Stock is illustrated on the site, and there is secure online ordering.

Bloomsbury Book Auctions

www.bloomsbury-book-auct.com

The website of London's only specialist book auction house contains full details of recent and forthcoming sales, including online catalogues and prices realized. You can bid via email and, if you wish to sell something, you will find advice on the procedure available from the site. You can also request a brochure via email, which explains all about Bloomsbury, or pay to subscribe to a "wants" list. To receive future details, email your postal address to them.

Bookshops in Hay-on-Wye

www.hay-on-wye.com/bookshops/body.htm

Hay-on-Wye in Wales is renowned for its second-hand/antiquarian bookshops, and this site acts as a good guide to them. Shops are listed alongside their addresses, telephone numbers, and links to their websites. You will also find a selection of links to bookshops from around the world here.

British Internet Bookdealers' Centre

www.clique.co.uk

Your gateway to the British book trade, this site offers details of and links to virtually every Internet-connected book dealer in the UK. There's advice on selling books on the Internet as well as links to book databases and resources, associations, libraries, and much more. You can also download the register of UK book dealers for offline viewing in e-book format, free of charge.

Classic Bindings

www.classicbindings.net

You can buy library furniture and accessories as well as books from this London dealer. Books are sold as collections to equip libraries and by the foot purely for decorative purposes as well as individually. Books are described in full, with prices. If you wish to buy anything, you can send them an email.

Dealer's Choice Books Inc

www.art-amer.com

This Florida-based book dealer has new books, videos, and CD-ROMS on art and antiques. They particularly specialize in books on art, with everything from

Bénézit to artists' signature books and auction guides. There are also sections on antiques, glass, porcelain, and furniture bronzes. You can order books through email, telephone, or fax and credit cards are accepted.

International League of Antiquarian Booksellers

www.ilab-lila.com

The League represents antiquarian booksellers in 20 countries around the world. Its website includes links to the sites of members from various countries including Japan, the UK, USA, Australia, Germany, France, and Korea. Information on forthcoming international book fairs are listed at this site, which also boasts a useful glossary of terms used in the book trade, advice for buyers and sellers, and much more.

Maggs Bros

www.maggs.com

"Serious about books without being stuffy" is the motto of Maggs Bros., purveyors of rare books by royal appointment. Their site shows some of the superb volumes for which they have been known since the 1850s. There are some real rarities here, and prices to match, though collectors of more modest means will find a good selection for under £50.

Peter Harrington

www.peter-harrington-books.com

The site of this leading London book dealer allows you to find out information on book-related events, as well as search through a database of stock. Download the current catalogue and see examples of the art of fore-edge painting (a form of book illustration). Send an email to them if you wish to purchase something.

Potterton Books

www.pottertonbooks.co.uk

New, second-hand, and antiquarian books on various aspects of art, antiques, and design can be bought through this site. Ornamental design sourcebooks and rare and unusual books are among the items for sale that can be ordered – and paid for – online, and a search engine allows you to search by keyword, price range, or both. Alternatively you can contact Potterton directly with your specific requests.

Rare Books Worldwide

www.worldbookdealers.com

Some of the world's top book dealers are represented on this site, which claims to be the most comprehensive source of the rarest books in the world. Shop online for your pick of more than 100,000 volumes covering 40 subjects and spanning five centuries. Browse through the latest dealer catalogues, look at the events listings, or read trade news stories and scholarly essays on various aspects of antiquarian books. There are also links to specialist services in the book world, a detailed glossary, and the chance to subscribe to a free email newsletter here.

Zardoz

www.zardozbooks.co.uk

Zardoz is Europe's largest out-of-print and collectible fiction book dealer. Its site has a sophisticated search engine, and there is also a useful list of books that Zardoz is looking to buy themselves. You can bid at online auctions via ebay or choose from a selection of books, which largely comprises crime, cult, and fantasy novels in paperback. The links page will put you in touch with other sites specializing in out-of-print and collectible fiction.

WORTH A LOOK

www.bookpalace.com
Popular culture, art books, and graphic novels.

www.hrkahnbooks.com
Canadian dealer offering rare books and manuscripts.

www.irelandbooks.com
One of Ireland's leading antiquarian book dealers.

www.kentrotman.ltd.uk
Dealer specializing in antiquarian books on military history.

BREWERIANA

Beer Can Collectors of America

www.bcca.com

This site is naturally strong on American beer-can collecting, but it is also of interest to international enthusiasts. There is a potted history of the beer can and an explanation of how the hobby began, and you will also find a wealth of links to breweriana and beer-related sites around the world. There is news of forthcoming "canventions" and you can even play beer games.

Beer Collectibles 1880–1960

www.breweriana.com

Items related to beer and breweries, mostly dating from 1880 to the 1950s, can be found on this site. There is advice on various topics, including the likely value of these collectibles, and you can also buy and sell through the site. There's a search engine to help you find different items for sale and you can

All things beer- and brewery-related from 1880–1960 can be found on this website.

then buy online. There are three ways that you can sell on the site: in some cases, they will buy your collection outright, you can also put it up for sale through the site to other collectors, or it can be offered at auction. You must contact them by email in the first instance if you wish to sell anything. There is also a "Brewery History" that is updated regularly.

Beery Bits and Bobs

www.breweriana.co.uk

This site has assorted items for sale online, including T-shirts, bar towels, ties, and lapel badges, as well as a wide range of beermats from the last 50 years. An extensive catalogue on the site is subdivided by category. While the collectibles shown are mainly British, there are some from other countries available here too.

Guinness Collectors' Club

www.guinnesscollectorsclub.co.uk

This site caters for all lovers of Guinness collectibles (or "Guinntiques", as they are called here). Buy, sell, and exchange items with fellow collectors, ask questions, and learn about this brewery's memorabilia. There are lots of facts, figures, and trivia, as well as links to the official Guinness site and to various breweriana sites.

Jan's Beer Pages

www.beercollection.net

A listing of email addresses of more than 1,100 fellow breweriana collectors around the world is one of the most useful elements of this site, which is as much for those who love to drink beer as for those who collect its artefacts. There's also a blacklist of online breweriana dealers who are allegedly not to be trusted, a gallery of beer posters for sale, and information on beer museums or "beer musea".

Pub Paraphernalia

www.pub-paraphernalia.com

Pub Paraphernalia is the site for lovers of the traditional British pub – wherever they may live. There are lots of collectible items, from glasses to bar towels and advertising items, which can all be ordered online and paid for with your credit card. A search facility enables you to look for items relating to specific breweries.

WORTH A LOOK

www.barmirrors.com
Collectible bar mirrors for online purchase.

www.bassmuseum.com
Beer museum based in Burton upon Trent, the UK's brewing capital.

craftbrewers.com/breweriananet
Includes classified ads for collectors.

CERAMICS

Andrew Muir

www.andrew-muir.com

Clarice Cliff and Art Deco pottery are the specialities of this dealer, whose site includes a selection of Clarice Cliff pieces for under £300 (see also Art Deco, pages 135–6). A search service enables you to look for specific patterns in stock, and a currency converter will help you with your online purchases if you are buying from outside the UK, where Andrew Muir is based. You can track down where the dealer will be exhibiting by consulting a fairs listing or let him have your views on the site by writing in the guestbook.

Banana Dance

www.bananadance.com

Ceramics of the Art Deco era are celebrated on this site, which features Shelley, Carltonware, Winton/chintz, Susie Cooper, and, of course, Clarice Cliff, along with some general antiques. You can buy any of these online via a secure server.

The site also features a list of forthcoming fairs where Banana Dance will be exhibiting, complete with stand numbers so you can track them down in person.

Box of Porcelain

www.boxofporcelain.com

The "collectibles" end of the porcelain market is catered for on this site, which boasts a large selection of Doulton and Beswick figures, Bunnykins, character jugs, and Spode paperweights. Some older Worcester porcelain is also stocked. There are also royal commemoratives and Warner Brothers figures, and you can order them online via a secure server (see page 161 for commemorative sites). Beswick and Doulton enthusiasts are offered a "finder" service – just fill in an online form with details of any items you want, and they'll try to find them.

Castle Bryher

www.castle-bryher.co.uk

This attractive specialist online shop was set up in 1999. It deals with a wide variety of ceramics, with prices ranging from £30–£3,000. Customers can browse the full catalogue of more than 1,000 entries, or search for specific items by keyword or maker's name. You can order your choice online using a secure server, and have it dispatched to you by courier. A number of well-known manufacturers are represented in the catalogue, including Royal Doulton, Clarice Cliff, Beswick, and Moorcroft.

Ceramic Search

www.ceramicsearch.co.uk

This site, run by Top of the Hill Antiques in Burslem, Staffordshire, offers a free service to those seeking rare or obscure items of pottery or memorabilia. Provide a few details to register, and you can then submit a request. You can also search the extensive "Wanted List" database to see if anything you have stashed away could be someone else's treasure. The site also has a detailed historical guide to Burslem, the birthplace of Josiah Wedgwood.

Chintz Net

www.chintznet.com

This site is designed as a major web resource for all lovers of chintz. You can use the links to visit the international collectors' clubs, find information about forthcoming collectors' events, order specialist books on chintz, or register your "wants". There's also on online mall where you can shop for chintz from selected dealers. You can subscribe to a mailing list to keep up-to-date with all the latest news as well, and you can even take a virtual tour around an enthusiast's home.

Clarice Cliff Collectors Club

www.claricecliff.com

This is the gateway for all things to do with the famed Art Deco designer. Shop online for original and reproduction Clarice Cliff pottery, as well as books. You can also read about Clarice's life and works, and exchange views with fellow collectors via a bulletin board. There is also valuable information on Clarice Cliff patterns and shapes and you will find links to a multitude of Clarice Cliff and Art Deco dealers, auctions, and museums.

Collecting SylvaC

www.sylvac.pwp.blueyonder.co.uk

Two keen SylvaC collectors have set up this site, which is intended as a centre for the exchange of information among enthusiasts. It includes important news, such as warnings of fakes in circulation, and you can post details of items for sale/wanted without charge. There are also online galleries of SylvaC, showing pieces and their markings, and a guest book and news page for collectors to pool their resources.

Goss and Crested China Club

www.gosschinaclub.demon.co.uk

Goss China collecting became a big craze in Victorian times, and many thousands of these ceramic items, which were mostly souvenirs, were made. Collectible examples are offered for sale on this site. Send enquiries by email if you are interested in purchasing, or if you have any Goss and crested items you would like to sell. The descriptions of the pieces also provide interesting historical background information, and there's a book list with thorough reviews of relevant titles.

Rodge's Antiques and Collectables

www.rodge.clara.net

Pendelfin, Hummel, Wade, Beswick, Carltonware, and Poole Pottery can be found on this site, as well as a variety of other ceramics and collectibles. There is an extensive online catalogue with prices in pounds sterling and US dollars, but you will need to email them for purchasing details as you cannot buy direct from the site. Also included here is an "Auction Assistant" (someone "in the know" who provides detailed advice on buying at auction), features on various collecting topics, and even jokes. There is a message board, enabling you to join a thriving online community of collectors.

The Royal Doulton Company

www.royal-doulton.com

The Royal Doulton factory has been responsible for some of the world's most popular ceramics collectibles, from character jugs to Beatrix Potter and Brambly Hedge figures. Royal Crown Derby is also owned by the company. You will find information on the company's history and details of how you can join the collectors' club here. The site also includes information on special events for collectors. There is a range of figurines, collectibles and tableware to buy online at this site, too.

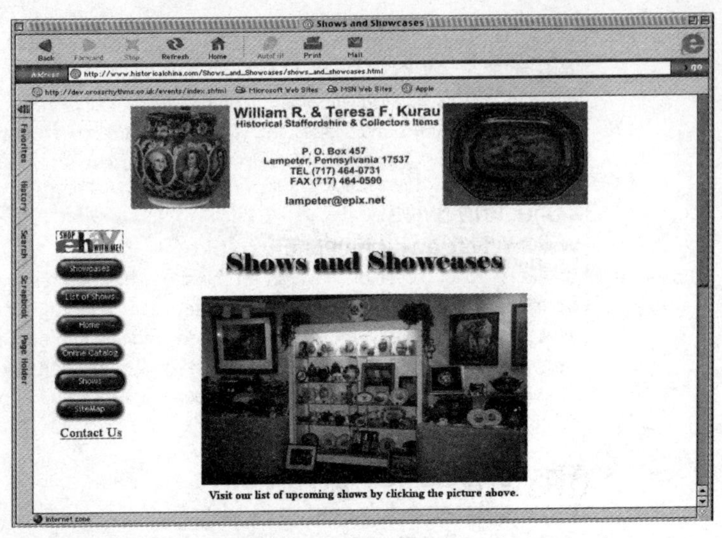

This American dealer's site has an online catalogue and a list of forthcoming shows.

When We Were Young

www.whenwewereyoung.co.uk

This site stocks current and discontinued ceramic collectibles that were originally made for children, but now they are also very popular with adults. Doulton and Beswick are well represented, and characters featured include those from *Alice in Wonderland* and the Beatrix Potter stories. Nursery china as well as ceramic figures are included, amid an assortment of other items such as silver spoons and thimbles (see pages 249–52 for other silver sites). A search facility will help you find what you are looking for, and you can buy online. There is also a variety of mailing lists, enabling you to get in touch with other enthusiasts in your particular collecting field.

William and Teresa Kurau

www.historicalchina.com

These American dealers specialize in historical Staffordshire, but carry a variety of other ceramics as well. The online catalogue is categorized into historical Staffordshire, cup plates, Liverpool, ABC plates, and miscellaneous, and they also sell Currier and Ives prints. There are detailed illustrations and descriptions of the items for sale; click on a price in the catalogue to link to their email if you wish to buy anything. Important out-of-print references for the subject are also for sale. The site provides a list of fairs that the dealer participates in, and a link to ebay, from which the company holds online auctions.

For sites specifically on pottery see pages 233–6, and for sites on porcelain see pages 226–8.

WORTH A LOOK

www.charltonpress.com
Online home of publishers of authoritative catalogues on 20th-century collectible ceramics.

www.members.tripod.com/~BeswickQuarterly
An online newsletter for Beswick collectors.

www.xs4all.nl/~andrewm
Dutch chintz site, available in English.

www.wadecollectorscentre.com
Wade for sale plus articles, links, and other features.

CIGARETTE CARDS

Cigarette Card and Trade Card Information Service

www.cigarettecards.co.uk

A specialist framing service for cigarette cards is one of the features of this site, which is run by a professional picture framer who also collects cards. He sells cards too, and you can shop online for them. Valuations are also offered through the site and there is a history of cigarette cards as well.

Franklyn Cards

www.franklyncards.com

Billed as the home of cigarette cards in cyberspace, the site is a useful web resource for this particular branch of collecting. Numerous cards, covering most popular subjects, are pictured on the site, but you must send an email to request prices and further information in order to buy anything. Regular auctions are also held on the site, and there is a full and informative list of FAQs too. You can also check on the catalogue value of your cards through this site in a price guide section.

London Cigarette Card Company

www.londoncigcard.co.uk

In spite of its name, The London Cigarette Card Company is based not in London but in Somerset in the west of England. The company was founded in 1927, and its website offers albums, books, and various accessories for sale, as well as the cards themselves. There are also details of the company's "live" and postal auctions and you can order hard copies of the latest catalogues and subscribe to a magazine, *Card Collectors' News*. Pictures of the company's showrooms are also shown on the site.

Murraycards (International) Ltd

www.murraycard.com

Shop online for cigarette cards featuring almost any subject you can imagine, from sports stars to military subjects, on the site of this London dealer which has stocks of over 25,000,000 cards. Some non-tobacco cards can also be found here, and you can buy albums to keep your purchases in good condition, as well as other accessories like framing kits, and a range of books on the subject of card collecting. The site also has details of the firm's regular auctions, and current special offers. There are links to other sites related to cigarette cards, and you can order a hard copy of their latest catalogue.

The Shakespeare Trading Company

www.shakespearetrading.btinternet.co.uk

Trade cards and postcards, as well as an extensive selection of cigarette cards, are offered by this site (see pages 229–30 for postcard sites). Popular subjects from animals and transport to sports stars are covered on the cigarette cards, and you can order them online (use the search facility to locate what you are looking for). Other features include links to various other hobbies sites and related web resources, plus links to tourist information sites about Stratford-upon-Avon, where the firm is based.

WORTH A LOOK

www.cardcreations.ndirect.co.uk

Dealers in tea and other trade cards as well as cigarette cards.

www.germancards.com

Site devoted to German cigarette cards, but available in English. Includes links to dealer sites and FAQs.

www.members.aol.com/noblegb/page/text.html

American site offering older cards and tobacco-related items.

CLOCKS AND WATCHES

Antiquorum Online

www.antiquorum.com

Based in Geneva, Antiquorum is well known in the antiques world for its specialist sales of fine watches and clocks. You can view sale catalogues online as well as place bids on items in forthcoming sales (which are listed in an Auction Calendar). It is also possible to bid in real time for certain auctions, but you must register first in order to do so.

Churchill Clocks (see page 154) have a range of longcase, wall, and other clocks for sale.

British Horological Institute

www.bhi.co.uk

This is the professional body for horologists, and it helps put the public in touch with specialist clock dealers/repairers. There are also hints and tips, informative articles from the society's online journal, and information on forthcoming fairs, exhibitions, and other events. Details of training courses and employment opportunities for horologists are included, as well as specialist books and videos for sale. There is a useful search engine that allows you to search all the references on the site using the keyword that interests you.

Charles Edwin Inc Antique Clocks and Barometers

www.charles-edwin.com

This dealer specializes in clocks and barometers and the extensive online catalogue has full and scholarly descriptions, as well as prices, for many items. Phone or email them if you are interested in purchasing something. A technical section answers such questions as how to move a mercury barometer safely, how to set a barometer, how to get your longcase clock ticking again, how the moon dial works, and how to determine the age and value of your clock. An extensive reading list is provided, together with a link to the online bookshop amazon.com. The dealer's show schedule is also included and there's a link to www.clockswatches.com, a research site for clocks and watches.

Churchill Clocks

www.churchillclocks.co.uk

An online valuation service for antique clocks is among the offerings of this dealer and restorer's site. This can be done by sending photos via email, although there is a charge for this service. Clocks for sale are also shown, along with their descriptions and prices. Send the dealers an email, and they will get back to you with purchasing details.

Derek Roberts

www.qualityantiqueclocks.com

You can hear (through WAV sound files) as well as see some of the clocks on the site of this UK dealer. A wealth of antique timepieces of all kinds can be seen, and features include a "clock of the month", which is described in lengthy and scholarly detail. An email will get you further details of any of the clocks shown that may interest you, and there are links to trade association and specialist horology sites.

Find a Clock

www.clockclinic.co.uk

The Clock Clinic offers clocks of all shapes and sizes on its website, and has a useful search engine that will help you seek out the works of specific makers. Photos of their stock can be enlarged for a clearer view. Phone, fax, or send an email if you want to buy anything. The site also includes details of the company's history and of its restoration services.

Historical Clock and Watch Research

www.clockswatches.com

This site is for anyone with a serious interest in horological research. It has a database of information on thousands of watch- and clockmakers and enquiries will provide you with links to websites, references to journals, and much more. Much of the information is obtainable free of charge, but you will have to subscribe on a pay-per-view basis for access to some parts of the site.

Horology – The Index

www.webcom.com/horology

This is a web resource that has links to a multitude of horological sites. These include academic sites such as those relating to the history of timekeeping, as well as commercial sites. There are also links to government organizations and museums around the world.

It's About Time

www.clocking-in.demon.co.uk

This site displays a vast array of antique clocks for sale. Longcases are particular favourites, and each of the images, which can be viewed in close-up, has a description and a price. Unrestored examples, which may be of interest to the enthusiast, are also available. Send an email for purchasing information, or if you would like to submit details of a "wanted" clock.

John Mann Antique Clocks

www.johnmannantiqueclocks.co.uk

This Scottish dealer boasts one of the largest stocks of superbly restored longcase clocks in Europe. It also offers moonphase, bracket, brass dial, painted dial, musical, and automaton clocks, all of the highest quality and with prices starting at around £3,000/$4,500. Copious notes on technical details and maker's history accompany good-quality pictures of the clocks. While many also have price tags, others are "price on application". Submit an email for further information on anything that interests you.

Kirtland H Crump Antique Clocks

www.crumpclocks.com

This is the site of a specialist in 200-year-old clocks, mostly from New England, but there are some European examples too. The pieces from the current inventory are all illustrated, and have detailed descriptions, although there are no prices given for them. Contact the dealer directly by telephone if you are interested in buying something. There is an extensive description of the repair and restoration services, as well as the appraisal services, offered. The site also gives details of its professional memberships of both antique dealers organizations and horological societies, with links to each one.

P A Oxley

www.british-antiqueclocks.com

The stock of a leading clock dealer is shown on this site, subdivided into categories such as longcases pre- and post-1800, wall clocks, and barometers. Full details including prices and provenance are given and, if you like what you see, you can send an email to them requesting details of how you can buy a particular item.

Pieces of Time

www.antique-watch.com

A vast collection of watches old and new and a wealth of horological information await the enthusiast on this site. Diagrams illustrate descriptions of various technical features, and there are also background details about many watchmakers. There are links to horological societies, museums, and various related websites. Watches are also for sale through this site although, if you wish to buy, it is probably better to ring them directly first to check the availability of stock.

Sugar Antiques

www.sugarantiques.com

Vintage Rolex and other quality watches are for sale through Sugar Antiques, which has a section in Japanese. Pocket watches and jewellery are also for sale, and are pictured alongside their prices and descriptions. Send them an email asking for further details if you want to buy anything, or to request a full list of current stock.

WORTH A LOOK

www.fineantiqueclocks.com
The site of a leading clock dealer.

www.kdclocks.co.uk
Longcases, bracket clocks, and more for sale.

COINS

A G & S Gillis

www.gilliscoins.com

This British coin dealer's site offers a large selection of coins for sale online. Ancient coins of the Roman, Anglo-Saxon, and Viking periods are particularly in evidence, as well as Greek and Celtic examples. These are all pictured on the site, and are accompanied by a range of antiquities including jewellery, which can also be bought online (see pages 200–2 for jewellery sites). You can email your requests to Andrew Gillis to see if he has what you are looking for – the feedback from a multitude of satisfied customers is proof that this service is trusted by coin collectors worldwide.

Airedale Coins

www.airedalecoins.com

The site of this dealer from Bingley, West Yorkshire, features an extensive list of coins, largely dominated by UK issues, although overseas countries like Mexico and Vietnam are represented too. Commemorative coins of all kinds are also very much in evidence (see pages 161–2 for commemorative sites). If you would like to buy something, you can print out a form from the site and send it to them through the post.

British Numismatic Trades Association

www.numis.co.uk/bnta.html

This specialist trade association has more than 70 members, and its website has a particularly useful list of top coin dealers from all over the United Kingdom. Full contact details are given for each dealer, with links to their websites where appropriate. The site includes brief details of the association's activities, including its anti-theft initiatives. If you are a dealer and are not listed, submit your details for free via an online form.

Chard

www.24carat.co.uk

This is the site of a UK dealer who offers jewellery as well as coins. The coin sections of the site offer useful information, such as a guide to coin grading and a guide to what makes a coin valuable. Some myths relating to coins are also dispelled. The site displays a variety of mostly British historic and current coins for sale, and it is possible to order them using a form that can be printed out and sent through the post.

Coincentre

www.coincentre.co.uk

Tokens, medallions, and banknotes as well as coins are offered on this site, where you can "pay by credit or debit card and start collecting straight away". Illustrations of individual coins are hard to come by, but coins are described according to a grading system. English coins are especially well represented, but the online catalogue has coins from all over the world.

Coincraft

www.coincraft.com

This large site belongs to a coin dealer who deals only with collectors and does not sell coins for investment purposes. The site includes useful information for the collector, such as a glossary of terms, and there are introductory articles on collecting different types of coins. As well as a wealth of historical information, the site offers British and world coins for sale, and you can buy directly online.

Coinlink

www.coinlink.com

As its title suggests, this is a web resource for coin collectors. It features information on associations, collectors' clubs, and forthcoming coin auctions. The site also includes advice on grading coins and warnings about stolen coins that could be in circulation. While much of the site is angled towards collecting American coins, the coinage of other nations is also represented, and the dealer's directory enables you to get in touch with numismatics specialists from around the world.

CoinZone

www.coinzone.com

This American site features online coin auctions, classified ads, and an online shopping mall for coin dealers. You will also find message boards to exchange views with fellow collectors, and a "coin learning centre", which features articles on various aspects of coins and coin collecting. There's also a guide to grading coins, as well as a magazine section for young collectors.

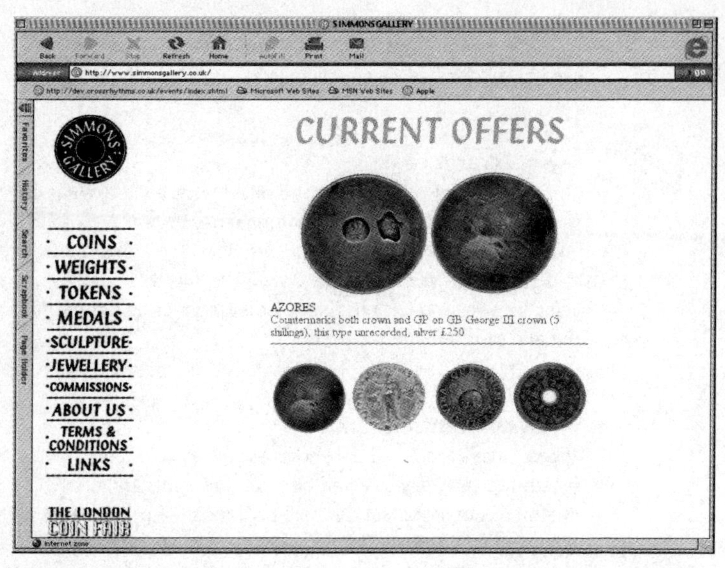

Simmons Gallery's site includes very impressive images of the items within their catalogue.

Jean Elsen s a

www.elsen.be

Jean Elsen is a leading Belgian firm that both auctions and sells numismatic items. Some medals are also included (see pages 212–13 for medal sites). A history of coins is a particularly useful feature of this site, including the coins of the Ancient Greeks, Byzantine coinage, and the ancient coins of the Far East. You will also find illustrated catalogues for forthcoming auctions and a list of coins that are available to buy at a fixed price. Ordering is through an email request – you will then be contacted with further information concerning payment details etc. An English version of the site is available.

Mike R Vosper

www.vosper4coins.co.uk

Mike Vosper is a UK dealer who specializes in Celtic and Roman coins. Later English, Scottish, and Irish coins are also offered, as are 17th-century tokens, and examples of all of these can be viewed on the site. Coins that have been illustrated on the site can be bought online with your credit card using a secure server. The site also includes some information on the history of coins, and researchers are invited to submit their work for publication on the web.

Simmons Gallery

www.simmonsgallery.co.uk

The site of London coin and medal specialists, Simmons Gallery includes not only details and pictures of the coins they have for sale but also gives advice to those who have something to sell. There are extremely detailed images in an online catalogue that is both educational and informative, and you can bid at a postal auction. In addition, the site has details of forthcoming London coin fairs and hotel booking information for visitors. (See pages 212–13 for a selection of medal sites.)

WORTH A LOOK

www.bexleycoinclub.org.uk
A collectors' club with useful information for the novice.

www.coinclubs.freeserve.co.uk
A site with information on numismatic societies, publications, and videos.

www.heavypen.com/coins/index.html
Detailed online article on collecting coins.

mywebpages.comcast.net/dougsmit
Non-commercial site on Greek and Roman coins.

COMICS

Books 'n' Comics

www.booksncomics.co.uk

This is a UK-based site featuring comics, graphic novels, and trading cards. Comics include most of the popular titles, especially American publications by Marvel and DC, and you can order online. Related merchandise, such as action figures, is also featured on the site and can be ordered in the same way. There is a Reviews page where you can add your own input.

Comic Art & Graffix Gallery

www.comic-art.com

Aiming to be the definitive resource for comic collectors, this site really does pack in a lot of information. Read about the history of comics, discover biographical information on artists and creators, and visit the site's virtual museum. American comics dominate the site and, if you'd like to buy some, you can visit the online store.

Comic Book Postal Auctions Ltd

www.compalcomics.com

Comic Book Postal Auctions Ltd started life as a mail-order service, hence the name. It's now firmly established online, and holds auctions every couple of months. The site has details of current and future sales and there's information about condition alongside each comic offered. Auction results are shown for the recent catalogues, which have included both British and American titles.

Comic Resources Site

www.comicbookresources.com

Updated daily, this is a site of news, views, and much more for comic fans. There are articles on various aspects of comics as well as bulletin boards and links to comic shops and websites. There is also a sophisticated search engine.

Comics for Sale Online

www.classicscentral.com

This Canadian website has an extensive list of comic books for sale. Covers are illustrated through the site, and you can order by email and then pay by cheque. Charts indicating the contents of each issue accompany some comics, and there's also a dictionary of the comics' artists.

European Comics on the Web

www.poeha.com/comics

If you are looking for particular information on European comics, you should find it here. Virtually every European nation is catered for, from Poland and Russia to France and Sweden. Comic festivals are also covered, and there are seemingly endless links to comic shops across the continent. However, not all the sites listed have English versions (although most do).

Grand Comic Book Database

www.comics.org

This ambitious project aims to build a database of all the comic books ever published throughout the world. The database includes story lines, artist details, and other information useful to comic book fans. The vast searchable database houses all the information so far online and, if you'd like to contribute, the site is appealing for helpers from various countries.

Hamer Auctions

www.hamerauctions.co.uk

Hamers publish an annual comic guide, and also organize twice-yearly comic auctions. They specialize in British comics like *Beano*, *Dandy*, and the *Rupert* annuals and there is a link to auctions of these items through ebay. You can also sign up online to the Hamer Book Club, which offers discounts to members.

International Comics

www.comics-international.com

This is the website of a magazine devoted to the comics industry. It includes news and reviews as well as information on festivals and various events and a Q & A page which you can email with any burning queries. Perhaps its most useful feature for the collector is, however, its directory. Included here are links to comic shops in the UK, the USA, and the rest of the world, as well as to the sites of mail-order specialists and publishers.

Lambiek.net

www.lambiek.nl

This is the online home of an Amsterdam comic bookshop, with an English version available. Established in 1968, Lambiek is probably the oldest dedicated comic shop in the world. Thousands of titles in various languages are stocked, as well as artworks from different comics. The site has a comics encyclopedia that offers biographies of artists from around the world, together with samples of their work. The bookshop has recently introduced an online shop to the site, for those who can't make it to Amsterdam in person.

WORTH A LOOK

webhome.idirect.com/~cancomic/webpagemine/index.html
Canadian comic site that also offers restoration services.

www.cartoon.org
A Florida museum of cartoon art from over 50 countries.

www.csnsider.com
News, views, and rumours from the world of comics.

COMMEMORATIVES

Political Memorabilia

www.geocities.com/CapitolHill/6030

This site offers a range of political souvenirs, memorabilia, and other commemoratives, and its particular strength is the badges and pins of various political parties. Although it is an American site, it does include a number of items from other countries, including the UK and Canada. Send them an email enquiry if you are interested in any of the items shown on the site, or if you have something you would like to trade.

Royal & Regal Memorabilia

www.royal-memorabilia.com

Royal commemorative items of all kinds, especially pottery and glass, can be found on this site. Commemoratives from the present day back to pre-Victorian times are available. You can click on a picture of a particular monarch to find commemoratives from his or her reign. Choose from around 2,000 items in stock and then shop online for them.

Royal Commemoratives & Collectables

www.royalcoll.fsnet.co.uk

Royal commemoratives and collectibles from the reigns of several monarchs can be ordered online at this site. Everything from Queen Victoria's Diamond Jubilee commemorative ceramics to items relating to the abdication of Edward VIII is included here. Items in the online catalogue are described in detail, with particular attention to their condition.

Royals of England

www.royals-of-england.com

More than 500 items of royal memorabilia can be seen and bought through this website, which includes Victorian items as well as more up-to-date collectibles that relate to Queen Elizabeth II's Golden Jubilee. There are mugs, plates, spoons, and thimbles, as well as newspapers and ephemera to be found here. The emphasis is on the affordable, as the site is keen to attract collectors who are on a budget.

WORTH A LOOK

www.heatons-of-tisbury.co.uk/commemoratives.htm
Goss china and other commemoratives.

COSTUME AND FASHION

The Costume Gallery

www.costumegallery.com

Founded in 1996, this site has a "Costume Classroom" where you can take online courses, as well as an online library which features numerous articles on the subject of vintage fashion. There's also a research service for writers and TV producers who are keen to get the authentic look for their productions. You will also find links to numerous relevant commercial websites, costume designers' sites, and much more.

Davenport & Co.

www.davenportandco.com

Vintage clothing and accessories of various types can be bought from this American dealer's site. There is a particularly good range of 1920s and 1930s hats, but everything from Victorian lingerie to 1970s polyester can be found here. There are special offers on damaged items, which might be suitable for repair or use as patterns.

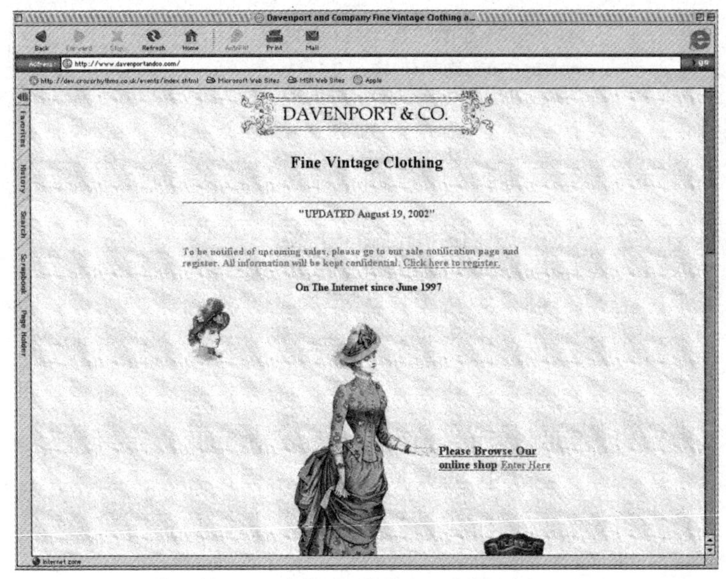

Davenport & Co. sell a wide range of vintage clothing on their website.

The Fan Museum

www.fan-museum.org

This is the site of the only museum in the world devoted to fans and fan-making (its physical site is in Greenwich, London). The collection comprises more than 3,000, predominantly antique, fans from various countries and periods, and several examples can be seen online. The site is educational, with useful information on the history of fans and the work of the museum's conservation department. There is also an online souvenir shop.

Heritage Studio

www.heritagestudio.com/costume.htm

This is a dealer's site with an eclectic range of vintage costume for sale. Items on offer include hats, shoes, underwear, and accessories, as well as military uniforms. There are links to the sites of costume dealers, museums, and militaria specialists (see pages 90–101 for relevant museums and pages 132–4 for arms and armour sites).

International Fan Collectors' Guild

www.hand-fan.org

Although the Guild is not a profit-making organization, you will find fans for sale on this large site, as well as links to commercial dealers. Various web resources are listed, and the site also includes some historical and cultural background, exploring such topics as the "language of the fan".

Joachim & Betty Mendes

www.mendes.co.uk

Dealers Joachim and Betty Mendes, based on the south coast of England, feature an extensive selection of costume on their website, largely from the Victorian era. There is a good selection of children's clothing, and miscellaneous textiles and lace. You can buy online, and there is a money-back guarantee.

The Museum of Costume

www.museumofcostume.co.uk

The Museum of Costume is based in Bath, England. On this site, you can learn more about the Fashion Research Centre, which has resources on costume from the 18th century to the present day. You can also explore the museum's collections online and follow a number of links to other costume sites.

Stitches in Time Vintage Clothing

www.stitchesintime.com

Browse through a series of "virtual showrooms" displaying costume and accessories from 1850 to 1970 on this site. All the items shown are for sale, and there are no reproduction items stocked here. Clicking on an item in the showroom will provide you with a larger picture and further information.

WORTH A LOOK

www.lace-bobbins.co.uk/links.htm
Links to various lace-related sites.

www.midnightgarden.com/costume
Costume site with an historical emphasis plus links.

COSTUME JEWELLERY

All About Costume Jewellery

jewelcollect.org

A bulletin board, an email discussion list, jewellery auctions, and an online collectors' club are featured at Jewelcollect, as well as links to various dealer websites. Do not join the email list unless you are serious about costume jewellery – your mailbox will soon be overflowing.

Cristobal London

www.cristobal.co.uk

Twentieth-century costume jewellery is the speciality of this site, which offers a selection of contemporary pieces for online ordering, as well as vintage items by the best-known names. Chanel, Schiaparelli, and Dior are all here, among many others, and the site also provides histories of famous firms and designers.

Everything Under the Sun

www.hostsite.net/everything

This site does indeed have "everything under the sun" but includes a great selection of signed and unsigned pieces of costume jewellery for sale. It is informal in style, and includes a section on "playful plastics", which has some very inexpensive pieces. More costly items in fine gold and silver are shown elsewhere on the site.

Forgotten Romance

www.forgotten-romance.com

This dealer site offers all kinds of collectible costume jewellery that can be ordered online. Pins, cufflinks, and various accessories are also included, and there's a bargain basement selection of pieces priced at less than £16/$20. The site also offers vintage linens, such as tablecloths.

Jewel Diva

www.jeweldiva.com

There is an emphasis on rare and unusual costume jewellery at Jewel Diva, an American site, and a large selection can be ordered online via a secure server. Stock includes signed and unsigned pieces and there are examples of Art Deco and Czech jewellery. There is a fine selection of Bakelite jewellery here too, as well as accessories such as handbags and hats.

Jewellery for "Stars"

www.moviestarjewels.com

Movie Star Jewels is the costume and vintage jewellery site for anyone who has ever wanted to look like a movie star of the "That's Entertainment" age. The site illustrates designer and signed pieces under the heading of "Leading Ladies" while those pieces that are "waiting to be discovered" are headed "Understudies". All the stock pictured is for sale through the site.

Liz Collectible Costume Jewelry

www.lizjewel.com

Antique, vintage, and modern collectible costume jewellery are all offered on this site, which boasts a particularly large selection of Bakelite and Art Deco pieces. Tiaras and even crowns are included for sale online, and the site also features a classified ads section.

Terezi Vintage Costume Jewelry

members.aol.com/terezij

A selection of pins, brooches, necklaces, earrings, and bracelets can be seen and purchased on this American site. Pictures and thorough descriptions accompany the stock, and matching sets as well as single items are offered. There is also a special section for silver and copper jewellery, and you will find plenty of links to other jewellery sites.

Valerie B Gedziun Designer Costume Jewelry

www.valerieg.com

Vintage costume jewellery, including a collection of rare Trifari from the 1930s and 1940s, can be found among the online stock of this specialist dealer. American and European designers are represented, and an extensive selection of stock is pictured on the site. A section on contemporary items is also included, and there are links galore to many other interesting sites.

See pages 200–2 for a list of jewellery sites.

WORTH A LOOK

www.alicejewels.com
Victorian, vintage, and ethnic jewellery.

www.bbbeads.com
Vintage and contemporary jewellery.

www.eternaljewels.com
Costume jewellery for sale.

DISNEYANA

For Disney Enthusiasts

www.disneyananet.com

Designed as a place for Disney enthusiasts to buy, sell, and exchange on the Internet, Disneyananet actually offers much more than that. There are also interviews with people who have worked on Disney films, and links to other Disney and similar collectible sites.

Learn about the Land of Disney

www.justdisney.com

Listen to the sounds of Disneyland, through downloadable WAV files, and learn about the background to your favourite Disney films at Just Disney. This site has little in the way of collectibles, but there's lots of information on the company's history and biographical information about Walt Disney himself, plus many useful links to other Disney sites.

Online Disney Directory

www.webdisney.com

WebDisney, a guide to Disney on the Internet, features more than 600 sites and the list is growing all the time. A search engine enables you to find the kind of site you are looking for as quickly as possible; as well as collectibles sites, there are also sites devoted to Disneyland and to Disney's films and TV programmes. Collectibles sites listed in the directory include auction sites, and there are also bulletin boards to put you in touch with fellow Disney fans.

Online Disneyana

www.disneyanacollectibles.com

A weekly contest with a chance to win Disney goodies is one of the highlights of this site, which features Disneyana old and new for sale online. Among the pieces included are some really unusual items that were originally intended for promotional use only. Pins, trading cards, figures, key rings, ceramics, posters, and many more items are available here.

Walt Disney Art Classics

disney.com/disneyartclassics

Walt Disney Art Classics is a division of the Disney Corporation. It is mainly responsible for producing collectibles relating to the Disney characters. On the site you will find posters, prints, and limited-edition collectibles galore. These include top-of-the range items by leading manufacturers. You can also search for retailers, both inside and outside the United States, and even join the Walt Disney Collectors' Society.

WORTH A LOOK

www.billbam.com/disney.html
A host of Disney collectibles for sale.

www.disneyselect.com
Fan site with Disney goodies including screensavers.

DOLLS

Barbie Collectibles Directory

you.barbiecollectibles.com

This is the official Barbie site and it includes a detailed history of the doll, complete with a Barbie chronology and Barbie trivia. While online at the site you can join the official collectors' club, shop for dolls and accessories online, and also discover how much the Barbie that you used to play with as a child might be worth today.

Bebes et Jouets

you.genie.co.uk/bebesetjouets

Only genuine antique French and German dolls are offered on this site, which carries no reproductions whatsoever. The site is divided into categories with headings such as "Yet more dolls", and "Dolls again", which suggests that this site is more about giving a flavour of stock carried rather than offering an online catalogue. However, if you are looking for top makers including Simon & Halbig, Jumeau, Bru, and Kestner, you will find them all here. You can email the dealers for more information and they will gladly email photos of any items and answer requests if you have something specific in mind.

A Century of Dolls

www.acenturyofdolls.com

Composition dolls are particularly favoured on the site of New York's largest doll and teddy bear shop (see pages 263–5 for further teddy bear sites). The site displays a selection of dolls by famous makers such as Kestner, Jumeau, and many others. Artist and limited edition dolls are also available. The site includes a list of artists and manufacturers, and there's an invitation to "tell us about your collection" – fill in the email form on the site if you feel so inclined.

Denise van Patten Dolls

www.dollymaker.com

This is an informative site that includes a history of various types of dolls as well as listing dolls for sale. The sales section includes both Barbies and antique and miniature dolls. There's also section on doll-making and an online bookshop.

Doll Collecting

www.collectdolls.about.com

There are over 700 doll-related sites to choose from here, with categories covered ranging from antique bisque dolls to Barbies. There is also a wealth of information on subjects such as doll-making and costume-making, news and views (you can sign up for a free email newsletter), interesting online articles, discussion groups on dolls, doll auctioneers, museums, and reference material.

Doll Magazine

www.dollmagazine.com

Doll magazine is a UK publication that caters for all collectors, whether their interests lie in modern or antique dolls. The website includes a number of online articles, but most are readable only to subscribers – you can subscribe online if you wish. Useful features of the site that are open to anyone include a listing of doll clubs to put you in touch with fellow enthusiasts, a listing of doll fairs, and competitions that you can enter online.

Dolls of our Childhood

www.dollsofourchildhood.com

The website of doll historian Judith Izen offers online shopping from a lengthy list of stock that includes Barbie and Sindy as well as much older dolls, including some lesser-known makes. Signed copies of Judith's books are available to buy, and you can email her any related questions. Toy catalogues and baby furniture catalogues are also available.

Ellen's Dolls

www.ellensdolls.com

This is an American doll retailer specializing in contemporary collectible dolls, including limited edition items, new artist dolls, and bears. Search a range of dolls by artist/manufacturer, and browse the catalogue of illustrated items to make your selection. You can pay by credit card online, or order by telephone or post. There is also a mailing list that you can join to receive notification of new dolls, special sales, and updates.

Netdoll

www.netdoll.com

Search for dolls by artist name, company, or theme on the site of this American dealer. Prices of some of the dolls featured on this site, all of which are available for online purchase, run into four figures, but others are much more affordable. In particular, a selection of damaged items may well provide some bargains. Dolls new and old and of various types are included, and the site includes message boards and a useful doll glossary. The home page even features three "Dolls of the Day".

Theriault's

www.theriault's.com

Theriault's specialist auction house started out more than 30 years ago. Today the firm is a legend among doll enthusiasts, and its site includes a chance for you to learn more about dolls through an educational section. You can also browse through the online catalogues of the firm's auctions, look through the auction schedule, and join in an online auction. You will have to register to use the majority of the site, but fortunately this registration is available free of charge.

Treasures and Dolls

www.antiquedoll.com

A vast array of antique and collectible dolls can be found on this site. All of them are for sale, and can be bought online with your credit card. All the most popular makes from every era are included. There is a particularly good range of Madame Alexander dolls, and there are also "celebrity dolls", including a Marilyn Monroe. This site also includes bears, both old and new, by top makers such as Steiff.

WORTH A LOOK

website.lineone.net/~rmaxwell
Dealer site with dolls, teddies, and much more.

www.dollmasters.com
Doll accessories and reference books.

www.dollshowplace.com
Dolls for collectors and dolls' house builders.

www.geocities.com/heartland/prairie/5543
Includes bulletin boards for various types of doll collecting.

www.hersmine.com
Doll dealer's site with a wide selection for sale.

www.members.aol.com/DCDolls/dcdolls1.html
Dolls of the 1950s.

ENAMELS

A La Vieille Russie

www.alvr.com

A fine selection of enamels can be found on the large site of this leading New York dealers, who are also known for their quality jewellery and objets d'art. A variety of Russian decorative items are the mainstay of the business, and works by famous names can be seen on the site. You must contact the gallery if you want further details, and to purchase items. The site also includes news articles, a calendar of related events, and a chance to "ask the experts" a question.

Andre Ruzhnikov

www.russianarts.com

The gallery of Andre Ruzhnikov actually specializes in Russian decorative arts of various types, but admirers of fine enamels will still find plenty to enjoy on this site. Numerous examples of the enameller's art are shown, and you can fill in an online form for further information, including prices.

Bijoux Extraordinaire Ltd

www.jewelryexpert.com/articles/enamel.htm

Information on the art of the enameller can be found here in the form of an extensive illustrated online article. The differences between the various types of enamelling, such as cloisonné, guilloché, and plique-à-jour, are all clearly explained here, and the examples that are shown on the site are also available for you to buy if you wish.

Halcyon Days

www.halcyondays.co.uk

Fine enamels, porcelain, and other objets d'art are the specialities of the London-based company Halcyon Days, who hold four royal warrants. Their website features an illustrated online catalogue, which provides in-depth descriptions and discussions of many of their pieces. Both antique and contemporary pieces are stocked by them, and either category can be bought directly online.

Taylor B Williams Antiques, LLC

www.enamels.com

This is the site of an American dealer, with a large online catalogue of antique enamels for sale. The dealer specializes in English enamels from 1750–1840. You cannot buy directly from the site, but email enquiries are encouraged. This site is also a source of general information on enamel as it includes a glossary, an article on the history of enamels, and a recommended reading list.

WORTH A LOOK

www.antiques21.com/Restoration.html

Before and after restoration pictures and enamel FAQs.

www.klaber.com

Enamels and porcelain for sale.

www.nga.gov/collection/gallery/medieval/medieval-main1.html

This link takes you directly to the enamels collection of Washington's National Gallery of Art.

www.speel.demon.co.uk/other/fisher.htm

The art of Arts and Crafts enamellist Alexander Fisher.

www.stpetersburgcollection.com

Limited-edition Fabergé eggs and objects.

EPHEMERA

Antique Paper and Ephemera X-Change

www.apex-ephemera.com

This web resource for ephemera enthusiasts contains links to dealers, and you can search for those who have a particular speciality, such as booklets or advertising ephemera. There are message boards to exchange views or trade with fellow collectors and you can email your requests to dealers.

The Card Mine

www.cardmine.co.uk

Trade cards, postcards, and assorted ephemera can be bought via this site, which features regular online auctions (see pages 229–30 for postcard sites and pages 151–2 for cigarette card sites). You will also find a wealth of links, subdivided into card and other sites. There is also an introduction to the hobby, and a card location service for those seeking something in particular.

The Ephemera Catalog

www.ephemeranet.com

Ephemera from the 19th and 20th centuries, subdivided into 85 specialist categories, can be seen and bought on this site. Categories include such esoteric fields as ballooning ephemera and there is a searchable database of items if you know exactly what you want. A number of different dealers operate through the site and you deal with them, not the site – no buyer registration is needed, but sellers must pre-register.

The Ephemera Society

www.ephemera-society.org.uk

The Ephemera Society is concerned with all aspects of the hobby, and its remit includes everything from bus tickets to letterheads and from birthday cards to menus. The society is an internationally recognized authority, and its website includes details of how to join, as well as a calendar of its own fairs and of related events. Anyone is welcome, although there is a fee, and you can join using an online form.

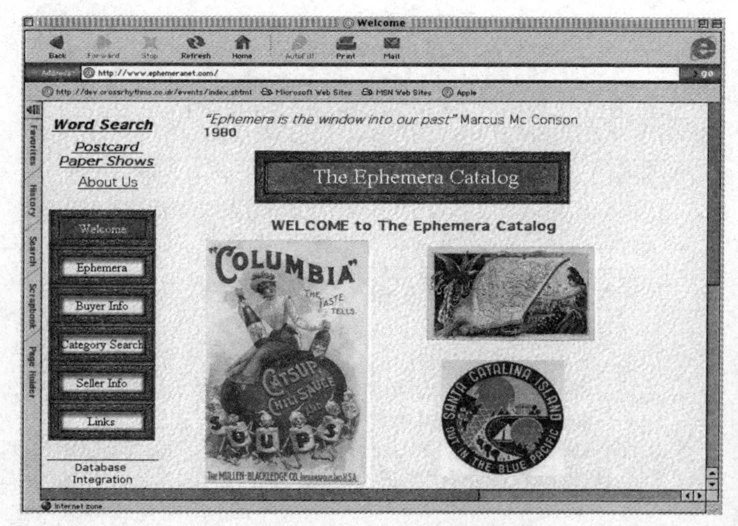

This huge ephemera site has an extremely useful searchable database.

Ephemera Society of America

www.ephemerasociety.org

The Ephemera Society of America's site includes examples of all different types of ephemera, from posters to cigar bands (see pages 231–2 for poster sites). There is also information on the history of ephemera given here, and you can join the society online.

Historic Newspapers and Early Imprints

www.historicpages.com

Informative articles on newspaper collecting are included on this site, which also offers guidance on likely values. The site explains how to spot reproductions, and includes information on related topics, such as the history of journalism. Historic papers, some dating back to the 17th century, can be bought through various online catalogues.

Ken's Paper Collectables

www.kens.co.uk

Ephemera ranging from TV and radio magazines to newspapers and theatre programmes can all be found on this site, and all items can be purchased by credit card via a secure server. Autographs, comics, and pop and sports memorabilia are also sold, and there's an email form to send details if you have something to sell. (See pages 159–61 for comic sites and pages 237–40 for rock and pop memorabilia.)

Lisa Cox Music

www.lisacoxmusic.co.uk

All manner of ephemera related to music can be found here, from scores and photographs to autographs of musical stars. There are early editions of the works of significant composers, and personal documents for sale (see pages 215–17 for related musical instrument sites). Download catalogues, search an online inventory, browse through recent acquisitions, or find information on forthcoming auctions. You will have to register to use some parts of the site, but this is free of charge.

Paper Antiques

www.paperantiques.co.uk

This is a web resource for the ephemerist, which contains links to dealers, societies, archives, and much more. There is a wide range of links, for example ones to a dance-card museum and another to match-cover collectors. The site also has links to dealer pages, and there is a question-and-answer page.

Roy Davids Ltd

www.roydavids.com

Manuscripts and autographed letters relating to art, history, literature, music, and many other fields are offered on this site, which also includes a lengthy and intelligent article on collecting manuscripts. Some of the items offered date back centuries and do not come cheap, while others are more affordable – all are accompanied by a detailed commentary that makes this a site for those who wish to learn as well as buy. If you do wish to buy, you can own something written by your favourite artist, writer, or composer.

The Scrap Album

www.scrapalbum.com

This site is designed as a tribute to old Victorian scrapbooks. Everything that might once have been pasted into those albums has now been "pasted" onto the site, including Victorian Christmas cards, Valentine's cards, and other ephemera. This non-commercial site also includes details of Victorian seasonal customs and links to various ephemera sites.

World of Playing Cards

www.wopc.co.uk

The home page of the English Playing Card Society is among more than 60 links to this site, which celebrates the history of the playing card. The site's purpose is educational rather than commercial, although several commercial sites are included among the links if you want to buy. As well as offering many colourful images of cards through the ages, the site tells us what a transformation card is, what Chinese playing cards look like, and when the Joker made its first appearance in a deck (see pages 269–72 for other games and toy sites).

WORTH A LOOK

www.celticpromotions.org.uk
Limited-edition phonecards.

www.scraplink.com
Links to scrapbook sites.

www.vintagelabels.org
Luggage label galleries and collecting advice.

FILM AND TV

The Big Picture

www.big-pix.com

This site offers movie posters and various memorabilia, mostly from the 1960s to the present. Stock includes press kits, buttons, and banners and you can buy online. Choose a category of film or just browse through the stock lists.

Buy Autographs Online

www.ctplatt.com

If you missed them at the stage door, you can still get your favourite star's autograph through Platt Autographs. The firm's inventory of 200,000 signed items includes material relating to royalty and politicians, as well as those from the entertainment world. Items are described in full, prices are given, and you can email, telephone, or fax for further details.

Collector's X-Change

www.f-t-l.com

Science fiction and fantasy TV and film collectibles are well represented on this site. Items for sale include autographs, toys, dolls, games, books, props, and comic books. There is a list of celebrity addresses and links to film studio sites.

Entertainment Collectibles

www.collectible.com

This site offers auctions and private sales of entertainment memorabilia of various types. The online inventory includes photographs of legendary stars such as Marilyn Monroe as well as props, autographs, and much more. TV- as well as film-related items are available for online purchase.

Film Star Memorabilia

www.starscomeout.com

Movie posters, lobby cards, and similar memorabilia are the mainstay of this site. A wealth of items can be found and there is a link to a site that offers reprints, although there are no reproductions here. Listen to a choice of film theme tunes while you browse and order online with your credit card.

Jim's TV Collectibles

www.jimtvc.com

A rich source of collectibles relating to a multitude of TV shows. This is the site of a California-based dealer, so the shows in question are mostly, though not exclusively, American. However, shows such as the *A-Team*, *Star Trek*, and *Starsky and Hutch* have an international appeal. Books, magazines, and toys are available for online purchase, as are TV soundtracks on vinyl.

Movie Memorabilia

www.moviemarket.co.uk

Billed as "the world's premier store for movie memorabilia", this site certainly has a lot to offer. There are posters, photographs, autographs, and assorted memorabilia relating to your favourite stars. You can shop online and, if you have something to sell, you can email the site with details – they are particularly interested in acquiring original posters in good condition.

ReelClassics.com

www.reelclassics.com

This site is for "reel" movie enthusiasts, and has lots of information on films and celebrities, including details such as celebrity birthdays. Of particular interest to collectors is the site's links page. This will lead you to a diverse selection of relevant sites, including those of autograph dealers, general movie memorabilia dealers, and specialist auction sites.

TV Toys

www.tvtoys.com

A wealth of toys, as well as books, games, cards, and other collectibles relating to favourite TV shows of the past can be bought through this site. There is also a library of articles on shows from *The Munsters* to the *Six Million Dollar Man*, and links to fan sites and to the official home pages of the stars.

A Wrinkle in Time

www.awit.com

This California-based dealer sells a wide range of TV and film collectible merchandise online, much of it being related to TV science-fiction and fantasy series. There is a list of cult TV and film memorabilia that is either available now, or can be obtained for you. Send them an email if you are looking for something specific.

For further poster sites see pages 231–2.

WORTH A LOOK

www.bartertown.org.uk
TV and film memorabilia for sale and wanted.

www.pittofhorror.com
Movie posters and memorabilia.

www.silentcinema.com
An index of silent movie collectibles.

www.solnet.co.uk/acme
Collectible toys, especially TV-related.

FINE ART

Art Around the Home

www.easyart.com

Using art in home-decorating schemes is a theme of this site, Easyart, which features articles on subjects such as framing. Its main purpose is to sell prints, including limited-edition prints, which it does through online ordering via a secure server. You can choose your print, plus a frame to go with it, before ordering. A wide variety of popular artists are represented, and you can read artist biographies and art history facts as you browse through the selection.

Art Connection

www.art-connection.com

As its name suggests, this is a gateway to art dealers, and is unique because many links to galleries are made by clicking on pictures of their stock, rather than their names. You can, however, scroll down lists of gallery names if you prefer to be conventional. You can also search the site by typing in the name of the gallery or artist you are trying to locate. Art fairs and restorers can also be found through this site.

Artfact

www.artfact.com

This site provides information on more than five million lots sold at auction worldwide since 1986. It is designed for art market professionals and features a searchable database of items, but anyone can visit the site. Search by keyword and/or price range, or use multiple word searches.

The Art Institute of Chicago

www.artic.edu

The Art Institute of Chicago is one of the USA's foremost museums and academic centres. It has fine collections of artefacts from many different cultures and periods, from European Decorative Arts to African and even Amerindian Art. The museum site contains visitor and student/teacher information, a calendar of events, details of exhibitions, an online library catalogue, and images of selected pieces from each of the collections.

Artline

www.artline.com

This site represents seven international art dealers associations – six based in the USA and one in London. Listings are categorized by gallery, artist, and association. The artists represented by the various galleries are listed alphabetically, with links to the relevant gallery, and detailed biographies. Photos of the paintings available for sale are also provided. You must contact individual galleries for more information about a piece if you are interested in buying it. There is also news of current exhibitions, as well as new artline.com members on the site, plus a calendar of major international art fairs.

Art on the Web

www.dart.fine-art.com

This is a fine art Internet database. The search engine offers various options to find works from a 37,000-strong selection from nearly 5,000 websites of dealers, collectors, and artists. You can buy or sell art through this site, or post messages on the bulletin board, and there's a simple guide to using the services.

Artprice

www.artprice.com

This French site, with an English option, allows you to search by artist for paintings coming up for sale in auctions around the world. You can also search through a database of art sold since 1987, and there's an analysis of the art market that includes price trends. The site is free for limited use, while paying subscribers have unlimited access. You can also buy a CD-ROM version of the database online.

Blains Fine Art

www.blains.co.uk

Modern and contemporary works can be seen on this website. The online inventory regularly includes works by artists such as Andy Warhol, Alexander Calder, John Piper, and Dame Laura Knight. You can browse through the selection, and send an email if you would like further details.

Bourne Gallery

www.bournegallery.com

The Bourne Gallery specializes in 19th- and 20th-century British and European paintings. Its website includes a search engine, which allows searches using keywords like "farm" or "beach" or, alternatively, the nationality, date of birth, or name of the artist, or the title of the work. More than 200 different artists are represented, and prices are listed. You can enquire by email if you wish to buy and there are regular online exhibitions.

Boydell Galleries

www.boydellgalleries.co.uk

The Boydell Galleries in Liverpool have been selling art since 1851. Their website displays watercolours subdivided by subject and painted by artists such as David Cox, Anthony Vandyke Copley Fielding, and John Varley (there are artists' biographies on the site). Prints and maps and scenes of old Liverpool are also for sale, although dealing is now done solely via the Internet and at antiques fairs. There is an email order form: you cannot buy online by credit card yet, but a fully-fledged online shopping system is in the offing.

Blains have an extensive selection of modern art works that are detailed online.

British Fine Art

www.britishfine-art.co.uk

In spite of this site's name, some European works of art are shown alongside British art, although the latter dominates. The emphasis is on affordable art of the 19th and 20th centuries, and the home page notes that while works by some Victorian artists, such as Atkinson Grimshaw, now command very high prices, there must be many lesser-known artists awaiting recognition. The implication is of course that some of them are on this site! Choose from a selection by subject or artist and see if you can spot a winner. If you think you can, fill in an online order form to buy.

Childs Gallery

www.childsgallery.com

This is the site of the longest-running commercial art gallery on Boston's Newbury Street, founded in 1937. The gallery specializes in 15th- to 20th-century paintings, prints, drawings, watercolours, and sculpture. There is a list of past and current exhibitions, a shows schedule, and publications available for sale. You can use the site's search engine to find a specific work or artist.

The Coeur d'Alene Art Auction

www.cdaartauction.com

This auction house from Reno, Nevada, USA, specializes in Western cowboy art and wildlife art by established contemporaries as well as past masters. Thumbnails of a selection of upcoming works are shown, along with descriptions. The site includes a catalogue order form and email address.

The Cooley Gallery

www.cooleygallery.com

This Connecticut gallery specializes in American paintings and works on paper of the 19th and 20th centuries. The website includes images from current and upcoming exhibitions and paintings in various categories, such as the 19th and 20th centuries, and contemporary artists. You can order hard copies of catalogues and the site also includes details of the gallery's appraisal service. Links include various art sites, including American art resources.

Daniel Katz

www.katz.co.uk

If it's sculpture rather than "flat art" that interests you, you'll find plenty of it here. Works in various media including bronze, metal, and terracotta are shown in an online catalogue – send an email enquiry if you are interested in anything. Works shown are all Old Masters from many different European countries and images are accompanied by a thorough and scholarly commentary.

Directory of Tribal Art

www.tribalartdirectory.com

This is an online source of information for those interested in non-Western art. The site includes news and features, details of forthcoming events, and a search facility. There is also a directory of dealers, featuring the top names in this field, which gives their full contact details.

Dulwich Picture Gallery

www.dulwichpicturegallery.org

Dulwich Picture Gallery in London was the first purpose-built art gallery in England, designed by Sir John Soane in 1811. It houses one of the finest collections of European Old Masters of the 1600s and 1700s in the world. If you cannot get to Dulwich, you can enjoy works by Murillo, Rubens, Poussin, Watteau, and many more online. If you can get to the gallery, the site will tell you all you need to know about forthcoming events, and there are details of the gallery's educational programme here too.

Emanuel von Baeyer

www.evbaeyer.com

Old Master drawings and prints at the quality end of the market are the mainstay of London dealer Emanuel von Baeyer, whose site shows numerous examples from the gallery's latest catalogues. Click on an image for an enlarged version and informative accompanying text. All are for sale, but prices of many works, as well as purchasing details, are only available on application.

Fine Art Trade Guild

www.fineart.co.uk

Established in 1847, the Fine Art Trade Guild is a leading British organization for those involved in the art trade. Its website features an online magazine, an exhibition for artist members, news of trade fairs, and much more. There's a listing of members, and the site also includes a bookshop and art-related consumer news and information.

The Fleming Collection

www.flemingcollection.co.uk

The Fleming Collection was founded by a London-based merchant banker, who was Scottish. In his honour, the collection amassed by the bank comprises works by Scottish artists or paintings with a Scottish theme. It could once only be seen by those who visited the boardroom, but now it is on show to the public at a new gallery in London, and via its online home. The website displays a selection of works from past, present, and forthcoming exhibitions, as well as giving an entertaining history of the collection and its founder.

Francis Kyle Gallery

www.franciskylegallery.com

Francis Kyle is a London gallery that handles the works of contemporary, mostly figurative, artists. Its website includes pictures and details of current exhibitions. As some artists are inspired by their predecessors, the site includes information about historical as well as current artists. You can search by category, artist, or keyword and then contact the gallery for further information.

Hilliard Society of Miniaturists

www.art-in-miniature.org

Named after the celebrated miniaturist, the society promotes the understanding of miniature painting, its history, and present form. There are online galleries (featuring works that are not necessarily for sale), and you will find information on miniaturist societies around the world, art materials suppliers, teachers, and much more. International exhibition details are also featured.

International Art Centre

www.internationalartcentre.co.nz

View lots from forthcoming sales and from recent auctions on this New Zealand auctioneers' site. There's also an online gallery with works at fixed prices, although you cannot buy directly online (you must submit an email enquiry). Modern and contemporary works, many by New Zealanders, dominate stock at auction and in the gallery, and you can read their biographies on the site.

International Print Center

www.ipcny.org

This is the website of a New York-based, non-profit-making organization that promotes the study and understanding of antique and contemporary fine art prints. The site has details of exhibitions organized by the Print Center, and these include historical information on prints and artists. The site has great links to museums, collecting clubs, dealers, and general print resources.

Irish Art

www.irishart.demon.co.uk

This site has information on Irish galleries and art shows, contemporary Irish artists, new prints, publishers, and more. You can also find out about online art shows, and join a mailing list if you wish to be kept up-to-date.

John Noott Galleries

www.john-noott.com

This is the site of a dealer who has four galleries, each with a slightly different speciality, from the contemporary to the art of the 19th century. The extensive online gallery includes biographies of artists. Prices are not always given, some are available "on application" and you must send an email or make a telephone call if you see something you like.

Kieselbach Auction

www.kieselbach.hu

The website of this Hungarian auction house, available in English, shows off a large selection of paintings from recent and forthcoming auctions. Many of the works are modern or contemporary, painted by Hungarian and other Eastern European artists. The site is particularly keen on feedback and provides online forms for you to register your views, or to place requests for items that may appear in future sales.

London Art News and Information

www.artlondon.com

Designed as a web portal to the London art market, this site has information on galleries and artists, news of art auctions, and a discussion board. There are also features on various artists and different aspects of the art world. You can shop from online galleries, or visit the online auctions. There are links to major international museums and institutions, dealers, galleries, and online resources.

Marlborough Fine Art

www.marlboroughfineart.com

The site of one of the world's leading galleries displays works by artists such as Raymond Mason, Paula Rego, Francis Bacon, Frank Auerbach, and many more. Biographies are included, and there are details of exhibitions and events at the gallery. Send an email for further details of works shown on the site.

The Metropolitan Museum of Art

www.metmuseum.org

Founded in 1870, the Metropolitan Museum in New York has a collection that now contains over two million pieces, both ancient and modern, from all over the world. Of these, the entire Department of European Paintings, plus more than 3,500 highlights from the other collections, have been reproduced online (although the museum states that they plan to add to this number in the future). Images can be viewed in a number of ways: by selecting a curatorial department from a list, by using the search engine, or by taking the director's own tour. Other features include the facility to create your own personal Met Gallery of your favourite pieces, an online shop, and information about visiting and special exhibitions.

Museé d'Orsay

www.musee-orsay.fr

Works by Cézanne, Renoir, and Manet are among those that can be seen on the website of this famous Paris museum, which is available in English. Biographical information accompanies the works on show, and there's also a history of the museum itself. An online shop offers gift ideas and stocks CD-ROMs and videos.

The National Gallery, London

www.nationalgallery.org.uk

Western European painting from 1250–1900 is housed in this major London gallery. The online version features illustrations of works by all the best-known names in Western art, accompanied by an informative text. Take a tour of current exhibitions, search the collections by artist or title, or browse through the online shop.

National Gallery of Victoria

www.ngv.vic.gov.au

The National Gallery of Victoria is Australia's oldest public art gallery. Its online version features drawings by William Blake as well as art ranging from Australian Aboriginal and Chinese and Indian art through to the Old Masters and French Impressionists. More than 500 works can be viewed online. You can order souvenirs such as greetings cards, books, prints, and art screen savers from the online shop by printing out their order form and sending it via post.

National Museum of Art, Osaka

www.nmao.go.jp

The website of one of Japan's major national institutions, with an English version available, features a selection of works from current and past exhibitions, complete with a commentary on the works and their contexts. There are links to the sites of the country's other national museums, making this a useful jumping-off point for exploring Japan's art collections.

National Museum of Western Art, Tokyo

www.nmwa.go.jp

Japan's only national museum devoted to Western art has a varied collection and works from the medieval period, through the Renaissance and Dutch Old Masters, to the French Impressionists are available online. You can view a selection offered, or search the database for something particular.

National Museums and Galleries on Merseyside

www.nmgm.org.uk

Based in Liverpool, the National Museums and Galleries on Merseyside is one of Britain's major regional public galleries and it has a particularly good collection of pre-Raphaelite art. The website offers a chance to view the cream of the collections online, including that of the renowned Lady Lever Art Gallery. There is a "picture of the month", in which an important painting is discussed, and there's also an archive of previous works that have had this honour.

National Portrait Gallery, London

www.npg.org.uk

The most comprehensive museum of its kind, the National Portrait Gallery in London was founded in 1856 to collect portraits of famous British people. Its website offers a database of the gallery's 34,000 works, 11,500 of which are illustrated, and you can search by artist, sitter, or portrait. Take a virtual tour and, if you're engaged in research, you can send an email query to the archivists.

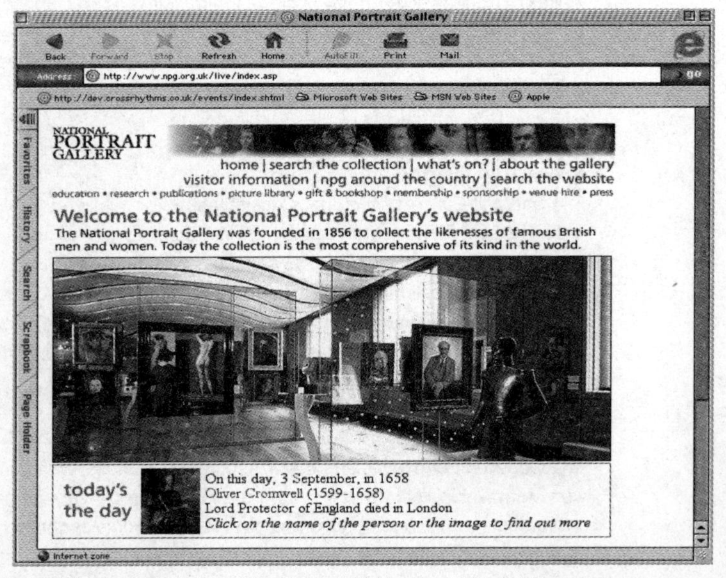

The National Portrait Gallery offers a searchable database of its 34,000 portraits.

Professional Art Dealer's Association of Canada

www.padac.ca

This leading Canadian association exists to promote art in Canada, especially its native art. Member galleries are listed by location, and there's a search engine to search for artists by name or by category (such as Impressionists, for example). Advice on seeking valuations can also be found.

Richard Green

www.richard-green.com

This top international dealer offers art ranging from 17th-century Old Masters to 20th-century British art. Richard Green's website has online versions of current and future exhibitions, which include discussions of artists and artistic movements. Send an email for full information, including prices for the pictures shown, or to join their informative email list that will send you details of their latest acquisitions as they arrive.

Russian Painting

www.rollins.edu/Foreign_Lang/Russian/ruspaint.html

This scholarly site is intended as a source of information for students and lovers of Russian art. The site tackles icons, 18th-, 19th-, and 20th-century art, and has essays on the key artistic movements. There are biographies of artists and topics such as restoration are also included.

Sims Reed Gallery

www.simsreed.com

Chagall, Matisse, Victor Pasmore, and David Hockney are just a few of the artists whose works are represented at this gallery and on its website. Of perhaps even greater interest to art lovers is the vast stock of art books available through the site. A sophisticated search engine allows you to find books by subject, artist, publisher, edition, and price range and you can buy online or send an email for further information if you wish.

Society of Fine Art Auctioneers

www.sofaa.org

The Society of Fine Art Auctioneers, or SOFAA, was founded in 1973 and has more than 40 members in various parts of the UK. Its site is a good source of information on local auctioneers in the country, as it has links to all the websites of its members. There is also a section that is devoted to news about the society and archivists.

Society of London Art Dealers

www.slad.org.uk

The website of London's top art dealers includes extensive information on each of their galleries, and links to the site of individual members. You can search by artist, gallery, or category (such as Modern British, Victorian, etc).

Tate Gallery

www.tate.org.uk

The ability to search a database of 50,000 works and more than 8,000 images is one of the most useful features of the site of this major British institution. As well as the Tate in London, there are sister galleries in Liverpool and Cornwall, and there are links to these sites, as well as to the new Tate Modern. The collection comprises British art from the 17th, 18th, and 19th centuries as well as modern art from all over the world. Researchers can contact the archivists and shoppers can buy books, posters, postcards, and slides online.

Tokugawa Gallery

www.tokugawagallery.com

This is the site of a specialist dealer in Japanese woodblock prints. The text, available in English, explains how these prints were made and offers biographical information on the artists responsible. Historical context is also provided with a discussion of how this art form developed. Prints are for sale in an online gallery and can be bought directly through the site.

Learn how Japanese woodblock prints are made on this informative website.

Van Gogh Museum

www.vangoghmuseum.nl

Available in both Dutch and English versions, this is the site of the Amsterdam museum that is devoted to Van Gogh and his work. You can take a "virtual tour" around the museum and the site also has an online shop as well as details of permanent collections and special exhibitions. An unusual feature is the page that explores the museum's architecture and provides biographical details of the two architects who designed it.

Virtual Uffizi

www.arca.net/uffizi

The complete catalogue of Italy's famous museum on the Internet. View works by artists such as Titian, Botticelli, and Leonardo da Vinci in a room-by-room tour or search for artists and follow links to full biographies. There are also links to other galleries and places of interest in Florence. If all this has whetted your appetite, you can book a tour of the real thing – you can also check out the museum's official website (www.uffizi.firenze.it).

Walker Galleries

www.walkerfineart.co.uk

Based in Harrogate in the north of England, Walker Galleries was founded in 1972. The gallery specializes in 19th- and 20th-century British and European art, many examples of which can be enjoyed through this site – or a hard copy of a favourite is yours if you request it by email. Contemporary ceramics are also on show. Biographical information on artists is given alongside images, and subject matter ranges from landscapes and still lifes to marine art. Send an email for further information if you want to buy.

Wiseman Originals

www.wisemanoriginals.com

Based in London and New York, Wiseman are leading international dealers in modern art. Their website features numerous pictures of the works on offer in the galleries, by artists such as Matisse and Miró. Descriptions and prices are given and there are online versions of current exhibitions.

World Art Treasures

www.bergerfoundation.ch

This Swiss site celebrates art from various world cultures. It is academic in its approach, and features examples of the art of countries and cultures such as China, Japan, Egypt, and Thailand as well as Europe. Various historical periods are covered, and there are scholarly essays on art-related topics.

World Wide Arts Resources

www.wwar.com

This US website includes everything "arty". There are details of contemporary and earlier artists, museums, galleries, art history, education, antiques, performing arts, classified ads, resumé postings, arts chats, and arts forums. A subscription to the online art newsletter will keep you up-to-date with events in the art world. Online exhibits are listed by subject matter, country, or medium, or alphabetically, and an agencies list includes groups and societies for artists and writers as well as professional organizations. The antiques that can be seen on this site are listed with brief descriptions and links to the related dealers and their websites. There is so much to discover here that this is a site you could move into for a couple of days and not get bored.

WORTH A LOOK

www.acga.com.au/G/GalleryGondwana/g.html
Australian Aboriginal art.

www.artcyclopedia.com
A resource for finding online images of specific paintings.

www.barber.org.uk
One of the world's finest small galleries, which houses art from the 13th–20th centuries.

www.godolphinfineart.com
Gallery specializing in artists from the west of England.

www.hazlittgoodenandfox.com
London art dealers founded in 1752.

www.monash.edu.au
Australian site with a good range of Japanese prints.

www.onthewildside.co.uk
Gallery specializing in wildlife art.

parallel.park.org/Netherlands/pavilions/culture/rembrandt
The site of the Rembrandt Research Project, which was set up some years ago to establish the authenticity of his work.

www.samsonart.ndirect.co.uk
Large site of a dealer in Russian art.

FURNITURE

Acorn Antiques

www.acornantiques.com.au

This Australian dealer's site includes useful historical background information, alongside photos and descriptions of stock, which explains the origins and development of various types of furniture. Stock is subdivided into categories such as bedroom furniture, library furniture, and so on, and, although you cannot buy online, prices are given in Australian dollars and you can email the dealer if you are interested in buying. Furniture shown on the site is mainly 18th and 19th century, and much of it is English or French.

Aveline

www.aveline.com

The website of this Paris-based gallery, available in English, is particularly useful for its informative articles on cabinetmakers and furniture-making techniques. It also displays an array of fine Continental furniture, with an emphasis on decorative pieces. There are gilded, marble-topped console tables, Italian commodes etc. Some of the items shown were originally made for European royalty and, if you would like to be their next owner, you can email the gallery to find out the full details.

British Antique Furniture Restorers' Association

www.bafra.org.uk

If you are looking for a properly qualified restorer or conservator, you'll receive help in finding one from this site. There are also informative articles on specific restoration projects and how the work was carried out. There are links to other professional associations, museums, and woodworking sites too.

Chiavacci Antiques

www.chiavacci-antiques.com

This Italian dealer, who is based in Florence, displays a fine selection of furniture and other antiques on this website, which is available in English. Furniture of the 18th- and early 19th century is particularly in evidence here and, as you might expect, there are many Italian pieces, as well as German and French items. You cannot buy directly online, but an email will get you further details of their stock. You can also subscribe to a mailing list, which will notify you of new stock as it arrives.

Clinton Howell Antiques

www.clintonhowell.com

This New York dealer displays a fine selection of English 17th-, 18th-, and 19th-century furniture on his website. A large quantity of stock is shown, subdivided by category and with full descriptions. No prices are given but you can email the showroom for full details. The pieces featured are in a range of woods: mahogany, rosewood, satinwood, and walnut, and some attractive decorative items are also included, from marble-topped tables to Gothic revival bookcases.

The Country Seat

www.thecountryseat.com

Admirers of good furniture design will find kindred spirits in the form of award-winning UK dealers Harvey Ferry and Willie Clegg, who run this website. It is devoted to "designer" furniture of the 19th century, from Pugin Gothic to Arts and Crafts, as well as 17th- and 18th-century pieces. The site lists some top makers and comments on their work. An email will get you further information on the examples of their work shown on the site, where you will find names such as Gillow, Lamb, and Wylie & Lockhead. Accessories such as ceramics, glass, lighting, and metalwork are also included, and there is a link to a website on Whitefriars Glass.

French Accents

www.faccents.com

French and Italian antique furniture from the 17th to the 19th century is featured on this dealer's site. Specializing in the top end of the market, there's an extensive online gallery that you can browse through or you can search the stock by keyword to find specific pieces more quickly – send the company an email enquiry if you are interested in buying anything. The site also features a useful glossary of antique terms.

Godson and Coles Fine Antiques

www.godsonandcoles.co.uk

This London furniture dealer offers a small stock of high quality 18th- and early 19th-century furniture and decorative items. Stock varies from Queen Anne burr-walnut chests of drawers and Chippendale-period chairs to Regency day beds. Click on the thumbnail images for a closer look, read the full descriptions and check dimensions. You cannot buy online, but you can contact the gallery by email to find out further information on any of the pieces shown.

John Bly Antiques

www.johnbly.com

John Bly is one of the UK's best-known furniture dealers, specializing in the top end of the market, and is a regular on the BBC's *Antiques Roadshow* – a page on the website chronicles his broadcasting career to date. The site also features information on his firm's design service, which specializes in Georgian-style interiors, and a selection from the current inventory. You can send an email if you are interested in anything that is shown, as you cannot buy online. However, you can buy some of John's books on antiques through a link to amazon.com.

Mallett

www.mallett.co.uk

Fine English and Continental furniture as well as paintings and glass and more can be found at the online showroom of this top London dealer (see pages 177–88 for fine art sites and pages 197–200 for glass sites). You cannot buy online, but the site does show off some stunning examples of furniture and describes these in full, also giving details of provenance. Elegant furniture of the Georgian era is particularly well represented. There is a sohisticated search facility enabling you to search by category, material, or style/period.

M Turpin Ltd

www.mturpin.co.uk

High-quality English furniture of the Queen Anne, Georgian, and Regency periods is particularly in evidence on the site of this London-based furniture dealer. A representative selection of stock is shown on the site, subdivided by categories such as tables. This is then further divided into console, dining, writing, and occasional tables. Accompanying text discusses history and provenance, but there are no prices, so you must email for further details if you wish to purchase something.

Peter Eaton Antiques

www.petereaton.com

This New England dealer specializes in American furniture from 1650 to 1820, with an emphasis on William and Mary, country Queen Anne, and Federal furniture from eastern Massachusetts, Connecticut and the Connecticut River valley. Services on the site include locating specific items, a photographic service, delivery including crating, and examining items at auction. The site has links to the Antiques Council and to Donald Sack Antiques, who carries comparable merchandise. You can buy directly from this site, but the dealer will want to speak to you first.

Pook & Pook Inc

www.pookandpookinc.com

This auction house based in Pennsylvania, USA, specializes in period furniture

High-quality English furniture can be found at M Turpin Ltd.

and accessories. Their website offers information on past and forthcoming sales as well as advice on buying and selling at auction. Illustrated catalogues are available online but if you wish to order a hard copy, there is an online form.

Scandinavian style

www.dmk.dk

Scandinavian design from 1920 to 1975 is celebrated on this Danish site (in English), which is strong on furniture with the classic lines of the modern age. Leading designers are well represented, and you can also choose glass and ceramics to go with the furniture. All items are for sale, and you must send an email for further information. Catalogues can, however, be bought online.

Seventh Heaven

www.seventh-heaven.co.uk

A good night's sleep in the style of our ancestors can be yours if you buy from this antique bed specialist. Most of the beds you will see on this site were made between 1820 and 1910 and there are examples with brass, cast iron, and wooden bedsteads. The website offers a comprehensive online brochure of current stock, and includes mattresses and bed bases as well as bedsteads. There's plenty of online advice, and you can order a hard copy of the firm's brochure. Email or telephone your enquiries if you like what you see.

Thomas Schwenke Inc

www.schwenke.com

This American dealer, who is based in Woodbury, Connecticut, specializes in American Federal furniture. The website includes an extensive online catalogue, mostly covering furniture, with descriptions and prices, although purchases should be made via email or telephone rather than online. There's also a chance to take a virtual tour of the showrooms. There are links to dealer organizations, resource sites, and www.sideboards.com, a specialist site devoted to that particular piece of furniture.

Tudor Antiques and Fine Arts

www.tudor-antiques.co.uk

A wide selection of furniture is shown on the site of Tudor Antiques, who specialize in furniture of the 17th to 19th centuries. Oriental as well as English and Continental pieces are included – you might find an altar table from Shanghai alongside a Sheraton-period sideboard. Close-ups are included of many items to give a better indication of quality, and you can send an email enquiry for further details and purchasing information. You can also register specific "wants", and they'll do their best to find them for you.

Wilsons Antiques

www.wilsons-antiques.com

Wilsons Antiques, based on the south coast of England, are specialists in

Georgian, Victorian, and Edwardian furniture in mahogany, walnut, oak, rosewood, and satinwood. Their website displays a sizeable selection of pieces, each with a short description, price, and dimensions. The selection is subdivided into categories such as dining-room and drawing-room furniture, as well as smaller pieces. You can use the online request form to ask for further information on how to purchase an item, or if you would like a specific item to be found for you. There is also a list of links to other antiques-related sites.

WORTH A LOOK

www.cavallo.co.uk
17th–19th century Italian furniture – view online and send an email for purchasing arrangements.

www.swedenantique.se
Swedish site featuring all kinds of furniture including Biedermeier.

www.yesterdaysdreams.co.za
South African site specializing in Victorian pieces. Online galleries display a wide range of stock, including French and English furniture.

FURNITURE: OAK AND COUNTRY

Alistair Sampson Antiques Ltd

www.alistairsampson.com

This London dealer specializes in town and country furniture and folk art and you will find pottery, paintings, brass, and treen as well as furniture on this site (see pages 233–6 for pottery sites, 177–88 for fine art sites, and 274–5 for treen sites). Oak is well represented here, and stock regularly includes pieces in an unusual style or form. Click on thumbnail images for a larger view of the items, and click again to contact the gallery if you're interested in anything.

Antique English Windsor Chairs

www.antique-english-windsor-chairs.co.uk

This website is devoted solely to that country furniture classic, the English Windsor Chair. A wide selection of these chairs is shown online, and accompanying descriptions point out various features including details of any restoration work that has been carried out. A detailed online enquiry form will get you further information if you need to know more or if you want to buy one.

Day Antiques

www.dayantiques.com

Day Antiques are based in the English Cotswolds and they specialize in early oak furniture, as well as tapestries, carvings, and treen. Stock items shown on this site are there as examples as much as offerings, since stock changes constantly. You must contact the gallery by email for further information of current pieces and prices. Items illustrated are mainly from the 17th and 18th centuries, and include practical pieces such as stools, chairs, and dressers.

Early Oak Antique Furniture

www.earlyoak.co.uk

Identify your antique oak furniture through this website by emailing a picture and as much information as you can to them. It's a free service, but valuations are not included. You will also find a history of oak furniture, and lots of pieces for sale. Each item of stock is illustrated and described in full, including details of the original use of the piece. Orders can be placed online, but payment must be made by cheque through the post or by banker's order.

Huntington Antiques Ltd

www.huntington-antiques.com

Huntington Antiques specialize in early period furniture, works of art, and tapestries from the medieval, Gothic, and Renaissance periods. Soothing music will accompany you as you browse through a selection of fine chairs, settles, dining tables and other pieces in oak and other woods. Items of stock are given full descriptions. You cannot buy online, but you can send an email to ask for pieces to be reserved, or for further information. There are also links to publications, trade associations, and international museums.

I & J L Brown Antiques Ltd

www.brownantiques.com

Regular shipments of antique English country and French provincial furniture are always arriving at the showrooms of this Herefordshire-based dealer, and stock is constantly changing. For this reason, there is no online catalogue at their site, although there is a selection of pictures of typical stock to give you some idea of what's on offer. There's also a "just in" selection of latest stock. Traditional farmhouse tables, French armoires, and English oak coffers are much in evidence here.

Paul Hopwell Antiques

www.antiqueoak.co.uk

Unusual items such as medieval parchment panels rub shoulders with more familiar items such as dressers and chests on the site of this oak furniture specialist. Browse through an extensive, well-illustrated online catalogue and fill in an online enquiry form if you wish to buy anything.

Red Lion Antiques

www.redlion-antiques.com

This site features a wealth of oak furniture as well as some pieces in other woods such as pine, elm, and walnut. Oak seems dominant here, though, and online stock is arranged into categories such as tables, bureaux, chairs, and dressers. Stock is well illustrated, with descriptions and prices in pounds sterling and US dollars – email or telephone Red Lion to order something. There are links to the sites of trade associations, publications, and resource sites here too.

RJG Antiques

www.rjgantiques.com

These New Hampshire dealers specialize in original painted furniture and accessories as well as top-quality folk art and working decoys. Everything sold is guaranteed. The site also sells supplies like stands for variously sized decoys, and a finish feeder that is perfect for dry painted surfaces. There are links to decoy publications, antiques dealers associations, a decoy auction house, and individual dealers. There is a form to register your collecting needs, and another for purchasing, but it is not a secure site, so you must contact them by telephone or post with your payment details.

Touchwood Antiques

www.touchwoodvibes.com

Touchwood Antiques favour an unusual and offbeat approach, showing off their wares through a series of images and brief captions that fade in and out of view. If you like the glimpses of early oak and country pieces, you can contact them via email for further information. As well as furniture, you will find metalware, tapestries, and treen (see pages 213–15 for metalware sites). Links unexpectedly include sites covering subjects like aromatherapy, alternative medicine, and music, which probably reflect the interests of the proprietors.

WORTH A LOOK

www.denzilgrant.com

Suffolk-based specialist in 18th- and 19th-century country and provincial French furniture, with a large online selection.

www.horizonantiques.com

American dealer who specializes in American antique oak from the 19th century.

www.jhillcountry.com

American specialist in European country antiques and accessories. The site features online shopping.

FURNITURE: PINE

Bygones of Ireland

www.anu.ie/bygones

Irish pine dominates this County Mayo dealer's site, but you will also find a few pieces from around the world. An extensive picture gallery shows examples of typical stock, and you are invited to contact Bygones for further information. Of particular interest is a page that shows the restoration of a traditional Irish dresser, describing the processes involved.

Claremont Antiques

www.claremontantiques.com

This website offers original antique pine furniture, including many items that still have their original paint finish. A large amount of stock is illustrated in colour with a description, but this is still only a representative selection. Visitors are invited to send an email or telephone for further pictures and the best prices available.

Heathfield Antiques

www.antique-pine.net

Reproduction and pine furniture made from reclaimed timber can be found on this site, together with antique pine pieces. Choose from a range of dressers, cupboards, tables, and many other items of practical furniture, and order them online. The site also includes a full company history and information on restoration services.

Mary Grace's Antiques & Country Pine

www.englishpine.com

This is the site of an American dealer who specializes in antique pine furniture. Here you will find English, Dutch, and Eastern European examples of armoires, hutches, chairs, etc. as well as a range of accessories such as antique kitchen scales and French posters. Browse through a varied selection of stock, and order a brochure online.

Parlour Farm Antiques

www.parlourfarm.com

Parlour Farm has large warehouse premises in the English Midlands and in Massachusetts in the United States. Their stock in trade is pine furniture, much of which is imported from Eastern Europe. Their website shows off a large selection of the stock, which is subdivided by category, and includes some interesting Russian pieces. Pictures are presented without accompanying text, but there are reference numbers if you wish to make further enquiries to the company by email.

Russian Antique Country Furniture and Accessories

www.pine.spb.ru

This is the site of a St Petersburg-based dealer whose stock includes a large range of mainly Russian pine furniture, although it does have other items such as Russian icons. Stock is dominated by 19th- and early 20th-century pieces, mostly in the original paint finish and priced in US dollars. The site also includes details of shipping arrangements.

Westville House Antiques

www.westville.co.uk

Furniture from the 18th and 19th centuries can be found on this site, which has a good selection of pine as well as some oak and mahogany. Online stock is arranged into categories, such as linen presses and washstands, and a click of the mouse will get you a larger and more detailed picture of each item. Prices are given, as are stock numbers to help with identification when making further enquiries.

Yellow Monkey Antiques

www.yellowmonkey.com

This New York dealer stocks mainly antique British and Irish pine, including painted as well as stripped pieces. A representative selection is shown on this website, which includes brief descriptions as well as providing useful definitions of relevant terms. Details of the firm's kitchen design service are also included. Send them an email for purchasing details.

WORTH A LOOK

www.potboard.co.uk
Antique pine from West Wales.

www.users.globalnet.co.uk/~tkcove34
Antique and reproduction pine furniture.

GLASS

Christine Bridge Antiques

www.antiqueglass.co.uk

This site has a vast array of glass for sale, helpfully subdivided into categories such as Irish glass, Art Nouveau and Art Deco, and decanters. You can send an email to check an item's availability, then buy with your credit card. A currency converter is included on the site. Also featured are details of forthcoming fairs.

Browse through an impressive selection of classic cranberry glass online at this site.

Classical Glass

www.gwi.net/~inventor

Victorian art glass is just one of the specialist areas covered by this site, which also offers paperweights and pottery. A large selection is shown and these can be bought online, as can a glass price-guide. Linked sites include perfume bottle dealers and glass museums. (See pages 221–2 for other paperweights sites and pages 233–6 for further pottery sites.)

Cranberry Glass

www.cranberryglass.co.uk

Cranberry glass is both colourful and collectible and, as this specialist site shows, it comes in all shapes and sizes. Familiar shapes, such as the "Jack-in-the-Pulpit" vases are here, as well as unusual shapes such as boots. If the classic raspberry colour is not to your liking, this site also features Nailsea and cameo glass in other hues. The website is designed to show off a special selection of stock and images are accompanied by catalogue numbers rather than prices – you can send an email enquiry for further details of a specific piece that interests you.

Glasgalerie Jan Kilian

www.glaskilian.de

This is the site of a German dealer whose bilingual site mostly offers glass dating from the 1850s to the present day (although there are some earlier pieces). Prices are shown in US dollars, but there is a currency converter. Preferred payment for online orders is by cheque or you can send your credit card details to them via fax. There are also links to dealers' sites, web resources, and articles about glass available here.

Glass Museum On Line

www.glass.co.nz

The main strength of this informative New Zealand-based site is a list of detailed articles on various aspects of the subject. There's a Glass Club message board where you can talk to other glass lovers, links to online auctions, and a chance to buy books directly online.

Historic Glasshouse

www.antiquebottles-glass.com

This website is largely for bottle collectors, but has much to interest the general glass collector too. Browse through an online inventory of collectible glass for sale and find out more about the history of glass. Marbles, paperweights, glass grenades, and inkwells are among the glass items included on this site, together with decanters, jugs, and other objects.

Just Glass

www.justglass.com

As its name implies, this site is dedicated to glass enthusiasts. It offers online auctions, with categories for most collectible glass from ancient through to contemporary Carnival. You can register for free if you wish to buy or sell, and there are no listing fees or commission charges involved. The site also features some useful resources for the collector, including a message board and chatroom, and an online mall.

Kevin A Sives Antiques

www.antiquez.com

This is the site of a US-based dealer who specializes in American blown glass, especially bottles and flasks. A selection of these can be seen and bought online. Items from the dealer's own collection are also featured, and there are links to glass, bottle collecting, and general antiques sites.

Somervale Antiques

www.somervaleantiquesglass.co.uk

A large selection of 18th- and 19th-century glass can be viewed on this site. Stock includes Bristol and Nailsea glass, and you will find decanters, wine glasses, scent bottles, and a miscellaneous section. Send an email if you want further details of any of the items shown.

The Woodsland Carnival Glass

www.woodsland.com/carnivalglass

This online meeting place for Carnival Glass enthusiasts offers the chance to sell your surplus pieces online and buy from fellow collectors. Post a "wanted" ad if you can't find what you're looking for, take out membership for "members only" features – that includes articles and access to a reproductions database – or follow a link to collectors' clubs worldwide.

WORTH A LOOK

www.artlieb.com
Scandinavian art glass for sale.

www.cmog.org
The Corning Museum of Glass, based in New York State, USA, which has an impressive online collection.

www.glassbooks.com
Specialist glass books for collectors.

www.whitefriarsglass.com
Site devoted to the important Whitefriars factory.

www.wotoandwife.bc.ca/vicglass.htm
Victorian glass available from a Canadian dealer.

JEWELLERY

Billy Rae

www.billyrae.co.uk

Georgian, Victorian, and Edwardian jewellery can be bought on this Scottish dealer's site, which includes a good selection of Scottish pieces such as provincial silver. If you have jewellery you wish to sell then simply email a picture, description, and price. A selection of Scottish silver can also be found on the site.

Buying Jewellery Online

www.jewelrymall.com

This is a web resource that lists links to jewellery sites according to the average price of stock, to avoid wasting your time if you're on a budget. You can also learn about gemstones: their history, significance, and how to look after them. There's even a humour section, with a "jewellery joke of the day".

Grays Antique Market

www.egrays.co.uk

Grays is one of London's best-known markets, and is where the trade as well as the public buy their antiques. While most collecting fields are represented, jewellery dominates, and this site will put you in touch with dealers of all kinds of stock. There are also links to other markets.

Irish Antique Jewelry

www.irishantiquejewelry.com

Irish jewellery has many followers, and if you would like to join them you can do so at this site. There's an online catalogue here and also special online offers. This site also has a trade-only section – useful if you are a dealer.

Jewellery Quarter

www.the-quarter.com

Birmingham's historic Jewellery Quarter is a key area in the UK trade. All the practical tourist information you need for your day trip is on this site – of course, there is a good list of jewellery retailers with contact details as well as details of other services such as jewellery repairers and locksmiths. There is an illustrated history section, and the "About Jewellery" page gives you the lowdown on diamonds, precious metals, etc, and even offers tips on anniversary gifts.

John Joseph

www.john-joseph.co.uk

John Joseph deals in jewellery from the Georgian, Victorian, Edwardian, Art Nouveau, and Art Deco periods. Stock is arranged according to the type of jewellery, so you can browse through images of brooches, necklaces, and bracelets from each era. Full descriptions and prices are included and the site is updated every two to four weeks as items are sold. Send an email if you are interested in buying any of the pieces that you see.

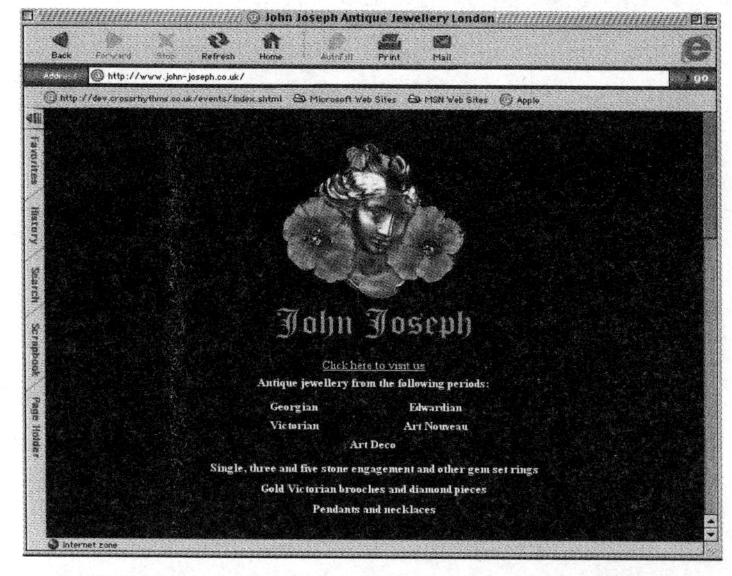

John Joseph deals in a range of antique jewellery, from Georgian to Art Deco pieces.

Online Antique Jewellery

www.antiquejewelryexch.com

This is an American jewellery site that offers an online store complete with its own "music while you shop" to enhance the shopping experience. The dealers who run the site are third-generation jewellers and they specialize in platinum. Jewellery from all the most popular periods, as well as some contemporary pieces, are stocked. Links are plentiful and, while they are not always directly antiques-related, they are interesting nonetheless.

Owlets of Hythe

www.owlets.co.uk

Shop online for quality jewellery by renowned makers such as Liberty, Cartier, Fabergé, and many others. Jewellery stocked is mainly from the Victorian, Edwardian, and Art Nouveau eras and all items are well photographed with full descriptions and background information provided. Details of various related services offered by this jewellery dealer are also included.

Regal Jewellery

www.regaljewellry.com

A large selection of Victorian and Edwardian jewellery features on this site, along with more modern pieces. Large-format images allow you to scrutinize the selection of antique rings, brooches, bracelets, and earrings in detail, giving a good indication of quality and, in some cases, even their hallmarks can be viewed. A click of the mouse will put items in your own online shopping basket, and there is also a search engine to allow you to find desired pieces more quickly.

See pages 146–66 for a list of costume jewellery sites.

WORTH A LOOK

www.brooksandbentley.com
Fine jewellery, collectibles, and handcrafted treasures.

www.dragnet-systems.ie/dira/antique
Irish jewellery dealer's site.

www.faycullen.com
US dealer's site with rings galore.

www.nbloom.com
Leading London jeweller offers online perusal of stock.

KITCHENALIA

Antique Mills Online

www.millmania.com

If you are interested in antique coffee grinders, or mills as they are also called, then this is the site for you. There's a large online catalogue of mills for sale (send them an email to receive purchasing information) or just browse through a private collection. You can also join the Association of Coffee Mill Enthusiasts – just fill in and post the printable form that is available on the site.

Antique Pressing Irons

www.uq.net.au/~zzbdavis

This is the website of a couple of keen collectors, and their collection of irons is displayed here. Discover the differences between flat sad irons, charcoal irons, and spirit irons, and view some examples of each. The site is a useful source of information, as it explains the history and origins of some of these irons. It also offers links to other kitchenalia sites, including those of museums – and did you know that there is a journal devoted to collecting irons?

Antique Stoves

www.antiquestoves.com

This site features various antique stoves, dating from 1750 to 1950. There are gas as well as wood- and coal-burning examples, and you can send an email if you are interested in buying any of them. You will also find information about spare parts and restoration, and there's a classified ads section where you can place anything you're selling and your "wants". On this site, you will also find "The Old Appliance Club", which caters for collectors of all appliances, including refrigerators and washing machines.

Barton & Barton

www.bartonandbarton.com

Specializing in 20th-century antiques, especially home furnishings of various kinds, this site boasts a large selection of kitchenalia. Subheadings include tea and coffee drinking, dining, and cooking. Stock will of course vary, but typically includes English enamel milk carriers, 1950s Italian biscuit jars, and 1920s French potato mashers. The site, which offers secure online shopping, is run by a mother and daughter team who live, respectively, in Provence, France and Surrey, England, which gives them the opportunity to search for stock from a wide area.

Cornish Ware by Gentry Antiques

www.cornishwarecollector.co.uk

The pottery of TG Green is instantly recognizable and is to be found in kitchens all over the world. Blue-and-white banded storage jars, spice jars, and the like are the factory's most famous products and they are well represented on this site. Other patterns, such as Domino Ware, are also included, and you can shop online. A book on Cornish Ware is for sale here and there are links to other dealer sites and to the site of TG Green pottery, which is still very much in business.

Irons and Other Kitchenalia

www.irons.com

This site is a useful resource for iron collectors, as it features an extensive bibliography as well as links to collectors' clubs, news of forthcoming auctions, and museums where irons can be seen. It's not just for iron enthusiasts, however, as there are also links to sites for washing machines, wood stoves, and other kitchenalia. Of particular interest here is the classified ads section, where advertisements can be placed free of charge.

Lee Maxwell's Antique Washing Machines

www.oldewash.com

This is the site of a museum in Colorado, USA, which is totally devoted to the washing machine. The site includes models from the early days, and there's a searchable database that allows you to locate specific machines. There are photos and even video clips on the site, as well as informative articles on the history of washing machines, the technology used to make them, and their social significance.

MC Antiques and Collectibles

www.mcantiques.com/kitchen.htm

Jugs, skillets, tins, and various kitchen-related artefacts are included among the online stock of this American dealer. There are several pages of kitchenalia to browse through, and ordering is done via an online form, which can be printed from the site, filled in, and then sent by post. The site also includes other items like advertising and packaging collectibles, as well as a few recommendations for further reading (see also advertising and packaging on pages 127–9).

Rookery Farm Antiques

www.antique-kitchenalia.co.uk

This is the site of a mother and daughter team who specialize in antique kitchenalia, most of which is English or French. Numerous examples of stock are shown, ranging from bread boards to coffee pots, as well as kitchen scales, coffee grinders, and much more. Objects shown are given as examples only, so you should contact Rookery Farm via email to receive the full information on their current stock.

The Toaster Museum Foundation

www.toaster.org

The Toaster Museum Foundation plans to open a permanent museum of those most ubiquitous of modern kitchen appliances. In the meantime, its website features photos and information on a huge range of toasters, some dating back to the early years of the 20th century. You won't find vintage toasters for sale here, although you can buy T-shirts and other merchandise online, but you will find a wealth of information on all the various makes and models. There are also illustrations, taken from old magazines, showing the toasters that the foundation would like to buy. This educational site also traces the history of bread, and the origin of the word "toast", which is taken from the Latin "to scorch, or burn".

WORTH A LOOK

www.antiquebottles.com.au
Australian bottles site that includes a selection of kitchenalia.

www.homegrownantiques.com/Miscellaneousglass.html
American kitchen glassware.

www.jonof.com/coppergallerypage.asp
Jelly moulds, flour sieves, scales, and much more.

LIGHTING

Antique Lighting – Karlucci

home1.gte.net/karlucci

A comprehensive stocklist is featured on this American site, which also includes a brief history of lighting in the United States. The site features antique lighting for sale from most periods, as well as bulbs and accessories, including some more unusual items. These include hand-painted bulbs that have been painted to match the colours of the original coloured bulbs of the 1930s.

Architectural Emporium

www.architectural-emporium.com

This site specializes in antique chandeliers, light fittings, wall sconces, and architectural antiques. Lighting is the mainstay of the business, and the online stock is subdivided into periods such as Victorian, Arts and Crafts, and Art Deco. No reproductions are offered, but the antique lighting can be ordered by credit card through the site.

Fritz Fryer Antique Lighting

www.fritzfryer.co.uk

This is the website of one of the UK's top lighting dealers. Fritz Fryer specializes in the period 1820–1950, but has a particularly fine Arts and Crafts and Art

Nouveau range. Many examples are pictured on the site and these have been stylishly and atmospherically photographed. More pictures show restoration work in progress, and there are full contact details for further information.

Hector Finch Lighting

www.hectorfinch.com

The site of this London-based specialist dealer includes images of a range of antique and contemporary lighting as well as a 360° view of the gallery. There are also accessories such as bulbs, hooks, shades, and chains on the site. You cannot buy directly online, but some information is given, and you can contact Hector Finch by email for more.

Howard's Antique Lighting

www.bcn.net/~iromla/front.html

Stock for sale on this dealer's site is divided by type (table lamps, floor lamps, etc) rather than period. Antique lighting from many different periods can be seen online, as can reproduction items. Enquiries and orders are welcomed via email.

International Guild of Lamp Researchers

www.dapllc.com/lampguild

This is the website of the International Guild of Lamp Researchers, a scholarly group of lamp collectors and enthusiasts specializing in liquid and gas-fuelled lamps. There is a detailed question and answer page, although it is made clear that appraisals will not be made over the Internet. There is also a list of lamp-collecting clubs, a useful lamp glossary, and a good links page.

Lamp Post

pages.prodigy.net/fritter/gaslite.htm

This is the site of a gas lighting enthusiast, and it begins with an appropriate poem called "The Lamplighter". The site also houses pictures of gas lights, a history of gas lighting, and a list of links. It is worth a visit purely for reference purposes since sites linked to include manufacturers of spares.

Lamparts

www.lamparts.co.uk

As specialists in the sale and manufacture of spare parts for lamps and lighting, Lamparts stock all kinds of accessories such as shades, brass pressings, and cotton-covered cables. Everything you will need for restoration projects can be found on this site, which is mainly of interest to the trade. Detailed drawings and photographs accompany stock lists, and a mail-order service is available.

Renaissance Antiques

www.antique-lighting.com

This specialist lighting firm is an importer, manufacturer, and restorer of antique and historical reproductions. Museums and film and TV companies which have used its services, including the BBC, are listed on its site. Stock is illustrated with prices, so you can shop online. The site also features "before and after" shots of recent restoration projects, and replacement shades and reproduction fittings can be bought here.

Sirlampsalot Publications

www.sirlampsalot.com

Reprints of vintage lamp catalogues are available through this site, which offers the opportunity for collectors to build up an invaluable library of specialist reference material. There's also a brief overview of lighting ephemera, with illustrated examples of trade cards and advertisements. Sites linked include that of the Historical Lighting Society of Canada, the International Guild of Lamp Researchers, and the Smithsonian Institute.

Vintage Lighting

www.vintagelighting.com

Electric, converted gas, and combination lighting from 1880–1940 can all be found on this Canadian site. All items are for sale, and prices are quoted in Canadian and US dollars. Stock is from various styles (there is a section devoted to Art Deco lamps), and is described in full with illustrations. The site includes a schedule of forthcoming shows in Canada, and links to lighting shops and interior design sites.

WORTH A LOOK

www.nauset-lantern.com

Marine lanterns are a speciality of this site.

www.rushlight.org

A society dedicated to all aspects of antique lighting.

MAPS

Altea Maps & Books

www.antique-maps.co.uk

Altea are based in the heart of the West End of London and this is their comprehensive site. An extensive online catalogue is the main attraction here. Hundreds of maps dating back as far as the 15th century are illustrated and described in detail, complete with information on the cartographers, and there are also atlases and globes. You can order online or register your "wants" if you can't find what you're looking for.

Barry Lawrence Ruderman Old Historic Maps and Prints

www.raremaps.com

Thousands of maps for sale from the 15th to the 19th centuries are illustrated and described online at this site. Maps of all parts of the world plus celestial maps are featured, and about 200 new ones are added each month. You can send an email postcard of some of the maps to your friends and colleagues, complete with a choice of accompanying music from Bach to Led Zeppelin.

Gillmark

www.gillmark.com

This map dealer has a particularly strong selection of English county maps. Maps from the rest of the world are also featured, and email requests can be taken for any maps not found on the site. For those that are, ordering is via a form downloaded and printed from the site.

Jonathan Potter Ltd

www.jpmaps.co.uk

You won't lose your way in map collecting if you visit the site of this top London map dealer. There is an introduction to the hobby, as well as biographies of the leading cartographers and detailed articles about various aspects of map collecting. Advice for the collector is also offered and selected maps from the thousands that are in stock at any one time are pictured and can be ordered online.

Lee Jackson Antique Maps & Engravings

www.btinternet.com/~leejackson

Prints as well as maps, showing everything from topographical images to portraits, are included on this antique map dealer's site. Maps of every continent and a great many countries are available for online ordering, most are illustrated and all are accompanied by informative descriptions.

Magna Gallery

www.magna-gallery.demon.co.uk/shop/index.htm

This is an elaborate site with a spoken introduction by the proprietor and lots of music, mostly by Vivaldi. Maps for sale are also featured, and each has a guide to condition and prices, and can be ordered by email. County maps of Oxfordshire are a speciality, but other English county maps and old maps of other parts of the world, from Texas to Australia, are included as well.

The Map House of London

www.themaphouse.com

A fully illustrated online catalogue offering maps from the past 500 years is one of the main features of this site. A vast inventory is stocked, and globes and prints are also included. Not all the stock can be seen online, but an email will get you further details of any stock that isn't shown.

The Map House has a large stock of items from the past 500 years.

Map World

www.map-world.com

This is the site of the London- and Cape Town-based map dealer. Relatively few maps are illustrated, but there's a useful potted history of cartography and technical definitions for those struggling with the difference between woodcut, copperplate, and lithograph.

Old Church Galleries

www.old-church-galleries.com

Maps from 1580 to 1900, by leading cartographers, are the stock-in-trade of this online London gallery, which also offers reproduction prints of the maps. Some 10,000 items are in stock, and about half are listed here. Few are illustrated on the site, but the gallery will email you a picture of any you might be interested in, and you can also order them via email.

Tooley Adams & Co

www.tooleys.co.uk

This is the site of the specialist map dealers founded by the late M V Tooley, author of many standard reference works on map collecting. Maps of all parts of the world, dating back as far as the 16th century, are illustrated and described in detail, and you can buy via post with your credit card, cheque, or banker's order. Travel books are also stocked here.

WORTH A LOOK

www.antiquemaps-online.com
Affordable maps from the 15th to the 19th centuries.

www.antiqueprints.com
The site of a UK specialist maps and prints dealer.

www.llgc.org.uk/dm/dm0067.htm
The map collection at the National Library of Wales.

www.postaprint.co.uk
Search a database of antique maps and prints and order them online.

MARINE

Andrew Jacobson Marine Antiques

www.marineantiques.com

This site includes an extensive online catalogue, which is subdivided by category. Choose from selections of scrimshaw, marine paintings, photos, and various artefacts. If you wish to order anything, you can send them an email. The site sometimes carries "special offers", and there are links to museums and maritime organizations.

Langfords Marine Antiques

www.langfords.co.uk

Animated ships' wheels and a picture of the proprietor greet visitors to this site. Online galleries are devoted to themes such as pond yachts, ships in bottles, instruments, and other marine items. Stock is shown with descriptive text, and you can email them for more information about anything you are interested in.

Maidhof Bros. Limited

www.seajunk.com

Unusual items such as movie props are featured on this site, which also offers an array of marine items. Most of the items on offer at this site have come from actual vessels, but these are augmented by general gift items with a nautical flavour. Everything, from watertight doors to sea chests and telescopes, is included, and you can shop securely online.

Mariner's Antiques

www.mariners-antiques.com

The sound of a cannon greets visitors to this site, which specializes in marine paintings and prints, nautical books, ship models, Royal Navy and shipping line memorabilia, and nautical antiques. Artists represented include well-known marine specialists such as Montague Dawson and the online selection of stock is extensive, although only a small amount is illustrated.

Maritime Antiques and Auctions

www.maritiques.com

Familiar items of nauticalia like divers' helmets and lamps can be found on this site, together with more esoteric items such as submarine launching tags. You can send an email if you want additional information about any items, and the site also lists forthcoming auctions and a list of "wanted" items. Other items include firehouse memorabilia such as old fire-fighting equipment and helmets.

Nauticals Ltd

www.nauticalantiquesltd.com

This American dealer, whose site includes an illustrated online catalogue, specializes in antique nautical items. The helpful descriptions of items include comments on their condition, and you can order by email. Items shown range from lamps and portholes to barometers and model ships.

The Olde Nautical Shoppe

www.oldenauticalshoppe.com

An eclectic range of marine antiques and artefacts awaits the enthusiast on this Florida dealer's website. There are books and charts as well as bells, lamps, instruments, and paintings, and new items are stocked as well as antiques. Everything is illustrated and you can shop online.

Peter Laurie Maritime Antiques

www.maritimeantiques-uk.com

This is the website of a dealer based in Greenwich, London, whose online selection includes naval regalia and weaponry as well as instruments and artefacts from scrimshaw to sea chests. There is a sizeable selection, and the provenance given with many of the items makes for interesting reading in itself.

Robinson's Nautical Antiques

www.ronrobinson.co.uk

Robinson's are specialist compass adjusters as well as retailers of marine antiques – you can enquire by email for further details about either. The site illustrates numerous examples of stock, along with their prices, and, while the popular, usual items are stocked, the site is also strong on more esoteric instruments. Unusual items such as telephones from ships' bridges are included.

Titanic Memorabilia

www.titanicmemorabilia.co.uk

Genuine coal from what is probably the most famous liner in the world is for sale on this site, which is dedicated to relics of the *Titanic*. The site has an online memorabilia shop, where you can buy everything from postcards, posters, and prints to books, reproductions of glassware as used on board, cups from recent expeditions to the wreck, and photographs of the vessel lying on the seabed. The more adventurous web surfer can also sign up for a diving expedition that will take them to see the *Titanic* in person. It is stressed, however, that these are not salvage expeditions and nothing will be taken except photographs.

WORTH A LOOK

www.anmm.gov.au
Australia's National Maritime Museum.

www.dolphin-quay-antiques.co.uk
An antiques centre specializing in marine artefacts.

www.lighthousedepot.com
Site devoted to lighthouse memorabilia.

www.ottocento.com
Italian dealer in marine antiques, site available in English.

MEDALS

Collect Russia

www.collectrussia.com

As its name suggests, this site specializes in all things Russian. Medals are particularly well represented, with orders and decorations from the Imperial and Soviet eras. There are also medals relating to other Eastern European countries and all are for sale online.

For Researchers

www.medal.net

MedalNet exists to help researchers of orders, decorations, and medals. There are listings of auctioneers, associations, and a "wanted" section for those wishing to buy. There are also links to websites of veterans' organizations and relevant archives and government bodies of many different countries.

Peter Morris

www.petermorris.co.uk

This site includes coins, tokens, and banknotes as well as medals (see pages 156–9 for coin sites and 244–8 for banknote sites). There are extensive lists of medals, with prices, from various countries from Belgium to Brunei. Not all the medals here are military – there are some like the Mongolian "Mother's Glory", which is awarded to a woman who has had eight children. Books on medals can also be purchased, and orders can be taken by phone, post, or email.

World Medals

www.worldmedals.co.uk

As its title suggests, the awards and orders of many countries are represented on this site, which has a search engine to help you find specific items. There are plenty of good-quality illustrations to accompany stock, and prices and guides to condition are given. Accessories such as replacement ribbons are also available. You can order via email, although this is not a secure site.

WORTH A LOOK

www.chapter-one.com/vc
Facts and figures on the VC, Britain's highest military award.

www.frontiermedals.com
Hong Kong-based dealer who offers a wide selection of world medals.

www.jcollinsmedals.co.uk
Medals for sale plus research services.

METALWARE

Christer Schultz Antiques

www.schultz-antiques.com

An eclectic mix of objects, ranging from fire irons and door knockers to coffee grinders can be found on the site of this dealer, who specializes in items in iron, steel, copper, and brass. Furniture and lighting is also shown on the site (see pages 188–93 for furniture sites and pages 205–7 for lighting sites). There is an extensive online catalogue that has prices in pounds sterling, US dollars, and euros, and you can send an email for purchasing details.

D M Govan

www.dmgovan.com

This site specializes in antique pewter, and includes a guide to looking after antiques in this metal, including advice on cleaning and polishing. There's also a useful history of pewter here. If you want to buy antique pewter, you will find a good selection online, but potential customers are advised to telephone to check the availability of stock. You can also send the company an email if you have something you wish to sell.

Eve Stone Antiques Ltd

www.evestoneantiques.com

Through this American dealer's site you can shop for antique metalware and also order tins of polish to keep it all looking good. You will also find historical information, such as the dates of the reigns of British monarchs listed here. Stock is subdivided by category (such as candlesticks, fire tools, etc) and is illustrated with prices and descriptions.

JAG Decorative Arts

www.jagdecorativearts.com

An assortment of metalware can be found on this site, and Liberty pewter is much in evidence. German copper items are also among the items featured, and most stock is from the Art Nouveau period (see pages 137–9 for Art Nouveau sites). There is a well-illustrated online catalogue, with full background details of the objects shown, and the site offers informative articles on various related topics. Furniture, lighting, and bronzes are also offered. Send an email request for further information if you would like to buy any of the items you see.

Patrick Reijgersberg

www.artonline.nl/reijgersberg

This is the site of a Dutch dealer, who is based in the historic town of Haarlem. His English-language site offers a particularly strong selection of metalware, although furniture, ceramics, and sculpture can also be found here. Brass

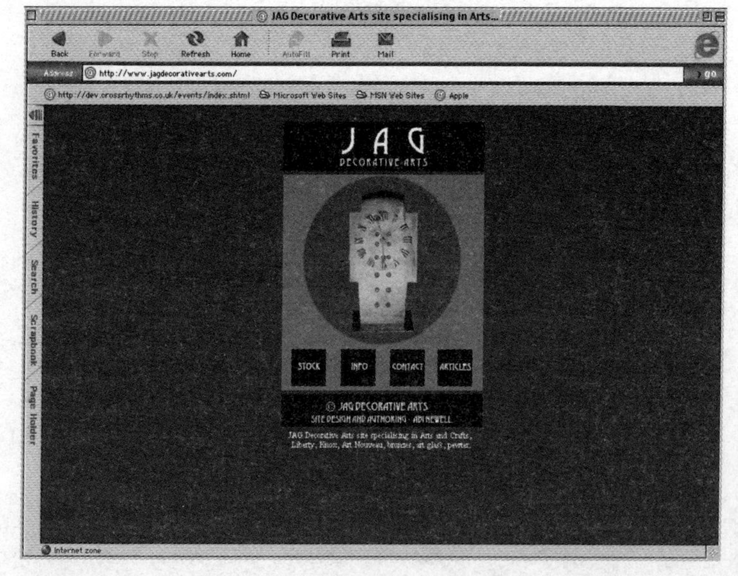

Metalware from the Art Nouveau period is much in evidence on this website.

candlesticks, pewter dishes, and bronze ewers are included among the stock shown on the site, and some of these items date back to the medieval period. Send an email for purchasing information.

WORTH A LOOK

www.kildare.ie/TimolinPewter
This is the site of Ireland's oldest pewter mill. Browse through an online catalogue and find information about, and the opening hours of, the company museum.

www.machumbleantiques.co.uk
The website of the chairman of the metalware vetting committee of the Bristish Antique Dealers Association.

www.pewter.co.uk
Collectible pewter tankards, flasks, and goblets for sale, plus a history of pewter can be found on this site.

MUSICAL INSTRUMENTS

The Complete Mechanical Music Links Page

www.geocities.com/heartland/ranch/9374/links.html

If you are looking for information on, or dealers in, all kinds of mechanical instruments, you will find everything you need here. The list of links is the main attraction of this site, but there are other features, such as a "piano room" where you can hear the sounds of the instruments of yesteryear.

For Violin Enthusiasts

www.scaramuzza.com

This is the site of Scaramuzza, a music shop that is based in Cremona, Italy, which is the home of the violin. The shop offers new instruments for sale as well as a full range of restoration facilities, but you cannot buy items directly online. There are links to relevant sites including the International Violinmakers' School of Cremona.

Greg's Antique Piano Page

www.oldpianos.com

This site has a fine collection of antique instruments. Photos and detailed discussions of each piano can be found, and there is a useful selection of links to other musical instrument sites too. There is also a free-of-charge classified ads section available for those wishing to buy or sell pianos.

Guitar Base

www.gbase.com

Visit this site and you can search through a database of 24,000 guitars from more than 300 dealers by make, model, or year. Guitar Base claims to have the largest used and vintage guitar inventory on the web, and the site also offers articles on guitar-collecting, interviews with top guitar players, and bulletin boards to share your views with fellow collectors.

Musical Box Society of Great Britain

www.antique-dealers-directory.co.uk/MBSGB

This society is devoted to mechanical musical instruments of all kinds, from barrel and pipe organs to mechanical singing birds. There are currently around 500 members, and you can add to their ranks by joining online. A small selection of instruments is shown on the site.

Palm Guitars

www.palmguitars.nl

This Dutch dealer, whose site includes a wealth of information (in English) on instrument makers and their histories, offers Western and ethnic musical instruments of various kinds, as well as guitars. If you are interested in buying anything, make an enquiry and you will be emailed an exact description of the item in question, plus additional photographs. Various accessories, including spare parts ideal for restoration projects, can also be found here.

The Piano Page

www.ptg.org

Lots of interesting information about pianos can be found on the site of the Piano Technicians' Guild, which is based in Kansas, USA. There's a history of the piano, a virtual piano museum, and information on manufacturers. The site also has news from the piano industry and details of conventions.

Piano World

www.pianoworld.com

This American site boasts nearly 1,000 pages of information on pianos, with a directory of piano professionals (although most of these are in the United States), tips on buying and valuing pianos, a chat room and reviews, FAQs, etc. You can buy sheet music and piano CDs, among other things, and even download a piano screen-saver for your PC.

Players Vintage Instruments

www.vintageinstruments.com

Mandolins, banjos, and other stringed instruments are featured on this site, which has an extensive online inventory for sale. Each instrument is discussed in detail, and is accompanied by several photos of it, and there are links to various instrument and musician sites.

Search the largest vintage and used guitar inventory at www.gbase.com.

Shrine to Music Museum

www.usd.edu/smm/witten.html

The important Witten-Rawlins collection of stringed instruments can be seen on this American academic site. There's a virtual tour of the museum, biographical information on famous makers, and a history of instrument-making. The collection includes guitars, violins, and various other instruments dating from the 17th century.

WORTH A LOOK

www.hidehitters.com

Vintage drum site.

www.vintagemandolin.com

Enthusiast's site that buys and sells mandolins.

ORIENTAL

Barry Davies Oriental Art

www.barrydavies.com

Barry Davies is one of the world's most respected Oriental art dealers, and his website includes an extensive online catalogue. Stock includes everything from sword furniture to porcelain, and objects pictured are accompanied by extensive and informative text. Further enquiries about the items shown on the site can be made by email.

Brian Harkins

www.brianharkins.co.uk

A well-designed page with pictures of current stock is just one of the features of the site of this London Oriental art dealer. A variety of items can be seen in bronze, lacquer, bamboo, and porcelain. Contact information and brief details of future exhibitions and the gallery's opening hours are also given, and a full catalogue can be ordered via email.

Hanshan Tang Books

www.hanshan.com

Hanshan Tang is said to be the West's foremost bookseller specializing in the arts of Asia. The visitor to this website can indeed browse through a vast selection of titles and search by subject, author, or keyword. The site includes brief but helpful comments on each volume, and you can order via email. There are also some useful links listed for specialist Oriental art magazines, societies (such as the International Netsuke Society – see below), and resource sites. (See pages 142–5 for book sites.)

Huang Imports

www.huangimports.com

Antique Chinese furniture is the mainstay of this gallery, which displays a wide selection of pieces for online ordering. Cabinets, chests, tables, and screens are among the offerings and you will also find accessories such as hat boxes and bamboo baskets. A search facility will help you find specific items and you can join an online mailing list to be kept informed of stock as it becomes available. (See pages 188–93 for furniture sites.)

International Netsuke Society

www.netsuke.org

This is the site of an international society with over 600 members in 31 countries. The FAQs will certainly help those who are new to netsuke, but even enthusiasts may learn something. A glossary of terms is similarly educational. There is also information about the society's journal and forthcoming netsuke conventions and events as well as links to the sites of various netsuke dealers around the world and also to museums and auction houses.

Jcollector

www.jcollector.com

A vast online catalogue of items for sale is the main feature of this site, which is devoted to Japanese and Asian antiques. Everything from fine porcelain to samurai swords can be found here, and objects are accompanied by details and several photographs; you can buy them via a secure order form. The site also has informative articles and features on various aspects of the arts of Asia.

Kyoto National Museum

www.kyohaku.go.jp

Admirers of Japanese art and artefacts will love the chance to browse through the collections of one of Japan's top institutions. A fine range of pieces, including ceramics, sculpture, textiles, paintings, and calligraphy, are all represented on the site, as well as Asian art in a broader sense (such as works from the Indian subcontinent). An English language version of the site is available, and the full descriptions that accompany each image help to put objects into their cultural context. The online catalogue currently features more than 2,000 works of art, but the collection has more than 5,000 and there are plans to put them all online.

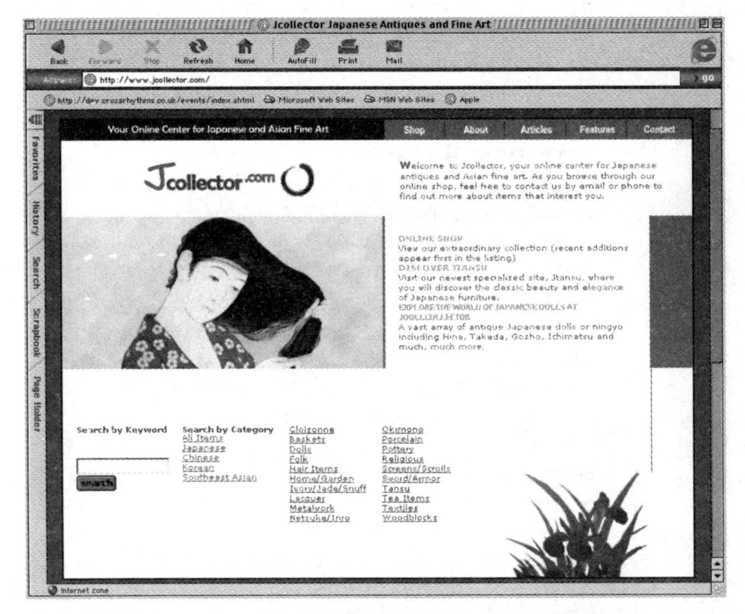

Search Jcollector's extensive catalogue by category for Japanese or Asian antiques.

McFadden Antiques

www.mcfaddenantiques.com

This Pennsylvania dealer has an extensive online catalogue. Oriental antiques is the mainstay of the business and includes porcelain, lacquer, metals, and other items, with Chinese and Japanese offerings. Coins, books, art and autographs, ceramics, and miscellaneous items are also included. The last category is extremely diverse – it includes everything from quilts to Roman glass. Dealer discounts are offered with proof of resale number. All the items on the site are pictured, and many are shown from multiple viewpoints. Purchases can be made by email.

The Oriental Corner

www.theorientalcorner.com

Woodblock prints, netsuke, bronzes, and many other examples of the arts of Asia can be seen at the extensive online gallery of this Californian dealer. There are details of the gallery's valuation service, and a guest book where you can register your specific interests.

Orientations Gallery

www.orientationsgallery.com

This New York-based gallery specializes in Japanese works of art, and takes a scholarly approach to collecting. The online gallery includes detailed discussions of items illustrated, putting them into their historical and cultural context and giving information about the artists. There's also a search engine and, while it's not possible to buy online, email enquiries about any of the items shown on the site are encouraged.

Roger Keverne

www.keverne.co.uk

Roger Keverne is a leading specialist in Chinese ceramics and works of art and the author of what is perhaps the definitive work on jade. Of particular interest on his site is a guide to Chinese dynasties and their dates. There's also a large online exhibition with lots of pictures and information, including references for further reading.

Silk Road Gallery

www.silkroadhawaii.com

Japanese dolls and porcelain, Chinese snuff bottles, and Tang pottery horses can all be found in the online gallery on this site. On the left-hand side of the home page are two lists – covering Chinese Art and Japanese Art – click on whichever interests you to see what types of antiques are available. For example, under Japanese Art can be found furniture, netsuke, okimono, sculpture, textiles, lacquer etc. Just click again to view the available stock in each category. This site is run by a leading Asian arts dealer in Hawaii, and you can send an email for further information on the numerous items illustrated.

WORTH A LOOK

www.asianartinlondon.com
The website of London's annual Asian art festival.

www.berwald-oriental.com
Browse through the catalogue of a leading dealer.

www.randdorientalart.com
Japanese, Korean, Chinese, and Thai art can all be found here.

PAPERWEIGHTS

Allan's Paperweights

www.paperweights.com

An informative and educational site that offers online "tutorials" on collecting paperweights and quizzes to test your knowledge. There are also paperweights for sale, which include examples from all the leading factories, as well as books, including authoritative works like the Selman price guides.

Caithness Glass

www.caithnessglass.co.uk

The site of this well-known paperweight manufacturer provides an insight into how they are made. There is also a chance to view the visitor centre, and to see a selection of products. The items are not sold directly online, but you can find a list of stockists on the site.

Glass Paperweights

www.paperweightsonline.com

This American dealer's site offers more than 400 weights for online purchase, plus accessories such as self-adhesive "feet" to stop your weights from sliding about on the shelf. There is also a useful glossary of terms, advice on photographing your paperweights, and an assortment of links to glass and general antiques sites.

International Paperweight Society

www.selman.com/ips.html

Learn more about paperweights and their history, as well as about the artists themselves, on this site, which also offers you a chance to join the society. The site is linked to that of the specialist paperweight auctioneers L H Selman, and you can download their catalogues from here. Also featured is a page of paperweight trivia, and even paperweight humour!

Sweetbriar Gallery

www.sweetbriar.co.uk

More than 1,500 paperweights are stocked by this leading Cheshire-based dealer, whose site shows weights from just about every manufacturer you can think of. Stock includes American, Venetian, British, French, and Chinese weights, both antique and modern. A range of inexpensive through to costly items is included, and there is a currency converter on this site too. You must order over the phone or send an email enquiry, as there is no secure server for buying directly online. The site also includes a wealth of information and news from the paperweight world.

WORTH A LOOK

www.wheatonvillage.org
Paperweights and glassware.

www.whitehouse-books.com
Book site with a good paperweight/glass section.

www.wpitt.com
American dealer of both antique and contemporary weights.

PENS

Battersea Pen Home

www.penhome.co.uk

This dealer has put a wealth of information on collectible pens online that you can peruse at your leisure. Choose from an extensive selection of vintage and modern pens, books, and accessories and buy them online. There's information on London antique markets and hotel listings, with prices and details of the London Pen Show. The site also includes a complete guide to the condition of pens on the site.

David Nishimura

www.vintagepens.com

A list of FAQs to help the nervous novice is one of the most useful features of this American dealer's website – buying pens on the web is one of the subjects covered. There's a glossary of terms, and a range of specialist books is reviewed and can be ordered directly online. You can also buy and sell pens on this site. Detailed advice on spares and repairs is available, and there are email contact details for various pen specialists. These include a dealer who even sells pen repair videos…

Glenn's Pen Page

www.marcuslink.com/pens

This site houses Internet pen links to dealer and collector sites, those sites devoted to specific makers, and bulletin boards. The site also includes articles on interesting topics such as a behind-the-scenes visit to a pen factory. You will also find advice on what to look for when buying a pen, and a discussion of the merits of different types of ink.

Jim's Fountain Pen Site

www.jimgaston.com

Information for the novice and the more experienced pen collector can be found on this site. Detailed FAQs should answer most of your questions, and there is advice on what to buy and how to look after your pens. View Jim's own extensive personal pen collection, and consult a list of useful links to over 50 pen sites.

The Nibster

www.nibs.com

A mail-order nib repair service is offered on this American site, which has "before" and "after" pictures to prove it. Other types of pen restoration are also undertaken. There's a guide to nib values and nib repair tools are also sold. Samples of calligraphy are shown as well, and there's help and advice for writers who happen to be left-handed.

Pen Auction Site

www.penbid.com

Billed as the world's first and only web-based, real-time, exclusive auction site for writing instruments, Penbid includes a complete tutorial for beginners and auction rules. Search for lots by description or seller, submit questions to the vendor, and view feedback from other users.

Pen Collectors of America

www.pencollectors.com

This US collectors' site offers you the chance to submit your own pens for inclusion in its online museum as well as to contribute articles on pens for surfers to enjoy (the site has many articles on the history of pens, and on various pen makers). Among the links are sites that, although not directly related to pens, discuss materials used in their manufacture, such as Bakelite.

Pendemonium

www.pendemonium.com

Pens by various makers are available to order via this American site, which also offers a vast range of writing accessories. These include replacement parts, nibs, blotters, and sealing wax, as well as pen storage cabinets. A catalogue, including an ink colour chart, can be sent to you by post.

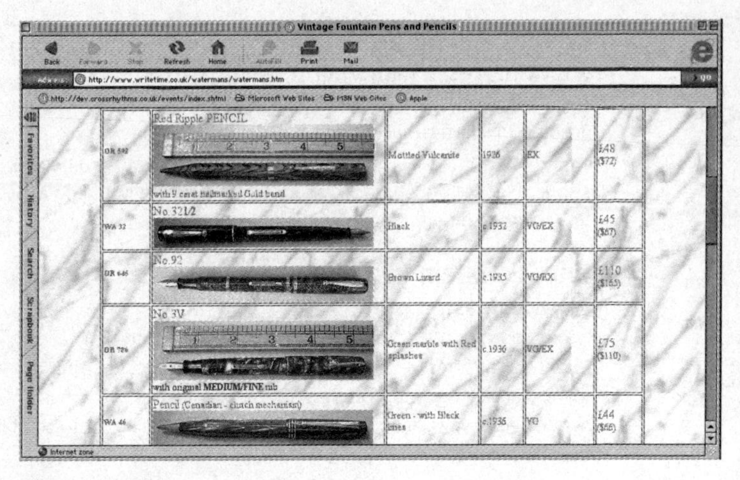

Writetime illustrates examples in detail, with information, date, and price.

Writetime

www.writetime.co.uk

Vintage pens and pencils are for sale on this site, some already restored while others are still in unrestored condition. Stock is fully illustrated and listed by maker, and "company histories" of the makers are included. There is also a section on rare and unusual pens, including some examples that, as yet, have not been identified.

Zoss Pens Mailing List

www.zoss.com/pens

As its name suggests, this is a mailing list designed to put pen collectors in touch with each other as well as give them more information about their hobby. It works by automatically emailing new messages to all the subscribers. A full explanation of the concept is given together with FAQs. Those on the list often trade between themselves, and joining the list is free of charge so it is worth doing. The site also includes news and press releases on some of the latest limited-edition pens.

WORTH A LOOK

home.tvd.be/sf15332

A bilingual Belgian site with a truly international range of pens.

www.old-pens.co.uk

Pens for sale, plus a restoration service.

www.penfriend.co.uk

The site of the world's largest independent pen restorer.

PHOTOGRAPHY

Bygone Photos

www.bygonephotos.com

Originals and reproductions of antique photographs are for sale on this site. Subjects include scenes of rural England and Scotland, female fashion photographs, royalty, and "cheeky Edwardian photographs" featuring nudes of that era. Ordering is via a printable form through the post. The site also offers you the chance to send in your own vintage photo to be displayed on the web for all to see.

Carole Thompson Fine Photographs

www.southernphotos.com

This is the site of a Tennessee-based dealer, whose stock is particularly rich in images of the American Civil War. Individual photographs and albums are available for ordering online. Credit card transactions are not accepted via the web, although you can pay by cheque, bank transfer, or credit card by post or telephone. The site also offers a history of Civil War photography and links to American Civil War sites.

Fox Talbot Museum

www.r-cube.co.uk/fox-talbot

William Henry Fox Talbot invented the positive/negative process, and is known as the father of modern photography. This is the website of the museum devoted to him in Wiltshire, UK. Photographs can be seen on the site, but its main appeal lies in its authoritative text on Fox Talbot and his achievements.

Learn About Photographers

www.masters-of-photography.com

From Fox Talbot to Man Ray, enjoy the work of the masters of photography on this site. There is a vast gallery of photographs, and you can zoom in for a closer look at each one. There are scholarly articles on the photographers and their techniques as well as details of books that can be bought via the Internet bookstore amazon.com.

Old Photo Album

www.city-gallery.com/album

Designed as a resource for genealogists, this American website has a wealth of mainly family photos from a bygone era. You can share your own old photos with the site too, and users of the site are invited to help identify them, or just comment on them.

See science and technology, pages 242–4, for vintage camera sites.

WORTH A LOOK

www.lcweb.loc.gov/rr/print
Library of Congress Prints and Photographs Reading Room, USA.

www.packer34.freeserve.co.uk
This vast site, devoted to the 1951 Festival of Britain, includes a multitude of vintage photographs.

www.rainyday.net/dd/library/photos.shtml
An online collection of old photographs and postcards.

PORCELAIN

Adrian Sassoon Gallery

www.adriansassoon.com

This London gallery specializes in Sèvres porcelain and shows off a sizeable selection of quality pieces on its website. Contact the gallery online for further information or if you wish to purchase an item. There's an archive of sold objects and general information on Sèvres itself. The site also offers contemporary glass and ceramics.

AntikWest London

www.antikwest.com

Chinese and Japanese porcelain are the specialities of this Swedish firm, whose site includes a large selection, priced in US dollars. You can send an email to reserve your chosen piece. The site also features information on fairs and a selection of books, some of which are in Swedish, although many are available in English.

Cathcart's Antiques

www.cathcartsantiques.com.au

This Australian dealer's site specializes mainly in English 18th- and 19th-century porcelain and pottery (see pages 233–6 for pottery sites). The site acts as an online showcase, featuring an extensive gallery of pieces in stock. These are shown with a "price code" rather than specific prices, but you can enquire by email for further details. Stock is particularly strong in blue and white Worcester but Oriental and Continental pieces can also be viewed here.

Chinasearch

www.chinasearch.uk.com

If there are pieces missing from your best dinner service, Chinasearch will try to find matching pieces to replace them. The firm deals with all the most popular

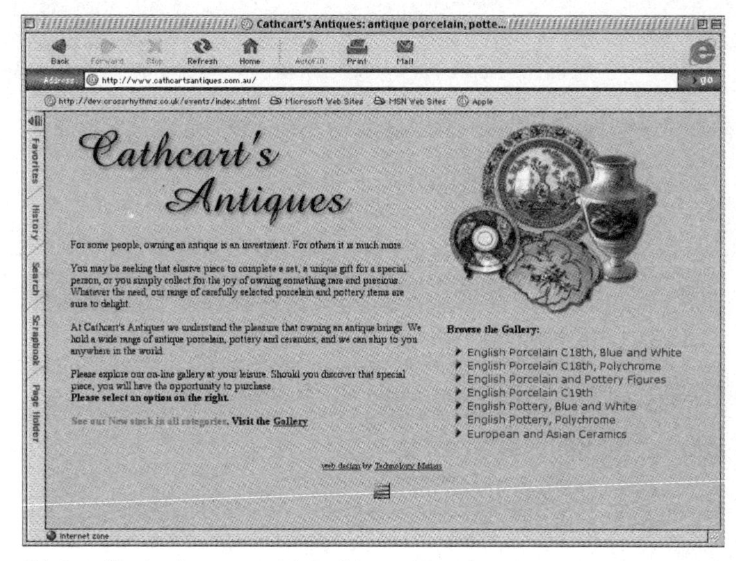

This Australian site showcases mainly English porcelain and pottery.

patterns and makes, from Worcester and Midwinter to Denby and Coalport. Register your requirements free of charge online.

E & H Manners Ceramics and Works of Art

www.europeanporcelain.com

This London dealer offers ceramics from the 16th to the 19th century, specializing particularly in the rarer porcelains of the 18th century. Pieces shown on the site are accompanied by detailed text that addresses topics such as questions of attribution. This text is also backed up by academic references. Prices are not given so you will need to enquire by email, telephone, or post for further information about the pieces that interest you.

Irish Belleek Porcelain

www.ladymarion.co.uk

A detailed price guide to Belleek is one of the many useful features of this site, which also includes a guide to marks, numbering systems, and other identifying features. You will also find Belleek for sale (although you must enquire by email if you want to buy anything), and links to collectors' societies, as well as a link to the site of the Belleek factory.

Meissen

www.meissen.de/engl

This website, which is given in both English and German, is that of the renowned porcelain firm Meissen. It includes a history of porcelain manufacture and the crucial part played by Meissen in its development in Europe. There are details of the company's museum and of the official collectors' club – members can buy exclusive items through the club. There is also a list of Meissen stockists around the world, complete with addresses.

Roderick Jellicoe

englishporcelain.com

This is the website of an English dealer who specializes in 18th-century English ceramics, and who is an authority on Liverpool porcelain. The site displays examples of pieces produced by many factories, from Lowestoft and Bow to Worcester and Chelsea, and also includes informative descriptions. You can make contact by email if you are interested in purchasing any of the items shown and require further information.

Royal Worcester

www.royal-worcester.co.uk

This is the official website of the celebrated porcelain factory that dates back to 1751. The site features a detailed history of the factory, information on the company museum and its collections, and the newly relaunched collectors' society. You will also find information on new products and a list of various stockists worldwide, complete with contact details and information about the Royal Worcester factory visitor centre.

Stockspring Antiques

www.antique-porcelain.co.uk

This is the site of a London-based gallery, which specializes in fine English porcelain. Stock is subdivided into categories such as 18th-century figures, and the site also includes pictures and commentary from the gallery's recent exhibitions. Contact the gallery for information on pieces shown on the site, or to order a catalogue.

WORTH A LOOK

www.antique-porcelain.com
London dealer who specializes in Oriental porcelain.

www.chinapatterns.com
Canadian tableware-matching service.

www.4limoges.com
A selection of Limoges boxes for sale, and a history of the porcelain.

www.royalworcester.freeserve.co.uk
A selection of mainly Worcester pieces from a dealer who is actually based in Worcester.

www.westwalesantiques.co.uk
Specialists in Welsh porcelain such as Swansea and Nantgarw.

POSTCARDS

Buy and Sell Your Postcards Here

www.collections.co.uk

Collections is the place to buy and sell postcards, telephone cards, stamps, and related collectibles. You can place orders via email, and the site also includes a good selection of links.

The Collector's Centre

www.collectors.demon.co.uk

Cigarette cards as well as postcards can be found on this dealer's site (see pages 151–2 for cigarette card sites). It has a beginner's section of Edwardian postcards to start you off and if you want to order, telephone with your credit card at the ready or fill in, print, and post the form on the site.

Days Past

www.argonet.co.uk/users/sunnyfield/dayspast

This dealer site has a particularly good selection of postcards of local scenes from around Britain. Other subjects include royalty, glamour, aviation, and politics. All items are illustrated, and you can order online by credit card.

Jim Mehrer's Postal History

www.deltiology.org

Postal history, as well as postcards, is covered by this American site, which is quite extensive. It also includes dealer pages as well as show information and a bibliography with a detailed commentary on the available literature. There's news of online auctions and some other, more unusual, inclusions, such as the offer of a "postmark calendar" – as the name suggests, it is a calendar featuring old postmarks. Payment is by cheque through the post, but potential customers outside the US should send an email enquiry first.

Postcard Collectors' Resource Site

www.postcard.org

This collectors' web resource has information and links on clubs, societies, and sources of postcards on the web, including auctions and dealer sites. Sources of postcard supplies, such as albums and so forth, are also listed here. You will find "personal pages" devoted to the specialist interests of collectors too – these range from postcards of bridges to baseball stars and nudes.

PostcardMall.com

www.postcardmall.com

This site bills itself as a "one-stop cyberspot for finding purveyors of fine postcards and deltiology supplies" – which just about says it all. The online mall features dealers in postcards and accessories. There's a classified ads section (there is a small charge for listing advertisements), and a collectors' page where you can list your contact details for fellow enthusiasts. You can also buy and sell via online auctions.

Postcard Pages

www.postcard.co.uk

This is the site of the Postcard Traders' Association, which represents the UK's foremost dealers in this particular field. The site includes news of forthcoming events, advice to collectors, and plenty of links to, among others, the websites of collecting clubs and societies. There are also "for sale" and "wanted" ads posted on the site.

Postcard Resources

www.u.arizona.edu/~jmount/postcard.html

This is a web resource featuring links to all kinds of postcard-related sites. These include museums, publications, newsgroups, and a glossary of postcard terms as well as the usual dealer, auctioneer, and collector sites.

Sidney Fenemore Postal History and Postcards

www.sidneyfenemore.co.uk

This is a large dealer's site with an extensive online gallery of postcards, all of which are for sale. The site also includes an "e-zine" that focuses on postal history. Links are subdivided by category to allow the visitor to go straight to specific sites.

T Vennett-Smith

www.vennett-smith.com

T Vennett-Smith is a leading British specialist auction house, offering postcards, cigarette cards, and ephemera (see pages 172–4 for ephemera sites). You can order hard copies of their auction catalogues and some of these are also shown on the site. You can carry out keyword searches of the online catalogues, or ask to see just the illustrated lots. There's advice for buyers and sellers here too, and you can send bids via email.

WORTH A LOOK

www.beverevivis.com/postcards
Postcards made from original paintings.

www.csgb.co.uk
The website of the Cartophilic Society of Great Britain.

www.marylmartin.com
The site of a supplier of albums and various other accessories for the postcard collector.

POSTERS

À L'imagerie

www.alimagerie.com

This is a French vintage poster site, which can also be read in English, with a large selection of posters. These are subdivided by category and orders can be placed by fax or post, with prices given in euros. Most subjects are covered, including transport, propaganda, sports, entertainment, and theatre.

Buy French Posters

www.affiche-francaise.com

Not surprisingly, Affiche Française is particularly strong on French posters. A vast array of examples, including all the most popular types, can be seen on the site, which is written in English. You can search for specific examples, and send an email for further information if you wish to order.

Gallery of Vintage Posters

www.vintageposterworks.com

This site is an online gallery of posters from the 1870s to the 1950s. All are original and can be ordered online and sent on approval. Subjects covered include advertising, travel, and entertainment, and there also is a condition guide so you should know what to expect when buying from the site.

I Desire Vintage Posters

www.idesirevintageposters.com

Desirable posters are easy to come by on this Canadian dealer's site. Images of 20th-century advertising from the Art Deco era are well represented here and there's also a "poster of the month" feature, which highlights a particularly interesting item in stock. You can buy through the site with your credit card, but send an email first for details of shipping arrangements.

International Poster Gallery

www.internationalposter.com

Vintage and modern posters from around the world can be found on the site of this American dealer. Features include a "poster of the day", an introductory article on posters, and a guide to values. There is also a search engine, which searches through 3,000 items on a poster database to find you what you are looking for.

The Nostalgia Factory

www.nostalgia.com

More than 35,000 items can be bought through this site (if you have the wall space!) Movie posters are the site's speciality and you can search a database by film title, director, year, star, and even composer. The site has a useful guide to condition and puts you in the picture about poster sizes and how they vary between countries. Lobby cards and other collectibles are available as well as posters. You can shop online and pay with your credit card.

Philip Williams Posters

www.postermuseum.com

French travel posters and Dutch posters are among the separate categories included on this site, which houses all the most popular poster-collecting fields such as Soviet propaganda and entertainment posters. Detailed descriptions and historical background information accompany stock, and ordering is through a form printed from the site – although an online ordering system is on its way.

Rozelle Cooper Poster Collection

www.rozellecooperposters.com

This site is a particularly rich source of posters from the Art Nouveau and Art Deco eras (see pages 135–9 for Art Deco and Art Nouveau sites). Click on thumbnail images of stock for larger pictures and descriptions, then send an email for payment details and shipping arrangements.

Vintage Western Movie Posters

www.vintageposters.com

Although this dealer's site would seem to be of most interest to Western movie buffs, it has something to offer the general poster enthusiast too. In particular, there is a wealth of information on the history of posters and a glossary of terms.

Yaneff International

www.yaneff.com

This is a Canadian gallery offering rare 19th- and 20th-century posters online. Artists such as Toulouse-Lautrec and Alphonse Mucha are among those whose work is represented. Other features include a detailed history of the poster and there are also links to information on poster books and other relevant sources on the web.

WORTH A LOOK

www.barewalls.com
Claims to be the largest Internet art print and poster store.

www.gal-123.com
A Swiss poster specialist with more than 10,000 original items.

www.ivpda.com
An international poster dealers' association.

www.plakatauktion.de
German poster auction site, which also links to an American site.

POTTERY

American Art Pottery Association

www.amartpot.org

This site is dedicated to lovers of American Art Pottery, from Abington to Zark by way of Cincinnati, Rookwood, and just about anything else. Here you will find advice, warnings about fakes, reviews of books on the subject, an online discussion group, and much more. The site also includes links to dealer sites.

Andrew Dando of Bath

www.andrewdando.co.uk

This site has a selection of pottery and porcelain dating from before 1870, and all of it is for sale. The online catalogue is subdivided by categories, including lustre ware, 18th-century English porcelain figures, early Staffordshire, and Continental pieces. The stock is well illustrated with descriptions and prices. You can order online, but should check that the item is still available first. This site also features useful advice on restoration, and tips on how to detect whether pieces have been restored.

Gladstone Working Pottery Museum

www.stoke.gov.uk/museums/gladstone

A wealth of information on most aspects of pottery and the potteries region of the English Midlands can be found on this site. It is designed mainly for educational purposes, and is especially useful for its extensive bibliographies. There is also a history of pottery as well as information on identifying pieces.

Howards of Aberystwyth

www.antiquepottery.co.uk

This dealer has a wide range of Staffordshire pottery (especially figures), lustre ware, creamware, and Welsh ceramics (for ceramic sites, see pages 147–50). The site shows a selection of books on Staffordshire, as well as the pieces themselves. Use the online enquiry form to get further details if you wish to buy either. Stock is divided into various categories, and pieces are described in full with fixed prices given for most. Many descriptions include references to academic works and historical background information.

Janice Paull

www.btinternet.com/~janicepaull

This is the website of a dealer who specializes in Mason's and other English Ironstone. Jugs, mugs, dinner wares, and ornamental wares for sale are all shown on the site, as well as inkstands and miscellaneous items. Enthusiasts will, however, find this site particularly useful for its information on marks, numbering systems used, etc, as well as its historical information.

Jonathan Horne Antiques Ltd

www.jonathanhorne.co.uk

London dealer Jonathan Horne holds one of the most comprehensive stocks of early English pottery in the world. Medieval pottery, English delftware, tiles, and much more can be found on his website. If you wish to buy, enquire by email first to check an item's availability. If you want to find out more about this subject, the site includes a list of recommended reading, with reviews of the books shown.

Keystones

www.keystones.co.uk

Keystones specialize in Denby Stonewares, and their site contains lots of information on identifying pieces. There is a gallery of pottery that is for sale and you can send an email enquiry if you would like to buy anything that you see. You can also register with an online matching service for discontinued tableware, find out more about books on Denby, and, for a small fee, also subscribe to a Denby newsletter.

Min's Antiques Intl

www.minsantiques.com

This is the site of a Canadian dealer who specializes in Moorcroft Pottery, as well as stocking Royal Doulton, Royal Albert, Belleek, and Art Glass. Moorcroft dominates the site, and the online selection is accompanied by brief background descriptions and prices but you will need to enquire by email or

This site includes a history of the Moorcroft company and you can also buy pieces online.

telephone if you wish to purchase anything. "Wants" can also be registered, and there are links to Canadian gateway sites, publications, and fairs sites.

Moorcroft

www.moorcroft.com

This is the official site of the Moorcroft Pottery, and it includes a company history. It also points the visitor to further sources of information, such as books and videos. Examples of the works of various Moorcroft designers are shown, you can buy through online auctions, and there's information on how you can join the collectors' club.

Pottery Auction

www.potteryauction.com

This site holds an online pottery auction, featuring mainly late 19th- to mid-20th-century pottery and related wares and the auctions last for 3–14 days. There is a host of other things to be found here, such as an active chatroom where information is exchanged. The "Pottery Forum" is a place for enthusiasts to post questions, which other readers will answer if they can. There is also a "Daily Headline News" link to current news stories, most of which are home- and garden-related – an unusual inclusion on a pottery site. An extensive list of pottery collector's clubs and organizations includes links to sites where available.

The Transferware Collectors Club

www.transcollectorsclub.org

This US site is a forum for those with an interest in transferware to share information. (Transferware is printed pottery that has had its image bonded on top of the glaze during firing.) The site is for collectors, dealers, and scholars alike, and focuses on wares produced between 1760 and 1880. Membership benefits include a newsletter and information about conventions, regional meetings, exhibitions, and seminars. The newsletter is posted online, and contains scholarly articles about various aspects of the subject. This also provides information about the annual meeting, which includes lectures and a dealer's sale as well as an auction. The online bulletin board is a place where you can post questions about your own pieces in the hope that somebody will be able to answer them. There are also some links to members' own websites, which include "Friends of Blue" – the English counterpart and inspiration for the American club.

Wedgwood

www.wedgwood.co.uk

A highly detailed history of the Wedgwood factory is one of the highlights of this famous company's site, as is a biography of its founder. There is a page of Wedgwood FAQs, links to feature pages showcasing particular ranges like Sarah's Garden or Contrasts, and an online magazine. You can also join the

Wedgwood International Society (a kind of collectors' club) online. Current Wedgwood products are detailed in the extensive product portfolio and can also be bought from the online store.

WORTH A LOOK

www.drawrm.com/pottery.htm
Continental and American Art Pottery.

www.poolepottery.co.uk
The official website of Poole Pottery.

www.quimperfaience.com
The official site of the French pottery Quimper.

www.wemyss-ware.co.uk
Wemyss ware site.

RAILWAYANA

For Railway Enthusiasts

www.railwayanapage.com

A non-commercial site for railway enthusiasts. There's news of the collecting scene, and specialist auctions, as well as general information. While this is a British site, contributions from around the world are welcomed. There's also a useful bibliography for those seeking relevant offline reading material.

Railwayana and Model Railway Home Page

www.irishrailwayana.com

This site is largely devoted to Irish railwayana, but also has plenty to interest the more general railway enthusiast. There are pictures of signs and tickets and also a links page with some unusual railway sites.

Railwayana Collectors' Network

www.trainweb.org/rcn-uk

Join email contact lists for collectors of railwayana here. Subscribers can place sale/wanted ads, ask for information, publicize events, and view a picture gallery that includes enamel signs, car and wagon items etc. There are also FAQs.

Railway Carriage Prints

www.carriageprints.com

The site of Greg Norden, author of a book on railway carriage prints, has information on this and other railway ephemera, and offers railway greetings cards for sale. Carriage prints surplus to Norden's own collection are also offered for sale, though they cannot be bought directly online – you must email your interest first, and then pay via post. There are also links to other railwayana sites here.

Yesteryear Railwayana

www.yesrail.com

Railway books, illustrations, and ephemera are the stock-in-trade of yesteryear railwayana. The site has information on the business, which deals exclusively through mail order rather than having a physical shop. You can consult their stock lists of everything that is available – these are not illustrated but do contain full descriptions and prices.

WORTH A LOOK

www.bhamrailwayauctions.co.uk
Leading British railwayana auctioneers.

www.gwra.co.uk
Railwayana auction site.

www.rail-sales.co.uk
Railway-themed items and memorabilia for sale.

ROCK AND POP

Awesome Beatles Catalogue

www.awesomebeatles.com

Memorabilia, books, and records, including some rare items, relating to the biggest band in history await the browser on this site. Search through a private Beatles collection that is not for sale, or browse a catalogue of items that are. There are also particularly useful FAQs relating to various aspects of Beatles collecting that are worth perusing here.

Beatcity

www.beatcity.co.uk

Beatles memorabilia is the speciality of this site too, but other pop items can also be found. Stock includes 1960s music magazines, autographs, rock and pop auction catalogues, a wide range of accessories, and many more unusual items – such as an inflatable Paul McCartney that dates from around 1965. You can order directly from the catalogue online or, if you have something to sell, email the full details of the item to the site.

This website specializes in posters of rock 'n' roll legends such as the Rolling Stones.

Bojo's Beatles Memorabilia

www.zbzoom.net/~bojo

This is the site of one of America's leading Beatles memorabilia specialists. Old and new items relating to the band can be found here, including trading cards, dolls, toys, and magazines, and you will be entertained with appropriate music as you browse. There's online ordering, and Bojo's are keen to hear from anyone with any sort of Beatles memorabilia for sale.

Classic Legends – Posters

www.classiclegends.com

This site specializes in posters relating to the biggest names in rock 'n' roll. Original concert posters and similar items advertising artists such as the Grateful Dead, David Bowie, and Santana can be seen online, as well as bought. Search by artist for your favourites, or join the mailing list for news of items as they become available. (See pages 231–2 for other poster sites.)

Elvis Memorabilia

www.elvisly-yours.com

Elvis souvenirs and memorabilia galore can be found on this site – these range from phone cards right through to coffee mugs. You can order all the items online, and there's also a list of links to Elvis fan and memorabilia sites. The site also offers Elvis puzzles and a chance to find a pen pal who shares your Elvis interests.

eRock

www.erock.net

eRock is a rock memorabilia auction site. You can bid for items relating to the Beatles, Elvis, the Rolling Stones, and other artists too numerous to mention. There are more than 300 links to sites dedicated to various artists and you can chat to fellow enthusiasts online.

Graceland

www.elvis.com

This is the official online site of the home of Elvis. There's Elvis news here, a complete biography of the King, and you can also book tickets to visit Graceland. An online shopping mall offers music, clothes, accessories, and collectibles of all kinds, and you can even listen to Elvis songs while you browse. There's also a "Graceland cam" that enables you to see what's going on at the home of the King.

The Hillbilly Cat and Me – Collecting Elvis

home1.gte.net/eap

This is the site of an Elvis fan whose collection is proudly displayed online. It is particularly useful for its Elvis collectibles price guide and its list of books on Elvis, which be ordered through the site. There's also an Elvis database, and links to various fan sites.

Rock Memorabilia

www.rock-memorabilia.net

If you've ever wanted to own a jacket, guitar, microphone, or album that has been autographed by your favourite bands then this site gives you your chance to acquire one. Shop online from a wide selection that incorporates Country artists such as Garth Brooks as well as BB King, Peter Frampton, and Phil Collins. All items that are bought from the site come with a certificate of authenticity.

Visionary Rock

www.visionaryrock.com

Backstage passes, autographs, programmes, and even guitar picks are among the items in this vast online catalogue of memorabilia. You can search by artist or by type of item and you can also buy online. All kinds of bands – from Aerosmith to ZZ Top via Whitney Houston, Elvis Presley, Neil Diamond, Deep Purple, and Little Richard – are represented. If you can't find what you are looking for, simply submit your "wish list" to the site and you will be notified as soon as something is available.

WORTH A LOOK

members.aol.com/elvisnet
Elvis fan site with merchandise for sale.

www.concertposters.com
Not just posters, but other rock 'n' roll ephemera too.

www.doors.com/rock_mem
Records, CDs, and gold discs are a speciality of this site.

www.rarebeatles.com
Songs, pictures, and stories of the Beatles.

www.rockarchives.co.uk
Music magazines of yesteryear, plus posters and programmes.

www.yk.rim.or.jp/~y_satou/beatles
Japanese Beatles fan site.

RUGS AND CARPETS

Achdjian

monsite.wanadoo.fr/achdjian

This is the site of a leading French dealer (available in English), offering online exhibitions of rugs and carpets. Items displayed on the site are discussed in some detail, and descriptions include a commentary on the various decorative motifs that have been used in the designs. You must, however, make further enquiries if you are interested in buying anything that has been shown. The site also includes views of the gallery and there are details of major international fairs where the gallery exhibits.

Anglo-Persian Carpet Company

www.world-rugs.com/anglopersian

This is the online home of one of London's first specialist rug shops, which opened in 1910. An online gallery displays the firm's entire inventory, and there is also a "reception area", which allows the visitor to ask questions or obtain further information on items before purchasing them directly online.

A Zadah Fine Oriental Carpets

www.zadah.com

This London gallery deals mainly with designers and decorators, although individual enquiries are welcomed. The site offers a small but representative selection of stock, including European as well as Persian and Central Asian items. Send an email for more information about any of the items that you see.

Khalil Antiques and Oriental Rugs

www.khalilrugs.com

Advertise your rugs for sale on this site, or email pictures to be valued. You can also sell direct to the gallery or, if you want to buy, you will find a large selection of rugs in several online galleries.

The Lenkoran Gallery

www.lenkoran.co.uk

Antique Persian, Caucasian, Anatolian, and even Scandinavian rugs and carpets can be found on this site. Pre-Colombian weaving is also included among a varied mix of stock for sale. There is a search facility if you know what you want, and an online form for detailed enquiries. Email them if you wish to buy.

Richard Purdon

www.purdon.com

The site of this established rugs and carpets dealer includes a selection of stock, mainly from the Near East and Central Asia. There are also pictures of items on show at the gallery, and, if you are interested in the stock shown, an email enquiry will get you further details. There is a small but well-chosen selection of links to the sites of other rug and textile dealers.

Samarkand Galleries

www.samarkand.co.uk

Browse through a fine selection of tribal rugs and weavings on the site of this internationally renowned dealer. The site includes a gallery history, together with online versions of recent exhibitions. There is also a selection of current stock on view; click on an image for a closer look, and send an email if you wish to purchase anything.

Sanaiy Carpets

www.sanaiy-carpets.co.uk

This is the website of a London-based dealer who offers Persian, Caucasian, and Anatolian rugs, carpets, and flatweaves – as well as European tapestries. A mixed selection of online stock is accompanied by brief descriptions, and further information is available from the gallery via an online enquiries form. There is a short company history as well as links, mostly to the sites of other antiques dealers.

The Tribal Eye

www.tribal-kilims.com

Antique rugs, kilims, and other tribal weavings are the specialities of this New York dealer, whose vast array of stock is featured online. Browse, make sales enquiries by email, and learn more about this area. The site includes some useful definitions for the uninitiated, and suggests some useful publications. There is also an extensive links page to other related sites.

WORTH A LOOK

www.floorbiz.com/flooring/rugs/antique.htm
A useful antique rugs web resource, especially for the interior designer.

www.frankames.com
Specialist in decorative and unusual rugs.

www.paulhughes.co.uk
Carpet and textile specialist with a good line in Pre-Colombian works.

SCIENCE AND TECHNOLOGY

Antique and Classic Camera Web Site

members.aol.com/dcolucci

This is an enthusiast's site that includes pictures of classic cameras from the proprietor's collection, as well as manufacturers' catalogues. Technical information is provided with the pictures and there's a long list of links to the sites of collectors, dealers, and manufacturers. (See pages 225–6 for related photography sites.)

Antique Telescope Society

www1.tecs.com/oldscope

This is a non-commercial website that is devoted to the preservation of historical instruments and the promotion of interest in the history of optics and astronomy. The site includes articles on the care, cleaning, and restoration of old telescopes as well as links to websites with further information on telescope makers and other web resources. There is also an elaborate virtual museum here.

Antique Typewriter Collecting

www.typewritercollector.com

A pictorial gallery of early typewriters, information on books about typewriters, and a typewriter timeline are among the many features of this site. If you have an old typewriter and want to know when it was made, this site will help you to find out. There are no vintage typewriters for sale, but typewriter ribbons and accessories are available for purchase and you can email the collector who runs the site if you have something you want to sell.

Arthur Middleton Antique Scientific Instruments

www.antique-globes.com

Globes, planetaria, telescopes, sextants, medical instruments, and barometers can all be seen in Arthur Middleton's comprehensive online catalogue. Historical and scientific information is included in each of the stock descriptions. Send an email if you would like to buy something and, if you are from a TV or film company, stock is also available for rent as props.

James Kennedy Antiques

www.jameskennedyantiques.com

This is the site of an American dealer who specializes in scientific, nautical, and medical instruments and accessories. An online catalogue is divided into categories such as calculators, meteorology, globes, orreries, and surveying equipment. Stock is accompanied by pictures with full descriptions and exact details of shipping costs.

Medical Antiques

medicalantiques.com

A large private collection of medical antiques is the main feature of this site. Artefacts shown all pre-date 1900, and each one is photographed and discussed in detail. All types of instruments are included, from spectacles to amputation saws. There's practical advice on topics such as starting a collection and how to date such antiques.

Old Radio Digital World

www.etedeschi.ndirect.co.uk

Anything to do with historical and collectible electronics is the theme of this picture-packed site. Read the latest news in the vintage technology world, a biography of Marconi, or browse through the for sale/wanted ads. There's also an online museum and plenty of links to related sites.

The Old Telephone Company

www.theoldtelephone.co.uk

Old telephones, fully restored and in working order, are offered for sale on this site. They are each illustrated and informative text provided. Spares for old telephones are also available, as is a small selection of phone-related advertising memorabilia. A list of FAQs includes answers to technical questions such as different phones' compatibility with various telephone systems.

The Telecommunications Heritage Group

www.thg.org.uk

Researchers, collectors, historians, and users of vintage telecommunications technology are catered for on this site. There are articles on various aspects of the subject, news, views, and details of places of interest, all of which are accompanied by links to websites where available.

Vintage Cameras Ltd

www.vintagecameras.co.uk

Lenses, accessories, books, and cameras (of course) can be found on this site, which covers photography from its early days right up to the present day. There are only a few pictures of the stock, but there are detailed stock lists available that provide prices and a condition guide. Ordering should be done via email, fax, or telephone.

WORTH A LOOK

www.hrsa.asn.au
The Historical Radio Society of Australia.

www.magiclanternsociety.org
This is the official site of the Magic Lantern Society of the United States and Canada.

www.mtn.org/quack
Online museum of failed and highly questionable medical gadgets.

www.temeraire.co.uk
Scientific instruments and marine artefacts.

SCRIPOPHILY AND BANKNOTES

All About Money

www.collectpapermoney.com

The answers to most questions about banknotes can be found on this site, and there is also a particularly useful section for the novice that gives explanations of technical terms. Collecting tips include advice on storage and there's a list of FAQs. If this does not answer your own questions, you can send an email query. Another useful feature is a banknote identifier, which shows common symbols on notes and their country of origin. This is a non-commercial site, but you can buy related books via a link to the online bookshop amazon.com.

A Banknote Affair

www.west-banknotes.co.uk

This is the website of a British dealer who specializes in British banknotes. You can shop securely online at this site for books relating to the hobby, albums, and, of course, the banknotes themselves. The online list of notes includes Scottish, Irish, English, Isle of Man, and Channel Islands issues. There is a newsletter, advice for new collectors, and information on forthcoming fairs.

Bank of England

www.bankofengland.co.uk/banknotes

The Bank of England's website includes useful information on the history of the banknote. The site also explains how they are produced and printed, and what factors influence design decisions when new notes are created. You will also find information on the bank's museum and archives, including news of forthcoming exhibitions.

Collectible Stocks and Bonds

www.oldstocks.com

Old stocks and bonds from a variety of industries are featured on this site, which offers online shopping. There is also a page that explains the attractions of collecting these items to the unconverted, and there are links to various dealer sites and collecting societies.

Collecting Banknotes

www.banknotes.com

As the name suggests, this is a site that is dedicated to banknotes, although some coins and stamps are also featured here (see pages 156–9 for coin sites and 260–2 for stamp sites). You will find more than 2,000 notes pictured on the site, and many of these are for sale. There is an online ordering system available, but payment must be done the old-fashioned way – by post. The site also has articles on collecting, a chat room, and a "Hall of Shame", which names alleged rogue dealers.

CSA Collectors Page

www.csacurrency.com

This website is for those with an interest in the bonds, certificates, and currency of the Confederate States during the American Civil War. Stamps, coins, and flags are also included here. The site has advice and warnings about fakes, and explains how you can spot the genuine article. There is a selection of Confederacy banknotes for sale online and you can also enquire by email if you wish to buy anything.

e-worldbanknotes.com

www.e-worldbanknotes.com

Banknotes from practically every country you could think of can be found on this site and you can buy them online too. Banknotes can be viewed by country, with or without accompanying images, or by price. Register your interests if you cannot find what you are looking for. An extensive list of links completes the site.

International Bond and Share Society

www.scripophily.org

This is the online home of the biggest collectors' society of its kind, which has members in 50 countries. Its website has information and advice for novice collectors, as well as housing an online gallery. You cannot buy the items that are shown in the gallery, but there is a page that includes links to specialist dealers and auctioneers.

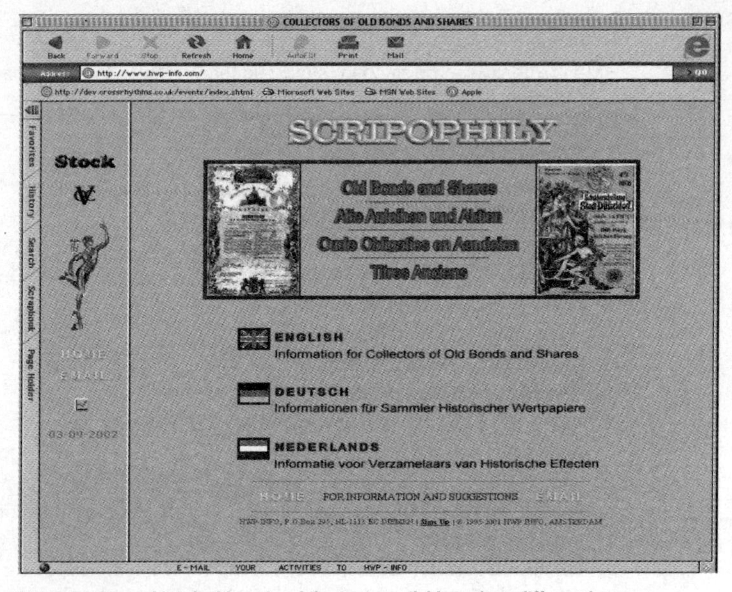

This extensive and invaluable scripophily site is available in three different languages.

Learn More About Scripophily

www.hwp-info.com

This simple but useful Dutch site, with versions in English and German, provides a wealth of information for those interested in this hobby at whatever level. You will find details about several collectors' societies and their meetings all over the world, forthcoming auctions, a list detailing what other collectors are looking for, and sources of information on scripophily. Of particular interest is a "top 15", which lists the highest prices paid for old shares and bonds at auctions in previous years.

R M Smythe

www.rm-smythe.com

One of the world's leading specialist auction houses, R M Smythe has been handling banknotes, share certificates, and related items since 1880. The company's website includes a full company history as well as giving information on forthcoming auctions. The company also has a retail division – you can shop online from a selection of stock or order the latest edition of their catalogue. The site also contains details of their fee-paying research service.

Scripophily.com

www.scripophily.com

A huge array of banknotes, share certificates, and bonds can be found on this site. Choose from oil, gas, and mining stocks, insurance certificates, war bonds, and much more. The stocks and bonds are all well illustrated, there is a search facility available, and you can buy directly online.

The Scripophily Exchange

www.scripex.org

This specialist online auction site, which is based in Poland, offers free buying and selling, although you must register before you can do so. Features of the site include a message board, for exchanging news and information with fellow collectors, and a gallery. The gallery features scans of various documents, and gives a commentary on them in English and Polish. There are also links to a selection of scripophily sites here.

Stock & Bond Auction

www.stockandbondauction.com

This is an interactive American auction site devoted to the collecting of antique stocks, bonds, and related items, covering areas from brewing to military. There is a brief history and explanation of scripophily for the uninitiated. Registration and bidding are free – if you wish to put items up for sale yourself there is even an introductory offer, with free credit, to tempt you.

StockOld Scripophily

www.geocities.com/WallStreet/6303

This Dutch site offers a gallery of bonds from a private collection, as well as a selection for sale. No prices are given, and visitors are invited to send an email to "make a deal". The site also features a list of books from the owner's library. These books are not for sale, but if you have a query, send an email and he'll look up the answer for you. You can't get fairer than that!

Stock Search International Inc

www.stocksearchintl.com

One of this site's main features is an online scripophily gallery, with share certificates and bonds for sale online, but there's much more on offer here as well. There are articles on the likely value of share certificates, and you can even scan in your own certificates and email them to the site for a free valuation. You can also take advantage of a research service that, for a fee, will enable you to see whether those certificates are still worth anything, beyond their value as collectibles.

The Right Note

www.therightnote.com.au

This is the site of Australia's leading banknote specialist and it therefore focuses on Australian currency. It includes articles on collectible banknotes and gives grading information. There is also an online catalogue, and ordering can be done via an online form that you must print out, then post or fax to them. A newsletter advises on current collecting trends.

WORTH A LOOK

www.husi.ch
A Swiss site with online shopping, auctions, and more.

www.spmc.org
Texas-based Society of Paper Money Collectors.

www.whaco.com
An organization for collectors of historic stocks, bonds, certificates, and autographs.

SEWING ACCESSORIES

Past Glories

www.tias.com/stores/pastglories

This site specializes in vintage needlework accessories and textiles, so thimbles, scissors, pincushions, and pattern books can all be found here. You can buy online, send an email if you require further information before purchasing, or sign up for email notification of new inventories and specials. You will also find related collectibles such as belt buckles and cummerbunds, handkerchiefs, and vintage textiles on the site. Look out for the special "sale" page, which has price reductions on various items of stock.

Thimbles, Etc

www.thimblesetc.com

This site specializes in thimbles, chatelaines, scissors, needle cases, and other sewing accessories, both for practical use and for the collector. Purchases can be made using a printable form that should be sent in the post and you can also buy display cases to house your collections. There's a "Thimbles of the Month" selection, highlighting collectible examples, and you can also send an email to request notification when new items arrive in stock or if you're looking for something particularly special.

Thimbles, Needlework Tools, and Hatpins

freespace.virgin.net/linda.pullen/homepage.htm

This is the site of a keen collector of all of the above, as well as lots of other related items, such as powder compacts. Part of her collection can be seen online and a small selection is for sale, although ordering must be done through the post. Among other features are sections on makers' marks and "Sewing Myths", but particularly useful is the extensive selection of links to other sites that offer information on collecting, as well as warnings of fakes.

Times Past Antiques

freespace.virgin.net/judy.pollitt

This is the site of Judy Pollitt, who trades from London's Portobello Road Market. The site focuses on unusual items and is intended as a web reference tool. Judy specializes in antique needleworking tools, especially thimbles, and current stock is pictured and described, although you cannot buy online. Browse through and send an email or fax for a condition report or price quote if something takes your fancy. There's also a library of items formerly in stock, and a link to Portobello Market's own site.

Vintage Sewing Machines

www.sew2go.com

This Canadian site is dedicated to vintage sewing machines, parts, and accessories. It displays a wide range of machines of all types, and there are useful charts to help you identify your own machine. You will also find a section on the history of the sewing machine, and a list of common technical problems and solutions. There are special features on paint restoration and how to pack sewing machines, written by devotees. Machines that are shown on the site are all available for purchase.

WORTH A LOOK

members.aol.com/jodeli/sew.html
A sewing-machine collector's site with images of a selection of machines.

members.aol.com/JSewCraftM/index.html
Online version of a Californian museum dedicated to sewing.

www.ismacs.net
The International Sewing Machine Collectors' Society.

SILVER AND PLATE

Argentum – The Leopard's Head

www.argentum-theleopard.com

On this American dealer's site there is a chance to learn about, as well as see, antique silver through extremely informative and in-depth articles on the subject. The current available stock is listed alphabetically and by category, and is illustrated along with the prices. Thorough descriptions are provided, which point out various aspects of each piece – including any negative points, which is extremely helpful to a buyer.

Daniel Bexfield Antiques

www.bexfield.co.uk

Daniel Bexfield is one of London's top silver dealers, and sells only solid silver (not plate of any kind) as well as jewellery and objets d'art. His site features some 10,000 images of items in stock, from ear-wax spoons to teapot stands, and you can order any of them online. It also includes features with advice on aspects of buying silverware. (See pages 200–2 for jewellery sites.)

Georg Jensen silver

www.thesilverfund.com

This site is of particular interest to 20th-century silver enthusiasts, as it focuses on the works of Georg Jensen. The site is available in various languages including German, French, Spanish, and Japanese as well as English, and includes an extensive inventory of stock that can be bought online. Separate areas of the site are dedicated to subjects such as jugs, jewellery, flatware, and novelty items. Information on how to identify Georg Jensen silver, including date marks, can also be found here.

Hallmark Database

www.collectiques.net/hallmarks

British silver is usually easy to identify because of the long-standing system of hallmarks. This site offers a thorough guide to these hallmarks, which should enable you to find out where and when your silver was made. The site is free of charge to use, and also covers gold and import marks for items imported into the United Kingdom.

Koopman Ltd

www.rareartlondon.com

The website of one of London's leading silver dealers includes an online inventory of the kind of fine-quality silver for which they are renowned. Click on the images for a closer look, as well as a description. Rare, unusual, and early items are included among the stock, and you can send an email for further information or to purchase something.

Louis Wine

www.louiswine.com

This site is that of a Toronto-based dealer specializing in antique silver and plate as well as jewellery. British, Irish, Continental, and American silver are sold, and, although you can order online, it is best to send an email to check the stock's availability first. The site also includes a search facility of their stock database.

Marks Antiques

www.marksantiques.com

An illustrated company history is featured on the site of this London silver dealer. They are the only antique silver dealers displaying their stock at Harrods,

Specializing in Georg Jensen silver, this site is truly multi-lingual.

and their inventory includes pieces by famous silversmiths such as Paul Storr, Paul de Lamerie, and Hester Bateman. You can shop online from an extensive catalogue of top-quality silverware, or search for specific items.

Nicholas Shaw Antiques

www.nicholas-shaw.com

English, Scottish, and Irish period silver can be found in quantity on this dealer's site. The available stock is subdivided by category, and small items such as nutmeg graters and vinaigrettes are included as well as larger pieces. There's a good selection of Indian colonial and Russian silver. You can also email the dealer to request further details about any of the items on the site or to make other enquiries.

Pillsbury-Michel Fine Silver

www.pillsbury-michel.com

This is the site of American silver dealers that sell antique silver as well as providing a silver-matching service for discontinued patterns, a bridal registry, appraisal services, and engraving. They are the exclusive sellers of the "Raj Cup" – a copy of a late 18th-century Anglo-Indian design used by the British in India. There is also an online form to fill out with your "wish list" and they will search for and locate rare items for you.

Spencer Marks

www.spencermarks.com

Full and enthusiastic descriptions accompany an array of silverware on this site, which offers silver to buy as well as books on the subject. Shop online and choose from a selection that includes 19th-century American silver, English pieces from the reign of George III, and Chinese export silver. As well as buying an item, you can also learn much more about it, as descriptions of stock include historical information and there is a large catalogue of past stock and other items. There is also the opportunity to add yourself to the Spencer Marks paper mailing list, which will mean you will receive catalogues, as well as email notifications whenever the site is updated.

William Walter Antiques
www.silver-antiques.co.uk

The online inventory of this London dealer is particularly strong on George III silver and old Sheffield plate. Click on any item in the stock list for a picture, price, and brief description, and send an email if you would like further information or want to purchase something.

WORTH A LOOK

www.thegoldsmiths.co.uk/AssayOffice/AssayOffice.htm
The website of the London Assay Office includes detailed information on hallmarks.

www.clearlight.com/~schredds
Georgian and Victorian silver and "inspired smalls".

www.silverman-london.com
Silver dealer's site that includes historical information on items.

SLOT MACHINES

Antique Slot Machines
www.antiqueslotmachines.com

This is the site of one of the largest slot machine specialists in the United States. There are no reproduction machines here; all are originals from the 1920s, 1930s, 1940s, and a few from the 1950s. The site includes a virtual museum with video clips. Machines for sale on the site include jukeboxes, gaming machines, and even cash registers. Enquiries can be made either by email or by telephone.

GameRoomAntiques
www.gameroomantiques.com

More than 100 web pages for coin-op enthusiasts can be found here. There are over 500 items from the stock of 50 dealers through this site, including pinball, popcorn, and Coke machines as well as jukeboxes and vending machines. You will find articles on collecting trends and how to repair your machines.

JRD Classics

www.jrdclassics.com

"Blueberry Hill" serenades the visitor to this site, which offers an online coin-op extravaganza. Pinballs, soft drinks machines, pool tables, and much more can be seen on the site. You must call or email for details of price and availability, or you can order a hard copy of the current catalogue.

Pinball Heaven

www.pinballheaven.co.uk

There is technical information, links, and old pinballs for sale at Pinball Heaven. Most of the machines shown are fairly modern, but even if you are a fan of older machines, you might find suitable parts from a long list of spares. Parts and complete machines can be shipped around the world.

Quality Antique Slots

www.sandiegoslots.com

This is the site of a California-based firm that buys and sells slot machines over the Internet. Stock lists are featured online with descriptions, and many are accompanied by photographs. You can request further information or enquire about selling your own machine via email. The firm also offers a repair service for damaged machines.

WORTH A LOOK

marvin3m.com/restore
A guide to restoring vintage pinball machines.

www.arcadewarehouse.com
Classic arcade games.

www.gaming-city.com/coinop28.htm
Antique gaming machines, Coke machines, and jukeboxes for sale.

SNUFF BOTTLES

Antique Snuff Bottle Gallery

www.cyberadx.com/sb-hist.htm

A brief history of snuff bottles introduces this California-based site, which also offers an online gallery. Each bottle can be viewed in a large format if you wish and is accompanied by a detailed commentary. Most bottles are not for sale, as they are from a private collection, but you will find a few that are. You must contact the owners of the site if you would like to make a deal.

International Chinese Snuff Bottle Society

www.snuffbottle.org

The site of this society includes a wealth of information, including FAQs and an explanation of the history of snuff bottles. You will find information on conventions, books for further reading (that can be ordered through the post using a printable form), and you can also search the site using keywords. Membership entitles you to three journals each year, a membership directory, and an invitation to the annual convention. There's an online membership application form, which you must print and post back to them. There is also an online gallery, as well as links to relevant dealers.

Nothing but Tea

www.nothingbuttea.com/snuff1.htm

The name of this site, "nothing but tea", is a bit of a misnomer. While tea-related items are the main attraction, there is also a fine online selection of snuff bottles – mostly from the latter half of the 19th century. Sign up online for an email newsletter and shop online for snuff bottles and, of course, tea and tea wares.

Robert Hall

www.snuffbottle.com

Robert Hall is one of the world's leading specialists in Chinese snuff bottles. His site includes a selection in porcelain, lacquer, glass, jade, and other materials. There's a brief history of the snuff bottle, and you can buy catalogues, many of which are now out of print, by email.

Snuff Bottle Store

www.snuffbottlestore.com

You can learn about Chinese snuff bottles as well as shop online here. There is information on the history of snuff bottles and the symbolism involved in their decoration, as well as a fine selection of them for sale. Stock is subdivided according to materials such as metal, stone, glass, and porcelain. There is a search facility, and you will also find past catalogues of specialist auctions for sale. Other Asian artefacts, such as netsuke and sculpture, are also included on this site.

Topper Gallery

www.topperart.com

A selection of snuff bottles can be seen on the site of this Canadian gallery along with a wealth of other artefacts from Asia, including netsuke and assorted Buddhist works of art. The online snuff bottle selection is not huge, but it only aims to show a small part of the gallery's total inventory. You may also send an email enquiry if you want more details of stock, to register your interests, or purchasing information.

WORTH A LOOK

www.chait.com

Specialist Asian arts auctioneer, whose monthly sales often include Chinese snuff bottles.

www.snuffbottleclub.com

Gives a history of painting on snuff bottles and collecting advice.

SPORTING COLLECTIBLES

Angling Artifacts

www.angling-artifacts.com

A whole host of links to the sites of international angling museums (including one in Tokyo) is one of the many attractions of this American site. It also offers a wide selection of reels, rods, tackle boxes, and even jewellery with an angling theme. You must submit an email enquiry before ordering, as many items go quickly and are offered on a "first come, first served" basis.

Antique Billiard Tables and Accessories

www.antiquebilliardtables.com

Lights, chairs, ball racks, and other antique accessories can be found on this site, as well as a selection of antique tables. The billiard tables shown all come with a full description, including provenance. You cannot buy directly online but there are contact details that explain how to get further information. The site is especially useful for its list of around 500 links to other billiard, snooker, pool, and related sites.

Canadian Golf Hall of Fame

www.cghf.org

Canada is the birthplace of golf on the North American continent, and this site is dedicated to the ever-popular game. It is the online home of an actual museum in Montreal, and you can take a "virtual tour" through a series of pictures of displays at the museum. There are 18 displays (one for each hole of a golf course!) and you can view antique equipment, clothing, trophies, and accessories from them, while learning about the development of the sport.

Cricket Books and Memorabilia

www.bowmore.demon.co.uk

As the title suggests, anything to do with the game of cricket can be found on this site. There are autographs of famous players for sale, and old editions of that cricket lover's bible, *Wisden's Almanack*, as well as programmes and other material. Sports such as boxing and golf are also represented on the site. Stock lists include full descriptions and prices, and orders are accepted via telephone, email, or snail mail.

Equestrian and Sporting Antiques

www.sportingcollection.com

Stirrups, bits, spurs, saddlery, equestrian books and prints, and even rocking horses can be found on this site. It is owned by a vet who was once a "horse-mad schoolgirl" and whose fondness for the four-footed beasts continues to this day. Most of the items shown are from her private collection, but she is prepared to trade some of them. The site is especially interesting for its historical information on subjects such as saddles and their evolution.

Golfingly Yours

www.golfinglyyours.com

Autographed photos of top players, antique clubs, and sketches of famous courses by those who designed them are among the collectibles you can buy on this site, which is guaranteed to please the most discerning golf enthusiast. Various modern and recent limited-edition collectibles rub shoulders with older items, and the older collectibles come with a guarantee of authenticity.

King's Golf and Sporting Antiques

www.sportsantiques.com

Golf is clearly the preferred game on this site, which offers various luxury goods as well as antiques, but antiques, artefacts, and memorabilia relating to various other sports are also included. In particular, there's a section on "English Sports", offering vintage cricket bats and balls, rugby balls, and polo equipment. There is also a selection of memorabilia such as autographs relating to sporting celebrities. You can shop online.

International Association of Sports Museums and Halls of Fame

www.sportshalls.com

This site puts the user in touch with sports museums around the world. Sports from archery to wrestling are covered, and you can search for museums by the sport or geographical location. Opening hours and admission prices of the various institutions are listed, as is a description of their collections and links to websites where appropriate.

Lion Street Books

www.boxingstuff.com

You will find plenty of boxing stuff on this site, which features extensive stock lists of books, photos, posters, and ephemera relating to the sport. There's a guide to the conditions of all the boxing collectibles, their prices are given in pounds sterling and US dollars, and you can buy them online with your credit card. The site also includes a section on wrestling and, if you can't find what you want, register a "wish list" and you'll be notified when they have it.

Mullock Madeley

www.mullock-madeley.co.uk

This is the site of a leading UK specialist auctioneer. Browse through catalogues of forthcoming specialist sales, which might be of anything from fishing tackle to aviation memorabilia. Golf, tennis, cricket, football, and rugby are particular specialities of this company. This is not an online auction, although you can submit email bids. The catalogues that can be seen on the website are thorough and there is an extensive online archive that should be useful for reference purposes.

Not just a bookshop, this site has various items related to boxing on offer.

Old Lures and Antique Tackle

www.oldlures.org

This is very much a site for the keen fishing enthusiast. It focuses on old fishing lures, or baits, and shows a variety of colourful examples. Advertising paraphernalia relating to these fishermen's friends can also be seen here and antique tackle and other fishing accessories are included too. This is the site of a collector who wants to add to his own collection, rather than sell anything. Visitors are invited to submit details of their own possessions for a free valuation, which may also come with an offer to buy, so it is worth doing if you have something to sell. Enquiries about any aspect of fishing collectibles are also welcomed.

The Olde Sport Shoppe

www.theoldesportshoppe.com

This California-based sporting antiques dealer offers a wide range of sporting collectibles online. Golf, basketball, baseball, badminton, tennis, and table tennis are among the sports represented. Fill in the online request form if you would like more details about items shown on the site, or if you want to buy something. The Olde Sport Shoppe also welcomes enquiries from those who have something to sell.

Online Sporting Memorabilia Auction

www.sportsauction.com

American sports such as baseball and US football feature strongly on this specialist auction site, but there's enough to interest users from other parts of the world too. Other sports covered by the site include boxing and hockey. Memorabilia on offer includes cards, photos, press passes, and various personal items of sporting heroes.

River & Rowing Museum

www.rrm.co.uk

Henley-on-Thames in Oxfordshire could be described as the spiritual home of British rowing, thanks to its world-famous regatta. It also has a River and Rowing Museum, and this is its official website. There are images of the galleries here and an historical account of the development of the sport of rowing. The site has a strong educational content, including information for schools, and there are links to sites dedicated to rowing history. This is a site that will be worth revisiting, as the museum has just received a grant to put more of its collection online.

Schotten Antiques

www.schotten.com

This is the website of a very well-known, UK-based, dealer in sporting antiques and memorabilia. Golf clubs and balls and tennis rackets are particularly well represented on this site but it also has a whole range of other things, including sporting trophies. Browse through an online selection, complete with photographs, and use the online form to order something, or send an email for further enquiries.

Sporting Memorabilia of Warwick

www.sportizus.com

Whether you are interested in motor racing, tennis, rugby, cricket, or any one of a long list of the many other sports that there are, you will find sporting antiques and memorabilia to suit you on this site, along with very good photographs, descriptions, and prices to accompany them. Stock lists are subdivided according to the sport in question and there's definitely an eclectic mix of items – you might find anything from a 1920s ball in the cricket section to a 1940s bicycle pump under cycling. All the items can be purchased directly online and there is also a keyword search facility for finding specific products more quickly. The site is particularly well maintained and it is also updated three times a week.

Sports Autographs

www.dspace.dial.pipex.com/town/terrace/od12/sports.htm

Autographs from the world of sports are offered through this site: athletics, boxing, cricket, football, golf, and motor racing are all covered. Check for an item's availability before ordering, as, although you cannot buy directly online with a credit card, you can buy via mail. The site also features a private sales area where individuals can buy and sell (there is a charge to sell, however, which will either be a flat fee or a percentage of the sale). The sale items are worth checking out, although these are not all sport-related.

Traditional Angling Products

www.traditional-angling.co.uk

If you thought that vintage fishing tackle was only bought for display, then think again. The site of this traditional tackle shop, based in Staffordshire, England, includes a gallery of fish caught by customers using tackle bought from the shop. There are also numerous brief online articles about traditional angling and equipment and there's a selection of books on offer. Modern tackle is also stocked here. You can order any of the items via email, telephone, fax, or post.

True Blue Collectables

www.truebluecollectables.com

This site bills itself as the place "where the legends live" and, with such a large online selection, it's easy to see why. Sports represented range from horse racing to cricket and from boxing to basketball and, if you request the monthly email newsletter, you can be entered into a draw to win autographs and memorabilia. Search the online catalogue and shop online, or follow the links to auction sites.

WORTH A LOOK

www.fantiques.com/sports/sports.html
Sporting antiques and collectibles for sale.

www.memorylnsports.com
Sports collectibles, autographs, and sound recordings of big events.

www.scottishmultimedia.co.uk/Writing/RacingBooks.htm
Antiquarian and secondhand horse racing and equestrian books.

www.sportingantiques.co.uk
Cornwall-based dealer in sporting antiques.

www.sportsartifacts.com
Memorabilia site that is particularly strong on baseball, but caters for many other sports too.

www.uk.cricket.org/link_to_database/SOCIETIES/ENG/CMS
Home page of the Cricket Memorabilia Society.

STAMPS

British Library Philatelic Collections

portico.bl.uk/collections/philatelic

The British Library Collections, some of the world's most important, are featured on this site. Background and historical information on the various collections is given, and many of the stamps are illustrated. There is information on gaining access to the physical collections for those who wish to visit.

Casper's Weird Stamps

www.raster.it/stefano/a

A fun site that offers the chance to "identify your weird stamps and at the same time help other people out". Its main feature is a gallery of stamps that are considered unidentifiable by their owners or, at least, are not featured in most standard catalogues. Submit your ideas, or a scan of any stamps you are unable to identify – someone in cyberspace might be able to solve the mystery.

Find That Elusive Stamp

www.stampfinder.com

Billed as the global stamp exchange, Stamp Finder includes a searchable database of stamps that can be bought online. There's an e-zine with news from the stamp world, a dealer's mall, and a "dealers only" area. There's also a calendar of events, and you can register your stamp "wants", receiving email notification of items as they become available.

Stamp2.com (see page 262) has 4,000-plus links and a wealth of articles, stamp news, etc.

For All Stamp Collectors

www.philatelic.com

A large stamp-collecting website that was established in 1994, philatelic.com offers an extensive range of services for the collector. There's a chatroom and bulletin board, an online mall, and lots of stamp-related software for sale. You can also send an e-postcard, or browse through links to a multitude of philatelic sites.

JJF's Philatelic Links

www.spacecovers.com/links/links_philatelics.htm

This site has a vast array of links to stamp sites. The links are divided by category and include several to related sites, such as postcard collecting. Each link is accompanied by a brief description of the site, so you will know what to expect before you visit them.

Peter's Stamps

www.petersstamps.com

A complete catalogue of all British stamps issued since 1924, including those of the Channel Islands and the Isle of Man, is the main feature of this site. There are also lists of stamps for sale, which can be ordered through the site, an extensive list of links to other philatelic sites, and a useful glossary of philatelic terms and abbreviations.

Resource Site for Collectors

www.stamplink.com

Stamp Link is a web resource for stamp collectors, and includes reviews of websites as well as links. Sites that are linked include auctioneers, clubs and societies, and dealer sites. New Zealand is especially well represented, as there is a page of links exclusively for sites that are either based in that country and/or are dedicated to its stamps.

Sandafayre

www.stampauction.com

A wealth of online reference material can be found on this site, which offers articles on philately including contributions from resident expert James MacKay. As its title suggests, there are also auctions and you can search lots for specific items, browse lots by country, or view lots as they appear in the catalogues. You must register to take part, but this is free of charge.

Stamp2.com

www.stamp2.com

With more than 4,000 links in total, this must be the most exhaustive stamp links site of all. The home page is enticing, with links to the latest "News and Headlines" from the stamp world as well as articles and other philately sites. There is information and advice on practically everything a stamp collector would need to know about – from issuing countries to types of perforation. The site also offers stamp trivia and the chance to get in touch with other collectors in the "Community" section.

Stanley Gibbons

www.stanleygibbons.com

The online home of the world's oldest stamp dealers offers the chance to shop for accessories like albums and magnifiers as well as the stamps themselves. There are online auctions, a free online newsletter, and details of events and special offers. Advice on your collection is available via email, and you can seek out information about particular stamps using the site's search facility.

WORTH A LOOK

www.gbps.org.uk
The Great Britain Philatelic Society.

www.linns.com
Web resource for all things philatelic.

www.philately.net
Stamps for sale plus web resources.

www.stampshows.co.uk
Information on UK stamp events.

TEDDY BEARS

Baba Bears

www.bababears.co.uk

Teddy bears from c.1904 right up to the 1970s can be bought from this site, as well as soft toys such as gollies and nightdress cases from the same era. British makes such as Chad Valley, Merrythought, and Farnell are well represented, as is the legendary German make of Steiff plus a selection of American bears. There are articles on bears, links to various bear sites and museums, and, if you are not sure if your pockets are deep enough to buy, you can pay for anything that takes your fancy in instalments.

Bears and Beyond

www.bearsandbeyond.com

This is a Canadian teddy bear Internet store that focuses largely on artist bears – German bears are a particular speciality. There's an A–Z of bear artists, a discussion forum, and details of news and events currently occurring in the teddy bear world too. There are also bear postcards that you can purchase directly online and you can find advice on various topics including designing your own bear web page as well.

Cyberspace Doll and Teddy Bear Show

wwvisions.com/craftbb/cyber

This site is made up of a series of bulletin boards that put teddy bear and doll enthusiasts in touch with each other and give them information on their hobby. Browse through for sale/wanted ads, locate sources of supplies and accessories, and exchange information on clubs, classes, and shows. (See pages 167–9 for other doll sites.)

The Great Teddy Bear Hug

www.teddybears.com

Information, addresses, and some links to websites of magazines, shows, and collecting clubs can all be found on this site. Details of books on teddies are also given, and there's a useful glossary. There is also a section on the International Golliwog Collectors' Club, including articles on these toys and details of how you can join the club.

Merrythought

www.merrythought.co.uk

The site of the leading English bear maker (established in 1930) includes a full version of the firm's current catalogue, and you can place orders online. Also included is a complete history of the firm, and a chance to join the Merrythought International Collectors' Club.

The Old Bear Company

www.oldbear.co.uk

This is the website of a shop that deals exclusively in old bears and soft toys. There are lots of pictures of bears and other animals for sale on the site by makers such as Steiff, Merrythought, Chiltern, and Chad Valley. These all come complete with descriptions, and you can order them directly via email. There is also a useful links page to various bear-related sites. (See pages 269–72 for toy sites.)

Steiff

www.steiff.com
www.steiffusa.com

A menagerie of soft toys awaits on this site, but it's for teddy bears that Steiff is still best known, and there are lots to choose from in the firm's catalogue. Discover the history of the teddy bear, read information on the Steiff Museum, or visit the Steiff Club pages, where you can contact like-minded collectors and buy, sell, or exchange bears. The site has two versions, one of which is tailored to users in the United States.

Teddy Bear UK

www.teddy-bear-uk.com

Biographical information on famous bears such as Pooh and Paddington (not to mention their creators) is featured on this site, which is a web resource for UK bear collectors. Find out how to identify and care for your bear, take a tour of the online museum, learn about bear makers and their histories, and even find out how to make your very own bear. There's an online shopping mall where you can buy online, a map with listings of bear shops, and links galore to clubs, societies, and bear repairers.

Teddy Bears Den

www.teddybearsden.com

This site focuses mainly on modern collectible bears, rather than older examples. The online shop has bears by some of the best-known bear artists from all over the world. You can also buy kits and patterns and learn about bear terminology and how to make a bear. Messages can be exchanged with other enthusiasts, there's a bear search engine, and you can send an email teddy bear postcard.

Teddy Bears on the Net

www.tbonnet.com

One of the oldest teddy bear resource sites, this one has been going since 1995. It provides information on bear artists, galleries, books, and also has a history of the world's favourite soft toy. Contact fellow collectors, find out information about the care and repair of these toys, or submit details and a picture of your bear for identification.

WORTH A LOOK

www.bearsbythesea.com
Californian bear site.

www.justbears.net
Toronto teddy bear shop.

www.theteddiestrader.com
Teddy club with items for sale as well as much more.

TEXTILES

Antique Quilt Source

www.antiquequiltsource.com

Based in the heart of Pennsylvania's quilt-making country, the Antique Quilt Source is America's largest mail-order antique quilt company, and it has been in business for more than 20 years. Most of the quilts were made between 1840 and 1940, and you can see a large selection of them online, alongside prices and detailed accompanying text. This makes the site a good pictorial reference source of quilt types. You can order a copy of the catalogue online, but if you wish to buy something, you should telephone them or download a postal order form.

The Honiton Lace Shop

www.honitonlace.com

Lace from the English town of Honiton is famous all round the world, and this shop, which is based in the Devon town, has a fine selection of it. The site shows images of the shop's interior and examples of stock, dating from the 16th century to the present day. Collars, handkerchiefs, bridal veils, and many more items are featured, along with their prices, and you can shop online. As well as Honiton lace, there's also a good selection of Continental lace items to choose from.

Joachim and Betty Mendes Antique Lace & Textiles

www.mendes.co.uk

This is the site of Brighton-based specialist dealers who offer lace, textiles, and fans to interested parties. Bedcovers, cushions, shawls, curtains, and many other items can be seen on their site. Pictures and prices of their stock are included, punctuated by informative snippets of textile and lace-making trivia. You should send the company an email for further details if you see something that you particularly like.

This American site has a wealth of antique lace and linen for sale.

Joanna Booth Antiques

www.joannabooth.co.uk

Fine tapestries, many dating from the 16th century, can be viewed on the site of this London dealer, who also offers Old Master drawings and sculpture (see fine art on pages 177–88). There are views of the dealer's gallery and there is also an online form for requests and feedback. You cannot buy online, but enquiries by email or telephone from potential buyers are welcomed.

M Finkel & Daughter

www.samplings.com

This American company is a specialist dealer in schoolgirl needlework. The online site offers samplers and silk embroideries for sale, with pictures that can be enlarged. Detailed research accompanies each offering. An article entitled "historical context" gives a brief background of the subject, but the descriptions of each sampler tell the real story. Excerpts from various publications give information about the owners of this business. There is a discussion of conservation, and a "resource" section provides links to online sites for genealogical research. There is also an extensive bibliography.

The Old Lace and Linen Shop

www.antiquelinen.com

This Florida-based shop boasts a vast array of antique textiles on its site, from bed linens and hand towels to runners, tray cloths, doilies, christening gowns, curtains, and much, much more. Stock pictured on the site is accompanied by informative descriptions. You can request further details by email if you would like to buy any of the items you see. You must, however, send payment for the items by post.

Pamela Simon Vintage Fabrics

www.vintagefabrics.com

Fabrics from the 1940s to the 1960s are the stock in trade of this American dealer, whose site shows various samples online; click on a sample to view the detail in a larger format. The site has advice for those who would like to order – the most important point is to make sure you know exactly how much fabric your project needs first as there is only a finite supply available. Payment is by credit card or in advance by cheque through the post.

Rocky Mountain Quilts

www.rockymountainquilts.com

Two hundred years of quilt making is celebrated at the online home of this American firm, which specializes in quilts from 1740 to 1940. A large selection of quilts can be seen on the site, but an even wider selection of pictures can be sent to you via email on your request. You cannot buy online, but can contact the gallery for details of any items you may be interested in. The site also has details of Rocky Mountain's quilt restoration service, which can be carried out through the post.

Stephen and Carol Huber

www.antiquesamplers.com

This is the site of one of America's foremost dealers in antique samplers and girlhood embroideries. It includes concise definitions of terms that apply to needlework: sampler, memorial, silk-embroidered pictures, canvaswork, stumpwork, etc. Also included is a list of fairs and directions to their physical shop, which is open only by appointment. A number of pieces in each of the categories they deal in are illustrated, along with full descriptions, sizes, and prices. Calendars are available for sale and each month is illustrated with a sampler and full description (useful to keep as a pictorial reference even after the year is over).

The Textile Restoration Studio

www.textilerestoration.co.uk

An insight into the work of the textile conservator/restorer is offered on this site. It is run by professionals in this field and, while its purpose is of course to advertise their own services, visitors should learn a lot themselves. A list of FAQs gives advice on some common restoration/conservation problems and you can browse through a catalogue of suitable products that are not usually available through retail outlets if you would like to "do it yourself". There's also information on lectures and courses if you would like to learn more.

Textiles, Rugs, and Tribal Art

www.cloudband.com

Cloudband.com is a large site dedicated to serving the needs of anyone with an interest in textiles (European and Asian), rugs, and tribal art (see pages 240–2 for rug sites). It offers a comprehensive range of services including an online shopping mall, which features several internationally known dealers. To interact fully on the site, you must first register via an online form, although this is free of charge. As well as the mall, other features include FAQs, lists of useful links, a discussion forum, a detailed online magazine, and the opportunity to subscribe to a monthly newsletter.

Vintage Textile

www.vintagetextile.com

Antique linen, lace, damask, silks, and much more can be found on the site of this New England-based dealer. You can shop online here from a large selection of towels, pillows, shawls, and curtains of yesteryear, some of which are still in mint condition. A collection of vintage clothing and costume is also shown and these, too, can be purchased through the site (see also pages 162–4 for costume and fashion sites).

WORTH A LOOK

www.artofp.com/persian_art.htm

Mostly Persian textiles in stock, with an overview of Persian art history.

www.needlearts.com/articles/articles.html

Articles on needlecraft can be found here, including some that describe the restoration of antique textiles.

www.textileconservator.pair.com

A US-based conservator offers advice and also shows examples of treatments.

TOYS AND GAMES

Alvin's Vintage Games and Toys

freespace.virgin.net/hidden.valley

This fun, quirky, imaginative, and rather noisy site is that of London-based Alvin's Vintage Games, who offer board games dating back to the 19th century. More recent examples from the 1950s, '60s, and '70s are also included, as are jigsaw puzzles and toys relating to Disney. There are also puppets galore, from Pinky and Perky to *Magic Roundabout* characters. You can buy online – items are illustrated with detailed descriptions – and there is a useful chart for working out postage rates to various parts of the world.

Barry Potter Auctions

www.barrypotterauctions.com

This is the site of a specialist firm of auctioneers whose interests lie in toys such as Dinky, Corgi, and Matchbox cars, as well as model railways. You can browse through the catalogues of their forthcoming auctions and buy hard copies online, as well as subscribe to a free email newsletter. All prices and estimates for the items are given in pounds sterling but, if this is not your currency, exchange rates can be found on the site too. There's also a shop, where you can buy items directly online.

Big Red Toy Box

www.bigredtoybox.com

This is a superb web resource for all toy lovers. The site's features include a highly informative toy encyclopedia, and a message board where you can post a question if you still can't find the information you want. Visit the Repros section to find reproduction replacement parts for a wide range of toys. There are also opportunities to take a look at fellow enthusiasts' collections, or buy and sell via the online flea market.

For Die-Cast Toy Enthusiasts

www.toynutz.com

Toynutz is the website of the Toy Car Collectors' Association, and it covers all popular makes and some lesser-known ones. There are nostalgic reprints of Husky, Corgi, and other makers' catalogues for sale, and showcases of classic die-cast toys. Links take you to stockists, manufacturers, toy museums, and clubs around the world, and there's even advice on how to start your own collectors' club.

The Forgotten Toyshop

www.forgottentoys.co.uk

Action Man is a firm favourite on the website of The Forgotten Toyshop. On this site you will find figures of this British answer to GI Joe as well as various uniforms and accessories. Visit the "wants" page to register your interests if you cannot find what you are looking for. If you do find something you like you can pay by various methods including cheques through the post and credit cards, although your details must be submitted via a printed form, faxed, or sent through the mail. Other items in stock include TV-related toys of various kinds and overseas telephone enquiries are welcomed (staff speak Japanese as well as English).

GPCC Toy Collectors Club

www.ultranet.com/~ed

If you remember your toys from the 1950s, 1960s, and 1970s, then this collectors' site is dedicated to helping you find them today. There are links to websites including auction and dealer sites, advice, and honest reviews.

Hasbro

www.hasbro.co.uk

The colourful UK site of the famous games manufacturer lists its current top sellers and recent additions on its home page. In the online shop section you can register your own personal profile, stating the age group you are interested in, and buy a huge range of products online. The "Gift Guide" will provide suggestions if you are stuck for ideas.

Hornby

www.hornby.com

The well-known British model railway manufacturer has its complete catalogue online, so you can browse through the firm's latest trains, track, and accessories. A company history is included, and you can also join the Hornby Club online. The site features competitions and links to the sites of railway companies.

John F Green Inc

www.greenmodels.com

Airfix, Tamiya, Revell – these are names that will be familiar to keen model-makers. Kits by these and many other manufacturers are available on the site of John F Green, who buys and sells mostly out-of-production kits. Some are from TV and film series, while others are World War II or classic ship models. Search for your favourites, and buy them online.

Master Collector Online

www.mastercollector.com

Describing itself as the ultimate source for doll and toy collectors, this site certainly has an impressive selection of links to the sites of toy dealers and manufacturers. It is particularly strong on dolls and action figures, but its main attraction is a classified ads section that thousands of collectors buy and sell on. You must pay for full access to this, which costs £5/$8 a month. (See pages 167–9 for other doll sites.)

Neatstuff

www.neatstuff.net

If your idea of neat stuff includes vintage board games, tinplate robots, and sci-fi toys, then this American site is for you. Examples of toys you thought you'd forgotten forever are pictured in all their glory, with detailed descriptions. You can order any of them online via a secure server.

Old Toy Soldier Home

www.oldtoysoldierhome.com

Britains, Mignot, and all the best-known toy soldier makers are represented on the site of this California-based toy dealer. And not just soldiers – knights, Romans, Egyptians, and accessories such as dioramas can be found here too. You can buy online, choosing from a wide range of figures, old and new. There are numerous links to toy dealers, clubs, magazines, and manufacturers, including some that may well be new to you.

Raving Toy Maniac

www.toymania.com

If your love of collecting action figures has become an obsession, then this is the perfect place for you. It's worth visiting the site just for the seemingly never-ending list of links to the sites of collectors' clubs, image archives, manufacturers, and toy dealers. This website also includes news from the toy industry, advice and hints for collectors, and visitors can buy the latest collectible playthings directly online.

Resource for Toy Collectors

www.toy-box.com

Toy Box is a useful resource for all serious toy collectors, but especially those who are engaged in research. It includes lists of all the main toy makers, information on trademarks used by them, and has a searchable database of manufacturers. There are also online auctions and a specialist bookshop available to peruse and buy from.

Tinplate Toys

www.sable.co.uk/tinplate

Describing itself as the essential site for all lovers of tinplate toys, new or antique, this site certainly has a lot to offer the enthusiast. You can buy from an online toyshop, or follow links to toy dealers from around the world. Other useful links are to hobby magazines and toy museums in the UK and Germany, as well as Japan.

Toydorado

www.toydorado.com

Toydorado is a German site (with a version in English) and it offers an extensive gallery of tinplate toys, including robots and space toys, die-cast cars, and much more. Details including size, history, and year of manufacture are included, and everything can be ordered online. A links page takes you to various dealer and collector sites, including sites dedicated to specialist interests such as Dinky, Matchbox, Space Toys, and so on.

Vectis

www.vectis.co.uk

Toys, especially of the die-cast Dinky and Corgi variety, are to be found in abundance on this specialist auctioneer's site. Catalogues from forthcoming sales are featured, and there's also a searchable database of past catalogues, which are invaluable for research purposes and up-to-date prices. There is a handy guide to the auction process, and you can bid via email. Vectis are also interested in hearing from anyone with toys to sell – there is a form you can fill in online with details of anything you may have to offer.

Vintage Toy Train Shop

www.vintagetoys.co.uk

Toy trains by makers such as Bassett Lowke, Hornby, and Bing are the speciality of this UK dealer, who also offers books on this field of collecting. You can shop online, but an email or phone call to check availability before ordering is recommended. Choose from a wide range of trains plus accessories such as figures and even spare light bulbs for your locomotive.

WORTH A LOOK

www.antiqueclocksandtoys.com

Dealer's site with wind-up tinplate toys, cast-iron money banks, and much more.

www.tqag.com

American auctioneer specializing in toys, dolls, and teddy bears.

www.viatek.net/antiques

Toy dealer's site that is particularly rich in old pedal-cars.

WINE AND WINE-RELATED ITEMS

Christopher Sykes Antiques

www.sykes-corkscrews.co.uk

Christopher Sykes Antiques are based near historic Woburn Abbey in Bedfordshire, England, and they deal in wine-related antiques of all kinds. Their website shows off a selection of stock that includes items such as wine cradles as well as corkscrews. Pictures shown are purely representative examples of stock, since turnover is high. You can, however, order a hard copy of the latest catalogue and the firm runs an efficient mail-order service.

Corkscrew Centre

www.corkscrewcentre.com

This is the site for anyone interested in corkscrews and similar wine-related collectibles. Shop online and choose from a vast selection by British, German, Scandinavian, Italian, and other makers. Items offered include the mundane as well as novelty items and there is a number of bottle openers and penknives as well as corkscrews. You can also add to your library, as there is a selection of specialist books listed here.

CorkscrewNet

www.corkscrewnet.com

This site is a web resource for all corkscrew collectors, featuring links to all kinds of related sites. There's a "Hall of Fame" on the site, devoted to those who have made an impact on this hobby, and links to societies in various countries. You will also find advice on caring for your collection, which includes hints and tips on cleaning.

The Kent Collection

www.claretjugs.com

A history of claret jugs and of wine itself is included on the website of this private American collection. Its main appeal, however, lies in its huge display of claret jugs of outstanding quality. Items in this collection are discussed in detail and you can choose to view the collection by historical period, style, or make. Unfortunately you can only look, as the items are not for sale, but you can contact the owner if you have a top-quality jug you wish to sell.

Patricia Harbottle

www.corkscrews.uk.co

Corkscrews, wine bottles, and wine-related silver are the stock in trade of this UK-based dealer. Corkscrews are particularly in evidence on this site, which has a good selection, and includes novelty examples. The site also has a search facility to find specific items and you can buy any of the items you find online by credit card, although send an email first to check their availability.

Schredds of Portobello

www.schredds.com/winelabs.htm

Schredds sell small antique silver, mainly 18th- and 19th-century pieces, and items range from caddy spoons to sugar tongs (see also silver and plate on pages 249–52). There is a sizeable selection of wine-related silver shown on this website and this includes neck labels, wine funnels, and coasters. You can buy an item through the site, but you must first send an email enquiry to the shop to receive the full details.

Winebid

www.winebid.com

Billed as the premier online wine auction site, Winebid offers a wide selection of fine and rare wines. Wines on offer are consigned for sale by private collectors, or directly by the winery itself. Register to bid, which is free, although you will be asked for your credit card details and proof that you are over 21. Bidders pay a buyer's premium, which is a percentage of the hammer price. Vendors also pay a premium on any items that are sold, although listing them is free. If you do not want to take part, you can browse the site for free, and search for results of recent Winebid auctions.

WORTH A LOOK

www.antique-wine.com
Vintage wine gift-sets to suit special anniversaries or birthdays.

www.btinternet.com/~chateauxwines
Bristol-based wine merchants with a good range of vintage tipples.

WOOD AND TREEN

Joel S Perkins & Son

www.joelsperkins.com

This American site specializes in antique wooden bobbins, and offers a selection for sale online. They come in various shapes and sizes, and some have been turned into candlesticks. The site also has a miscellaneous selection of other bygones including shoe lasts.

Manor Farm Barn Antiques

www.btwebworld.com/mfbantiques

Treen is well represented among the stock of this UK dealer, who also sells oak and country furniture and kitchenalia (see pages 193–5 and 203–5 for other related sites). You cannot buy online but the site features a selection of pictures of stock as examples and you can send an email for more details. The site includes a list of fairs where Manor Farm Barn Antiques will be attending, and you can email them to request complimentary tickets for any of these events.

Michael Wisehall

www.wisehall.com

This Dublin-based dealer sells 18th- and 19th-century furniture and metalware, but also carries a good selection of "interesting and unusual items", including a lot of treen. Typical stock might range from a fruitwood bottle corker to a wooden model of a coal truck. Send an email for more details about any item that interests you.

Nancy Neale Typecraft

www.woodtype.com

This unusual site is devoted to antique wooden type, of the sort used in printing advertising handbills and so on, dating roughly from between 1820 and 1940. Numerous examples of letters and typefaces are shown in walnut, mahogany, maple, birch, and cherry. The site also explains the history of these collectibles. They can be bought online and are marketed as unique gifts, especially suitable for anyone in the advertising or print business.

S Scott Powers Antiques

www.burlsnuff.com

This is the site of a New York-based dealer who specializes in treen and snuff boxes (see pages 254–5 for snuff bottle sites) as well as other small objects in materials such as horn. The site includes a definition of treen and a selection of objects for sale. You will find mortars, scent flasks, mangle boards, and various other wooden items on this site. Objects shown are given comprehensive descriptions, including information on their origins and uses. Send an email enquiry if you're interested in buying anything you see. You will also find a list of recommended reading and some of these books are also for sale.

WORTH A LOOK

www.kickingbullgallery.com

Native American and American folk art site with a good selection of wooden items for sale.

www.marquetrysociety.ca/Techniques.html

Information on Tunbridge Ware and how it's made.

www.mauchlineclub.org

Site dedicated to Mauchline ware.

GLOSSARY

Chat Live chatrooms let you "talk" to other people using your web browser in real time. You type your reply and then read the answers as soon as they are written. Chat forums are web-based bulletin boards. You leave questions and answers on a web page, and visit the site hours or days later to check out the replies.

Directory A massive list of websites, which has been organized into handy categories to aid searching.

Domain An essential component of a web address, the domain name of a site can offer substantial clues about its nature (see URL below).

Download When you open a web page in your computer's web browser program, you are actually downloading information onto your hard disk. This information will be automatically deleted from your computer after a certain period of time. You can also download files from the Internet, such as software drivers for your printer.

Emoticon A picture made out of text characters used to denote an emotion. They are handy to use to depict the mood you are trying to express, which can otherwise be difficult in an email. The smiley :) or :-) is one type of emoticon.

Encryption Used to encode information to prevent unauthorized access. All good online shops will use some kind of encryption to protect its customers' details from criminals.

FAQs Frequently Asked Questions. A list of answers to common questions about a site or subject that new visitors might ask.

Flash Software used by web authors to make their sites look nicer and possibly more interactive. If you don't have a Flash plugin installed, you won't be able to use the site as intended, although the more considerate web authors build in a basic version of the site for people with older Internet browsers.

Frames A technique used on websites that creates separate areas on a screen. All modern browsers support frames nowadays, as they are incredibly popular with web authors.

FTP File Transfer Protocol. A way of providing files that can be downloaded using either a web browser or a dedicated FTP program. You would also use FTP to upload your files when creating a website.

Gif A type of graphics file often used to create small pictures, logos, and buttons on websites.

Hacker Someone who can access computers using advanced networking techniques. They are far more likely to infiltrate the networks of large companies than your home computer.

HTML Hypertext Markup Language. The computer language that is used to create web pages.

HTTP HyperText Transfer Protocol. The software used to send web page information from the server to your browser.

Hyperlink A selected word or phrase, picture, or button that provides access to another part of a website when clicked with a mouse.

Internet A global network of computers, providing many services including the world wide web.

ISP Internet Service Provider. This is the company you use to gain access to the Internet. Home computers use modems to dial into the ISP, which then forwards information from the Internet onto your screen. When you send an email message, it leaves your computer and passes through the ISP onto the Internet, towards its destination.

Jpeg A type of graphic file that uses compression to allow the production of photo-quality pictures that download quickly.

Lurker Someone who reads messages posted in chat forums and on Newsgroups, without contributing. It is advisable to lurk for a while, before joining a new discussion group so that you can check whether or not it is suitable for you.

Mac A type of personal computer made by Apple.

Mirror A copy of a website. Mirrors of very popular websites are made all over the world, so that Internet users can use the closest one and therefore get faster performance.

Modem A device used by computers to establish Internet connections over a phone line. Most can also be used to send and receive faxes.

Newsgroups An area of the Internet consisting of thousands of very specific bulletin boards where people can share ideas and opinions.

Offline It is possible to download pages from the Internet onto your hard disk and view them after you have disconnected from the Internet. Doing this is called working offline.

Online When a computer is connected to the Internet, it is online.

Operating system The software that allows a computer to run programs like word processors, web browsers, and games.

PC The most popular type of home computer, PCs are made by a large number of different companies.

Plugin A piece of software that increases the abilities of a web browser program, allowing it to read more complex web pages.

Proxy A computer on the Internet that offers slightly better performance to certain websites. ISPs sometimes provide proxy servers to their subscribers as an optional extra.

Search engine A feature on some websites that attempts to index the websites on the Internet, providing visitors with the opportunity to search through its records.

Server A program on a computer that provides a service. Websites exist on web servers, email is dealt with by email servers, and files can be moved to and from FTP servers.

Shockwave As with Flash, a website that uses Shockwave requires you to install a plugin to reap the benefit of its features. It is normally used to improve a website's design.

Site A collection of web pages held under the same domain name. They are easy to find because they are all linked together in one place.

SSL Secure Sockets Layer. This security feature, which is found in all good web browsers, uses encryption to exchange information between computers. It is used by conscientious online shops to protect customers' details from the potential threat of criminals.

TLD Top Level Domain. The ".com", ".org", and ".co.uk" part of a web or email address.

URL Uniform Resource Locator. The technical name for a web address, for example, http://www.apple.com/press.htm, which is made up of the following components:

http:// – The network software used to distribute web page data.
www. – The first part of the web server's name.
apple – The name of the computer that holds the pages.
.com – The top level domain name (TLD).
/press.htm – A web page.

Virus This is a malignant computer program, more likely to be found hyped up in newspaper reports and Hollywood films than actually on your hard disk. Viruses are usually transferred when programs are downloaded, and are often received as an attachment to an email.

Web browser A program that displays web pages. There are different types and versions, although they all perform the same function. Later versions tend to work better with some websites. Microsoft's Internet Explorer and Netscape's Navigator are the most popular.

WAV files Sound files that can be downloaded from the Internet and played through your computer.

www The world wide web. Arguably the easiest part of the Internet to use, the web contains over a billion pages of information.

INDEX

A

D

E

F

G

H

I

N

O

P

T

U

V

ACK FORM

e sites described in this book have been thoroughly checked and were ect at the time of going to press, however, due to the very nature of the ernet, sites are changing constantly with new ones springing up daily. It is ievitable that many worthwhile sites will not have made it into this edition but there is always next time!

If you would like to suggest a site for possible inclusion in the next edition of *Miller's Antiques, Art, & Collectibles on the Web* or have any comments about the book we would love to hear from you!

Please photocopy this form and return it to:

Miller's / Antiques Web Guide
Mitchell Beazley
2–4 Heron Quays
London E14 4JP
UK

Alternatively, you can email us now (supplying all the information listed below) at: **millerswebguide@mitchell-beazley.co.uk**

Site name ______________________________

URL ______________________________

Subject area ______________________________

Brief Description of what the site offers and why you think it should be included in the *Miller's Antiques, Art, & Collectibles on the Web*

____

____

____

____